John and the Others

John and the Others

Jewish Relations, Christian Origins, and the Sectarian Hermeneutic

Andrew J. Byers

BAYLOR UNIVERSITY PRESS

© 2021 by Baylor University Press
Waco, Texas 76798

Cover and book design by Kasey McBeath
Cover image: Shutterstock/Ishaan Banerji

The Library of Congress has cataloged this book under ISBN 978-1-4813-1590-6.
Library of Congress Control Number: 2021938796

Printed in the United States of America on acid-free paper with a minimum of thirty percent recycled content.

Contents

Acknowledgments

I began writing this book before I knew I was writing it. At some point a few years ago, I recognized that a series of lectures, a handful of paper presentations, and a published article were collectively part of the wider project that became *John and the Others*. The lecture series were endured by students at Cranmer Hall, the theological seminary at St. John's College of Durham University. Their questions and questioning in undergraduate and postgraduate classes on the Johannine literature honed my thinking and surely prevented me from meandering too far (I hope!) down wayward paths. For their enthusiastic support and fellowship in learning, I am tremendously grateful. Two paper presentations served as testing grounds for many of the arguments and ideas found in chapter 2 of this book, "John and Other Jews." One paper was delivered at the Durham New Testament & Early Christianity Research Seminar, a community and context I have cherished for over nine years. The other presentation was in Cambridge, where I offered "Theosis and 'the Jews': Divine and Ethnic Identity in the Fourth Gospel" as the 2018 Tyndale New Testament Lecture. I am grateful to Ian Paul and Dirk Jongkind for the invitation and constructive interaction. In chapter 4, I reproduce most of an article that appeared in *Novum Testamentum*. I thank Cilliers Breytenbach and his colleagues on the editorial board for the permission to reuse here "Johannine Bishops? The Fourth Evangelist, John the Elder, and the Episcopal Ecclesiology of Ignatius of Antioch," *NovT* 60, no. 2 (2018): 121–39.

Once I realized I was actually writing *John and the Others*, I benefitted directly from countless conversations with colleagues and friends. John Barclay asked pointed questions in his matchless gift for providing accountability alongside warm support. Philip Plyming, Warden of Cranmer Hall, served as a lively and insightful host for a discussion on John and anti-Judaism that was recorded on the Talking Theology podcast. I am also grateful for the spirited yet measured interactions within the Johannine Literature Seminar Group of the British New Testament Society. Cranmer Hall colleagues Nick Moore and Richard Briggs encouraged me along the way and exemplified patient diligence amidst heavy teaching responsibilities. Matt Crawford heard out my general ideas on John and otherness over lunch at an SBL meeting, and I left feeling emboldened and inspired to keep plodding on.

A handful of gracious friends were kind enough to read portions of the manuscript as it neared completion. Luke Irwin, Francis Watson, Wendy North, David Lamb, Stephen Barton, and Andrew Lincoln constitute an intimidating list of readers. For their gift of time and feedback (both critical and supportive), I am so thankful. Any errors or misunderstandings that may surface in the book are most certainly my own.

The team at Baylor University Press has been outstanding. I am pleased that Carey Newman was willing to load the project onto his busy desk, and so grateful to Cade Jarrell for taking the baton and seeing the book to completion. His championing of my ideas has meant a great deal.

Having lived for almost a decade overseas, I find myself treasuring my family back "home" all the more. Such distance also deepens the appreciation of my adoptive church family at Kings Church Durham. With even greater appreciation I mention my wife, Miranda, and our four children. Academic books are professional products, but they emerge inescapably from relational fabric, from the messy entanglements of conversations in the car, at the breakfast table, by the bedside, and on the way to school and work. For my family in the States, my church in Durham, and for those in my home away from home, I express thanks for keeping me grounded. And Miranda, as much as I want to give you, my hands are quite empty—except for another book. I dedicate this one to you. It is not worthy.

Andy Byers
February 2021
Durham, England

Introduction

The Other Who Became Flesh

This book is about texts, but I open with an image. The photograph was taken on July 8, 2018, in Charlottesville, Virginia. The colors are vibrant. In the background are the reds, blues, and whites of a Confederate flag and the white star set within the navy of a Bonnie Blue flag. Both are born aloft by protesters at a Unite the Right rally. A red conical hood adorns a member of the Ku Klux Klan, his body sheathed in a matching red robe. A yellow banner reading "Police Line Do Not Cross" streams perpendicular along steel-gray fencing. A man dressed in black raises a Nazi salute, his arm looming over green grass. Their faces are white. Centered in the foreground is a police officer, calm and erect, guarding the makeshift barrier and positioned on the opposite side of the barricade tape. His face is black. Later that day, protestors would clash with counterprotestors, and police would fire tear gas.[1]

The photograph went viral a month later after a similar Charlottesville rally resulted in tragic violence.[2] The scene depicted on

[1] An account of the day's frightening events can be found here. Hawes Spencer and Matt Stevens, "23 Arrested and Tear Gas Deployed After a K.K.K. Rally in Virginia," *New York Times*, July 8, 2017, https://www.nytimes.com/2017/07/08/us/kkk-rally-charlottesville-robert-e-lee-statue.html (last accessed June 19, 2020).

[2] The photo was taken by Jill Mumie. For more details, see Andrew Katz, "The Story Behind the Viral Photo of the Officer and the KKK," *Time*,

July 8—reinforced by the range of colors—pictures the dynamics of "the other," a term used with increasing frequency to denote antagonized social distinctions in our politics of identity. The "Do Not Cross" emblazoned on the yellow police tape is unwittingly symbolic but perhaps as suggestive as the formal emblems and insignia of Southern American pride and white supremacy. Black/White, police/civilian, protestor/counterprotestor—these polarized categories of identity that collided in and around Justice Park in the summer of 2018 seem all the more crystallized after the violence, protests, counterprotests, and online vitriol of the summer of 2020.

"Othering" and the (Problematic) Discourse of Difference

The language of "the other" encompasses a comparative mode of identity construction. Jonathan Z. Smith writes that "othering" is "reflexive"[3]—those operating within the rubric of otherness feel self-knowledge is secured by comparatively delineating who they are not: "A 'theory of the other' is but another way of phrasing a 'theory of the self.'"[4] Someone (or some*thing*) other than our individual selves need not be understood as inherently threatening. In fact, the idea of "the other" can be viewed positively as an important source of meaning and purpose.[5] But with such a Cartesian emphasis on "the self" dominating contemporary modes of identity construction, the labeling of "the other" is largely perceived as a negative and fiercely polemical act in which alterity (i.e., "otherness") justifies the reduction of a different person or group to a prejudiced cast of traits, a composite stereotype easily dismissed or even attacked. At its heart, "the actions of othering are very much tied up with the

---

August 14, 2017, updated August 16, 2017, https://time.com/4899668/charlottesville-virginia-protest-officer-kkk-photo/ (last accessed June 19, 2020).

[3]   Jonathan Z. Smith, "Differential Equations: On Constructing the Other," in *Relating Religion: Essays on the Study of Religion* (Chicago: University of Chicago Press, 2004), 230–50 (here 232).

[4]   Jonathan Z. Smith, "What a Difference a Difference Makes," in *Relating Religion: Essays on the Study of Religion* (Chicago: University of Chicago Press, 2004), 251–302 (here 274).

[5]   Mark Freeman is seeking to recover this more positive construal of the other in *The Priority of the Other: Thinking and Living Beyond the Self* (Oxford: Oxford University Press, 2013).

misuse of difference."[6] Indeed, othering has become *the pathologizing of difference*.[7] Varying degrees of (negative) "othering" seem to be at work within the broader cultural spheres many of us inhabit. As individuals and social groups jostle all the more closely in a crowded, pluralistic world with blurred national boundaries and uncertain geographical borders, our contemporary construal of the self sometimes or even frequently relies on negative labelling. The "identity politics" of Western society tribalize ideological commitments and codify racial or cultural distinctives in such a way that those outside one identity are often disparaged and divided into a "them" that stands against an "us."[8] Powerbrokers may promote policies that reduce members of a social class, gender, or ethnicity into nonentities. The gaming and entertainment industries facilitate the concept of "the other" by creating easily disposable "bad guys," whether zombies, generic-looking soldiers, or monstrous creatures bearing little or no personhood. The hero who eliminates such foes is celebrated; the gamer who defeats them on the screen suffers no conflict of conscience. As our use of communications technology abets the harsh political discourse and the "take-no-prisoners" aggression toward those whose version of "justice" or "truth" challenges our own, the gulf widens between "Right" and "Left." News agencies, beholden to ideologically defined consumer markets (particularly in the United States), produce headlines and stories that tend to sharpen and delineate social boundaries.[9] Political parties

---

[6]   Letty M. Russell, "Encountering the 'Other' in a World of Difference and Danger," *HTR* 99, no. 4 (2006): 457–68 (here 459).

[7]   I am drawing the term "pathologizing" from one of the section titles in Travis D. Boyce and Winsome M. Chunnu, eds., *Historicizing Fear: Ignorance, Vilification, and Othering* (Louisville: University Press of Colorado, 2019).

[8]   Rabbi Jonathan Sacks points to the competitive nature of market forces and the Social Darwinian idea of the survival of the socially fittest as influences driving negative group interactivity. See his *The Dignity of Difference: How to Avoid the Clash of Civilizations*, rev. ed. (London: Bloomsbury, 2003 [2002]), 142–43.

[9]   See the reflections in Rolf Dobelli, *Stop Reading the News: A Manifesto for a Happier, Calmer, and Wiser Life*, trans. Caroline Waight (London: Sceptre, 2020 [2019]), esp. 43–46.

acquire loyalty by stoking fears of an easily identifiable (and thus caricatured) enemy. For those participating in this collective habitus, binary "othering" is the inevitable dark side of understanding and articulating who we. The result is the emergence of a "cancel culture" that cannot (or will not) tolerate difference. Within the more specific domains of the academy, "otherness" has become the object of sociological and cultural analysis.[10] As classicist Erich Gruen observes, "Scholarship regularly identifies the construction of 'the Other' as a keystone of collective identity."[11] Philosophers, anthropologists, psychologists, sociologists, literary theorists, and historians alike are wrestling within (and beyond) their fields over this language of alterity, difference, and identity.[12] The discourse of otherness is also taking up residence in the field of biblical studies.[13] This "theory of the other," however, risks certain

[10]   A seminal work featuring the binary nature of otherness is Fredrik Barth, *Ethnic Groups and Boundaries: The Social Organization of Culture Difference* (Long Grove, Ill.: Waveland Press, 1998). See the discussion of Barth's work in Thomas Hylland Eriksen and Marek Jakoubek, eds., *Ethnic Groups and Boundaries Today: A Legacy of Fifty Years*, Research in Migration and Ethnic Relations Series (London: Routledge, 2019).

[11]   Erich S. Gruen, *Rethinking the Other in Antiquity* (Princeton: Princeton University Press, 2011), 3.

[12]   Seminal works in the social sciences include Emmanuel Levinas, *Time and the Other: Lectures in Paris at the College Philosophique, 1946–1947*, trans. Richard A. Cohen (Pittsburgh: Duquesne University Press, 1990); idem, *Totality and Infinity: An Essay on Exteriority*, trans. Alphonso Lingis (Pittsburgh: Duquesne University Press, 1969); Jacques Lacan, *The Seminar of Jacques Lacan*, Book 2: *The Ego in Freud's Theory and in the Technique of Psychoanalysis, 1954–1955* (New York: W. W. Norton, 1988); G. C. Spivak, "The Rani of Sirmur: An Essay in Reading the Archives," *History and Theory* 24, no. 3 (1985): 247–72; also significant is the postcolonial work by Edward Said, *Orientalism* (London: Penguin Books, 1978). For a recent overview of the study of othering, see Travis D. Boyce and Winsome M. Chunnu, "'I Want to Get Rid of My Fear': An Introduction," in *Historicizing Fear: Ignorance, Vilification, and Othering*, ed. Travis D. Boyce and Winsome M. Chunnu (Louisville: University Press of Colorado, 2019), 3–16.

[13]   E.g., see Michal Bar-Asher Siegal, Wolfgang Grünstädl, and Matthew Thiessen, eds., *Perceiving the Other in Ancient Judaism and Early Christianity*, WUNT 394 (Tübingen: Mohr Siebeck, 2017); Aaron Kuecker, *The Spirit and the "Other": Social Identity, Ethnicity and Intergroup Reconciliation in Luke-Acts*, LNTS 444 (London: T&T Clark, 2011);

methodological pitfalls. The agents of othering under investigation may themselves become unwittingly othered as they are studied and objectified.[14] Furthermore, this mode of inquiry may promote negative ideas of otherness by reducing complex social dynamics into oversimplified categories for the sake of reaching manageable research goals. Preoccupation with the delineations of identity may unnecessarily magnify intergroup difference. When this is done, perhaps for heuristic purposes, studies tend to discover a disproportionate degree of alterity between the subjects observed and overlook the subtle yet equally important dynamics of negotiating difference. The social border lines are so highlighted that they seem impermeable to those categorized as equally monolithic outsiders.[15] Such an approach and its methodological hazards may

---

Anders Runesson, "Judging Gentiles in the Gospel of Matthew: Between 'Othering' and Inclusion," in *Jesus, Matthew's Gospel and Early Christianity: Studies in Memory of Graham N. Stanton*, ed. Daniel M. Gurtner, Joel Willitts, and Richard A. Burridge, LNTS 435 (London: T&T Clark, 2011), 133–51; Frank Anthony Spina, *The Faith of the Outsider: Exclusion and Inclusion in the Biblical Story* (Grand Rapids: Eerdmans, 2005); Ruth Sheridan, "Identity, Alterity, and the Gospel of John," *BibInt* 22 (2014): 188–209; Paul Trebilco, *Outsider Designations and Boundary Construction in the New Testament: Early Christian Communities and the Formation of Group Identity* (Cambridge: Cambridge University Press, 2017); David Frankfurter, "'Jews or Not': Reconstructing the 'Other' in Revelation 2:9 and 3:9," *HTR* 94, no. 4 (2001): 403–25; Rodney S. Sadler Jr., *Can a Cushite Change His Skin? An Examination of Race, Ethnicity, and Othering in the Hebrew Bible*, LHBOTS 425 (London: T&T Clark, 2005); see also the relevant essays in Laurence J. Silberstein and Robert L. Cohn, eds., *The Other in Jewish Thought and History: Constructions of Jewish Culture and Identity* (New York: New York University Press, 1994). One of the most sobering accounts of otherness in biblical texts is offered by Regina M. Schwartz, *The Curse of Cain: The Violent Legacy of Monotheism* (Chicago: University of Chicago Press, 1997).

[14] On this tendency, see the discussion in Lisa Isherwood and David Harris, *Radical Otherness: Sociological and Theological Approaches* (London: Routledge, 2013), 2–11.

[15] For a brief overview of othering, see Sune Qvotrup Jensen, "Othering, Identity Formation and Agency," *Qualitative Studies* 2, no. 2 (2011): 63–78. His definition is a helpful entrée into the topic: "I define othering as discursive processes by which powerful groups, who may or may not make up a numerical majority, define subordinate groups into existence in a reductionist way which ascribes problematic and/or inferior

have emerged, in part, out of a Hegelian dialectical philosophy that delights in setting up distinct binary antitheses.[16] Within the logic of a dialectical approach, a thesis is tested by an antithesis leading to a synthesis. When adopting a "theory of the other," however, the dialectical process is often stalled—by the nature of the task, focus lies ultimately on uncovering that which is antithetical. It is in the very nature of otherness that antithetical tensions resist the synthetic task.

Though influential studies and established methodologies affirm that identity derives from accentuating differences and decrying the identities of others, there are those voicing more nuanced understandings that complicate the polarizations.[17] More germane for the purposes at hand are the approaches by historians of the ancient world and scholars of religious studies. Judith Lieu has pointed out that "there can be other relationships with difference and alterity than the oppositional," though it is this "oppositional" feature "that has tended to dominate studies of identity and otherness in antiquity as well as in the present."[18] The observations by Gruen and Smith above are not endorsements for focusing primarily on the negative

characteristics to these subordinate groups. Such discursive processes affirm the legitimacy and superiority of the powerful and condition identity formation among the subordinate."

[16]   In addition to Jensen cited above, see Lajos Bron, "Othering, an Analysis," *Transcience* 6, no. 1 (2015): 69–90. For Hegel, see especially the section on lordship and servitude in Georg Wilhelm Fredrich Hegel, *The Phenomenology of Spirit*, ed. and trans. Terry Pinkard and Michael Baur (Cambridge: Cambridge University Press, 2018), 108–16.

[17]   E.g., the opening essays in *Grammars of Identity/Alterity—A Structuralist Approach*, ed. G. Bauman and Andre Gingrich (Oxford: Berghahn, 2004): Andre Gingrich, "Conceptualizing Identities: Anthropological Alternatives to Essentialising Difference and Moralizing about the Other," 3–17; and Gerd Naumann, "Grammars of Identity/Alterity: A Structural Approach," 18–50. See also the aforementioned study *The Priority of the Other* by Freeman. It is also important to note that, in popular culture, some story-makers complicate the concept of the other by personalizing characters or character groups who are initially objectified, then become endeared to the (entrapped) readers or viewers. Examples include the portrayal of the "Roaches" in the *Black Mirror* episode "Man against Fire" and that of "the others" in the series *Lost*.

[18]   Judith M. Lieu, *Christian Identity in the Jewish and Graeco-Roman World* (Oxford: Oxford University Press, 2004), 269.

elements of group difference. Gruen, for instance, challenges long-standing assumptions in *Rethinking the Other in Antiquity*, a study that "offers an alternative vision to the widespread idea that framing the self requires postulating the 'Other.'"[19] The contemporary imposition of a sharp dialectic onto ancient societies and people groups is grounded in a deconstructive bias: "To stress the stigmatization of the 'Other' as a strategy of self-assertion and superiority dwells unduly on the negative, a reductive and misleading analysis."[20] As Gruen argues throughout his extensive study, ancient peoples were conscious of intergroup differences, but they also actively entangled their own identities with the identities of others, generating fictive kinship ties, borrowing foundation stories, and imaginatively crafting connections across ethnic lines.

A similar case is made by Kostas Vlassopoulos in his study of ancient Greeks and Barbarians. He identifies the tussle between "two diametrically opposed approaches" to the study of people groups in antiquity: "One stresses conflict and polarity; the other stresses interaction, exchange and mutual dependence."[21] Taking the broader path, Vlassopoulos concludes his wide-ranging monograph declaring his aim to excise the polarizing interpretations contemporary scholarship often transposes onto the study of social identities:

> One of the major arguments of this book is the necessity of dissociating the history of the relationship between Greeks and non-Greeks from the context of Orientalism and the modern confrontation between West and East. This implies challenging the identification of the modern Western scholar and reader with the ancient Greeks, seen as the originators of freedom and science in their confrontation with despotic and religious-minded Orientals; but it also challenges the identification of

---

[19] Gruen, *Rethinking the Other*, 352.

[20] Gruen, *Rethinking the Other*, 356.

[21] Kostas Vlassopoulos, *Greeks and Barbarians* (Cambridge: Cambridge University Press, 2013), 4. Vlassopoulos takes a much broader approach, focusing on the dynamics of "globalization" and "glocalization" in the matrix of four "parallel worlds" (networks, immigrant communities, and the worlds of Panhellenism and other empires).

Greek attitudes towards Barbarians with the imperialistic and colonialist attitudes of the modern West.[22]

Though he acknowledges that strands of thinking and patterns of behavior have, over time, contributed in various ways to our world today, Vlassopoulos is clear that "the mapping of the modern distinction between West and East onto the ancient interaction between Greeks and non-Greeks is deeply flawed, because it is deeply unhistorical."[23]

Both Gruen and Vlassopoulos have recognized in their field of classical history a tendency that biblical studies must also challenge, and this is the categorization of early Christians, early Jews, and their Greek and Roman neighbors into tidily demarcated factions of "others." In this vein Tobias Nicklas helpfully remarks that

> working with group identities presumes that people in antiquity defined themselves in more or less stable ways, that they behaved according to their group's ethos in comparable situations, and only thought in patterns determined by their groups. At the same time, however, we regard it as self-evident that our own twenty-first century identities are complex, dynamic, and in part fragmented. Could this not also be the case for ancient people?[24]

In biblical studies, we must resist stretching oversimplified dichotomies across the canvas of ancient societies and their texts.

Among those ancient texts problematizing today's rigid construct of binary otherness are the Gospel and Epistles of John in Christian Scripture.[25] Into our agonistic societies, a Johannine voice

---

[22]   Vlassopoulos, *Greeks and Barbarians*, 321.

[23]   Vlassopoulos, *Greeks and Barbarians*, 321.

[24]   Tobias Nicklas, "Jesus and Judaism: Inside or Outside? *The Gospel of John*, the *Egerton Gospel*, and the Spectrum of Ancient Christian Voices," in *Connecting Gospels: Beyond the Canonical/Non-Canonical Divide*, ed. Francis Watson and Sarah Parkhouse (Oxford: Oxford University Press, 2018), 125–41 (here 126).

[25]   Without insisting on direct historical claims about his (or her?) identity, I use this traditional appellation to refer to the guarantor of the Johannine textual tradition and as the primary authorial voice underlying the Johannine writings. When speaking about specific texts, I roughly

may prove ameliorative. The Fourth Evangelist opens his account of Jesus with an alterity of a different kind: *in the beginning was the Other who became flesh.*

At the core of Johannine theology is a radical act of de-othering: the Incarnation.[26] Though the horizon between heaven and earth was more blurred in antiquity than in later eras that hardened the cosmic and secular divide (and eventually eliminated the former), passage between the two would have been the exception. In an early Jewish frame, the distinction between Creator and created was sharply drawn, and the most impassable barrier etched into the cosmos was between divine glory and mortal sinfulness. The most glaring "Do Not Cross" boundary demarcated the holy from the unholy. Yet John narrates the most astonishing of border crossings as the Logos enters a sphere of darkness, impurity, and sin. Though "flesh" does not bear the Pauline connotation of "sinful" in John's writings, the Incarnation of the Logos entails the (co-)Creator traversing into and physically inhabiting a created realm streaked with unholiness.

This divine figure of the Logos is presented both *as* God as well as *alongside* God. The two are one, yet also "other." In this divine alterity, otherness is not antagonistic. And through the agency of an-*Other* (another), divine entity, the Spirit, human beings are invited into this plural unity, this unified plurality. John celebrates the potential de-othering of divine and human society and envisions an "in-one-anotherness"[27]—what we might call a "perichoretic otherness"—in which difference is celebrated, embraced, and characterized by a love traipsing across boundaries and spanning

---

equate "John" with the Fourth Evangelist and the anonymous author(s) of 1 John, choosing to employ "the Elder" when referring specifically to the author(s) of 2 and 3 John. In this study, I am content to leave the complex (and ultimately inconclusive) debates about authorial identity unresolved.

[26] I recognize that feminist interpreters have seen the Incarnation as an act of gendered othering since John employs the masculine Logos rather than the Greek Sophia. On this perspective, see Isherwood and Harris, *Radical Otherness*, 12–16.

[27] This phrase is used to helpful effect by Richard Bauckham. See his essay "Individualism" in Richard Bauckham, *Gospel of Glory: Major Themes in the Johannine Theology* (Grand Rapids: Baker Academic, 2015), 1–19.

the greatest distance. The Johannine literature teems with theological wealth for societies ancient and contemporary that feel torn apart at the social seams. "The other" need not be othered.

This claim, however, will likely come as a surprise to many readers. The reason is because John's literary corpus is regularly charged with having an agenda of sectarian othering. I first came across the language of "othering" not while reading sociology, philosophy, psychology, political theory, or literary criticism (or even the news), but while reading a book on the Gospel of John.

In fact, John's Gospel features in the photograph I described above. The man bearing the Confederate flag behind the black police officer (who is ironically guarding the right to free speech) wields in his other arm a placard that reads "Jews Are Satan's Children." This slogan is vindicated with authoritative citations, with "John 8:31-47" and "John 10:22-33" listed first among other biblical sources.[28] Those citations, scribbled by hand with a permanent marker on poster board, beg the question: Did John sponsor a campaign of group delineation latent with the power to incite hate and sectarian violence?

The Scholarly Construct of Johannine Christianity: A Quick Profile

For those familiar with the field of Johannine studies, it is no secret that the reputation of the eponymous writer has a dark side.[29] Though the Fourth Gospel may be championed by theologians as an inspired text inviting human participation within the Trinitarian life and cherished by confessional readers as a narrative portraying divine love for "the world," many biblical scholars have come to view the Johannine writings as literary products of an introversionist sect that loved its own but arrayed

---

[28] I am thankful to my colleague Adesola Akala for pointing this out to me and for sending me the *Time* article cited above.

[29] Similar language can be found in Stephen C. Barton, "Christian Community in the Light of the Gospel of John," in *Christology, Controversy and Community: New Testament Essays in Honour of David R. Catchpole*, ed. David G. Horrell and Christopher M. Tuckett, NovTSup 99 (Leiden: Brill, 2000), 279–301.

itself against outsiders.[30] Theologians, churchgoers, and biblical scholars alike can readily acknowledge that these texts are acutely conscious of "the other," the person who lies beyond the limned boundaries of an esteemed in-group. Though many confessional theologians and churchly readers may perceive a hospitable and invitational stance toward these acknowledged outsiders, New Testament scholars have reason to be less enthusiastic, noting dangerous hermeneutical trajectories that the exercise of "othering" makes possible. Accusations are regularly made that John arises from an anti-society with its own anti-language expressing a worldview that is anti-Jewish, anti-Semitic, anti-ecclesiastical, and anti-hierarchical.

Indeed, within the discipline of biblical scholarship, the prefix "anti-" has become almost *Johannine.*

Perhaps my positive reflections above on John's "perichoretic otherness" and its potential for ameliorating divisive times constitute a delusional misreading of the Fourth Gospel. A brief survey of the consensus understanding of Johannine Christianity would suggest that such is the case. First, John seems invested in a dangerous program of othering a character group designated as "the Jews" (οἱ Ἰουδαῖοι). Though by no means an excuse for the stinging rhetoric, the general consensus—assumed throughout this study—is that the Fourth Gospel was forged in the furnace of inter-Jewish conflict. John is a Jewish writer with an audience of Jewish Christians whose theological roots are being ripped from their cultural soil and whose social bonds are being severed from cultic and civic life (whether this departure is self-imposed or imposed by others is one of the many ongoing debates[31]). The result is polemical language that is

---

[30] The term "introversionist" comes from Bryan R. Wilson's helpful taxonomy of the sect in *Magic and the Millennium: A Sociological Study of Religious Movements of Protest among Tribal and Third-World People* (New York: Harper & Row, 1973).

[31] Following the reconstructions offered by leading interpreters such as J. Louis Martyn and Raymond Brown, most scholars understand John's Gospel as arising from some form of social exclusion enacted by a more dominant group of fellow Jews. But this model has been challenged, with Adele Reinhartz and Raimo Hakola arguing that the Johannine believers initiated this severance of ties themselves. See Raymond E. Brown, *The Community of the Beloved Disciple: The Life, Loves, and Hates of an*

caustic and, to readers modern and ancient, disturbing. For many, among the most egregious acts of othering in religious history is Johannine; namely, that moment when Jesus says to οἱ Ἰουδαῖοι in John 8:44, "you are of your father, the devil."[32] It is on the basis of John's depiction of "the Jews" and his appropriation of Jewish religious ideas and symbols that Adele Reinhartz has recently labeled John as "thoroughly anti-Jewish,"[33] an accusation affirmed in that placard held up in Charlottesville, Virginia.

Secondly, these texts are viewed as standing in contradistinctive otherness to mainstream Christianity in the first and second centuries. Raymond Brown writes of the "one-upmanship of the Johannine Christians."[34] By

> counterposing their hero [the Beloved Disciple] over against the most famous member of the Twelve [Peter], the Johannine community is symbolically counterposing itself over against the kinds of churches that venerate Peter and the Twelve—the Apostolic Churches, whom other scholars call the "Great Church."[35]

Similarly, Robert Kysar accentuates the differences between John's Gospel and the Synoptic Gospels, and introduces it as a "maverick" text presenting a "heterodox form of Christianity" that "did not easily conform to the developing standard brand" of the wider

---

Individual Church in New Testament Times (New York: Paulist Press, 1979); J. Louis Martyn, *History and Theology in the Fourth Gospel*, 3rd ed. (Louisville: Westminster John Knox Press, 2003 [1968]); Adele Reinhartz, "The Johannine Community and Its Jewish Neighbors: A Reappraisal," in *What is John?* vol. 2: *Literary and Social Readings of the Fourth Gospel*, ed. Fernando Segovia, SBLSymS 3 (Atlanta: Scholars Press, 1998), 111–38; Raimo Hakola, *Identity Matters: John, the Jews and Jewishness*, NovTSup 118 (Leiden: Brill, 2005).

[32] All translations from biblical texts are my own unless otherwise noted.

[33] Adele Reinhartz, *Cast out of the Covenant: Jews and Anti-Judaism in the Gospel of John* (Lanham, Md.: Fortress, 2018), xxi.

[34] Brown, *Community of the Beloved Disciple*, 84. It should be noted, however, that Brown was reluctant to apply the term "sect" to the Johannine Community (88–91).

[35] Brown, *Community of the Beloved Disciple*, 83.

movement.[36] Though ever measured in his evaluations, D. Moody Smith is not conflicted in stating that Johannine Christianity's "relative isolation from other streams of tradition in the New Testament seems to bear witness to a path of origin off the beaten path" and betrays a "sectarian consciousness, a sense of exclusiveness, a sharp delineation of the community from the world."[37] Smith's successor as the George Washington Ivey chairholder, Richard Hays, observes that "the strongly sectarian character of the Johannine vision stands at the opposite pole within the New Testament from Luke's optimistic affirmation of the world and its culture."[38] For Harold Attridge, John's tradition stands as an "alternative to other forms of Christianity in the late first or early second century."[39] Bruce Malina and Richard Rohrbaugh understand John as the literary product of individuals who "stand opposed to society and its competing groups."[40] Ernst Käsemann is reliably blunt: the Johannine community is a "conventicle," and "from the historical viewpoint, the Church committed an error when it declared the Gospel to be orthodox."[41]

Clearly, the canonical writings superscripted with the name "John" in the Christian Bible feature the theme of otherness and have certainly been deployed, regrettably, as catalysts of negative othering. Though some may view John's Gospel as a salutary text staging what Christian theologians might hail as the greatest

[36]   Robert Kysar, *John: The Maverick Gospel*, 3rd ed. (Louisville: Westminster John Knox, 2007 [1993, 1976]), 2, 35.

[37]   D. Moody Smith, *Johannine Christianity: Essays on Its Setting, Sources, and Theology* (Columbia: University of South Carolina Press, 1984), 22, 2.

[38]   Richard B. Hays, *The Moral Vision of the New Testament: Community, Cross, New Creation; A Contemporary Introduction to New Testament Ethics* (New York: HarperCollins, 1996), 139. It is worth noting that Hays seems to have a more nuanced view of John in his *Echoes of Scripture in the Gospels* (Waco, Tex.: Baylor University Press, 2016), 281–345.

[39]   Harold W. Attridge, "Johannine Christianity," in *Essays on John and Hebrews* (Grand Rapids: Baker Academic), 3–19 (here 19).

[40]   Bruce J. Malina and Richard L. Rohrbaugh, *Social-Science Commentary on the Gospel of John* (Minneapolis: Fortress, 1998), 10.

[41]   Ernst Käsemann, *The Testament of Jesus According to John 17*, trans. Gerhard Krodel (Philadelphia: Fortress, 1978 [1966]), 76.

act of de-othering in cosmic history ("the Logos became flesh, and dwelled among us," 1:14), others (!) view John as guilty of an act of othering so virulent that it may have contributed to pogroms and genocide. How is it that the most significant text in defining Trinitarian theology can also be arrogated to justify ethnic violence? How can the same work bear such divergent legacies? How can this Gospel give way to a "poisonous *Wirkungsgeschichte*"[42] in which genocide seems almost plausible while also giving way to the cherished stream of tradition running through Nicea and Chalcedon and into countless pews via today's pulpits and seminary lecterns?[43] Does John portray the opening of a fissure within the perichoretic otherness of the Father, Son, and Spirit as a means of inclusion, or is he rhetorically chiseling a divisive fissure between an "us" and a "them"?

In spite of the more positive understandings of John the Theologian found in devotional literature, creedal formulations, and theological texts, he is known at times as John the Sectarian, and the interpretation of his Gospel and Epistles is governed in biblical scholarship by what I am calling a "sectarian hermeneutic." The notion that John is grounded in an alternative Christian vision and antagonistically opposed to those who refuse to embrace it (whether Ἰουδαῖοι, mainstream early Christians, or both) has become a rooted and virtually unassailable frame of reference for reading these texts. This sectarian hermeneutic is no mere fad. There is much to support the undergirding rationale, and its foundation has been tried and tested time and again without suffering any serious cracks. It is a paradigm that has been intellectually locked into place for several decades, its influences etched into the pages of multiple monographs and persistently codified in countless commentaries.

---

[42] Pheme Perkins, "Erasure of 'the Jews' in the Farewell Discourses and Johannine Epistles," in *The Gospel of John and Jewish-Christian Relations*, ed. Adele Reinhartz (Lanham, Md.: Fortress, 2018), 3–20 (here 3).

[43] Tuomas Rasimus acknowledges such divergent reception history in his introduction to Tuomas Rasimus, ed., *The Legacy of John: Second-Century Reception of the Fourth Gospel*, NovTSup 132 (Leiden: Brill, 2010), 1–16 (here 1).

These Things Are Written So That . . .

Though there is indeed what many would perceive as a dark side to John's theology of "the other," this book contends that the Johannine writings are not necessarily sectarian and they even hold challenge for our contemporary means of boundary construction, casting a salutary vision for how to be "other" without being "othered." I employ this language of otherness not as an expert in anthropology or social identity theory—methodological purists will surely find themselves disappointed. Though informed by current academic discussion, my usage is consciously less formal. As the ideas of "othering" and "the other" become more prominent in everyday discourse, I find it a helpful entry point of contemporary relevance into the topic of John's putative antipathy and insularity. My aim, however, is not to endorse binary oversimplifications but to complicate them, an approach also taken in Sung Uk Lim's *Otherness and Identity in the Gospel of John*.[44] John does engage in negative labelling, and he most certainly draws lines of partition—but as writers like Gruen and Vlassopoulos have found in their subjects of study, the lines and labels are more complex than a strict binary reading would suggest.

As a work of exegetical theology and theological interpretation, this book is in many respects an exercise in retrieval, a hopeful contribution to the current work of rehabilitating Johannine Christianity from the pejorative extremes of its sectarian reputation.[45] John's voice is certainly from the margins in the wider picture of the ancient Mediterranean world. Strikingly different from the

[44]   Regrettably, Lim's book appeared when my own manuscript was in production and I was unable to engage with his work. Please see his study for more on John and otherness: Sung Uk Lim, *Otherness and Identity in the Gospel of John* (London: Palgrave Macmillan, 2021).

[45]   See, e.g., Carlos Raúl Sosa Siliezar, *Savior of the World: A Theology of the Universal Gospel* (Waco, Tex.: Baylor University Press, 2019); David A. Lamb, *Text, Context, and the Johannine Community: A Sociolinguistic Analysis of the Johannine Writings*, LNTS 477 (London: T&T Clark, 2014); Michael J. Gorman, *Abide and Go: Missional Theosis in the Gospel of John* (Eugene, Ore.: Cascade, 2018); for a succinct presentation of Gorman's overall arguments, see his "John: the Nonsectarian, Missional Gospel," *Canadian-American Theological Review* 7 (2018): 138–62.

Synoptics, his own Jesus-story stands out as the "other Gospel" amidst the canonical Four within the narrower world of early Christianity. Yet in a day allegedly more receptive to marginal voices and minority reports, these writings deserve a fresh hearing in both the church and the academy. In ancient and contemporary forms of pluralism, Christian identity is helpfully articulated by clarifying who we are not, but the task is incomplete without affirming our affiliation with the one who says, "I am."

I have two related aims. The first is to limn a scriptural theology of identity and alterity based on the Johannine literature. But since this goal is obstructed by the longstanding sectarian hermeneutic in Johannine scholarship, that interpretive frame and its axioms must be carefully explored and, on several points, challenged. My second aim is therefore an attempted unsettling of the foundations on which these sectarian readings stand. Depending on the definition, "sect" may well be applied with relative accuracy to the social network that has John's voice in its ears. But how accurate are the unavoidable connotations of the term? I offer in the following chapter an all-too-brief account of this sectarian hermeneutic, the reference frame for thinking of Johannine Christianity, outlining its emergence and noting its primary coordinates. Throughout the book, I hope to blunt its edges, blur its frames, and complicate some fundamental assumptions. I do not intend to dismiss or overlook the differences between the Johannine literature and other early Christian texts, nor disregard wholesale the fruits of serious historical study that have contributed so much to understanding the fraught milieu out of which John wrote; my purpose, rather, is to honor the diversity in Christian origins without following the longstanding trend of rigidly construing *difference* automatically as *combative* or *competitive*.

In chapter 2, I consider "John and Other Jews," then "John and Other Christians" in chapters 3 and 4. Along the way, I will be challenging established presuppositions in order to make the case that John's collective portrait of the Jews, other potential outsiders, and troublesome insiders is to be understood within the wider theological vision of the divine inclusion of "the other" through the Incarnation's act of de-othering. John's othering is not ethnic, and "anti-"

is not necessarily a fitting prefix for describing his position toward other Christians. In chapter 5 I offer something of a synthesis by discussing the broader contours of the Other Disciple's theology of the Other. Though negative othering is certainly a feature of the Johannine literature, its conceptual anchor holds within the perichoretic otherness of the divine-human community, and the envisaged social disposition is one of testimony and invitation as well as resistance. John, the disciple who is both "other" and "beloved," is more concerned with the (missional) self-othering of his in-group than with a negative labelling of outsiders. The conclusion revisits the primary claims of the sectarian hermeneutic, and then considers how Christians might responsibly read John's writings as Scripture while living in a pluralistic age amidst "others," whether in the first, second, or twenty-first century.

1

Diversity as Enmity

The Sectarian Hermeneutic in Johannine Studies

Our default assumptions are ever lodged within hermeneutical circles that remain imperceptible unless we occasionally pause to take intellectual inventory. A degree of circular reasoning is inevitable when engaging texts, especially those whose origins are obscure. We read, make deductions, frame a paradigm, then reread from within that frame to test its potential for illuminating the work in hand. But some arcs in these hermeneutical circles are more responsibly crafted than others. The "sectarian hermeneutic" discussed in this chapter is an interpretative paradigm, a set of conceptual lenses through which the Johannine literature is read. The mode of reading the Gospel and Epistles of John as sectarian material is shaped in part by a complex range of influences and interests extrinsic to the actual texts, but it is also heavily anchored in Johannine writ. Here are five exegetical realities I will revisit in the final chapter that are intrinsic to John's writings and serviceable for the sectarian hermeneutic I seek to challenge:

1. *Difference*: John's Gospel is distinct from the Synoptics. When read in relation to the other three, this "other" Gospel seems out of place among Matthew, Mark, and

Luke, suggesting that Johannine gospel writing was a competitive act.

2. *Cosmological Dualism*: John erects boundaries and partitions humanity into two groups corresponding to the unbridgeable otherness of Light and Darkness. Human beings who are "from above" and "not of this world" are contrasted with those "from below" and "of this world."

3. *Harsh Polemics*: The Gospel's occasional sharp rhetoric seems to justify antagonism toward those on the wrong side of the dualistic divide.

4. *Insular Ethics*: The love commands in both the Gospel and the Epistles are often decried because their explicit orientation is toward "one another," with no corollary imperatives calling for a love of the neighbor or outsider.

5. *Charismatic Authority*: Since the Spirit-Paraclete is portrayed (at least in the Gospel) as an extradiegetic character who will guide believers after Jesus' ascension, it is often assumed that Johannine Christianity is unaccountable to ecclesial structures and hierarchies that soon developed within the broader traditions of the early church (to which a low-church "Johannine community"[1] would have been opposed).

Though my brief explanatory comments above evince certain assumptions in later scholarship deriving from later contexts, these five characteristics are certainly present within the texts (and at times magnified by their canonical relation to other early Christian writings). It is not necessarily a criticism, however, to assert that these Johannine features have not been interpreted within a hermetically sealed chamber but from within the swirling eddies and currents of Western intellectual traditions in modernity,

---

[1]   Texts do not emerge out of ahistorical vacuums, even if details of the historical contexts out of which the Johannine texts arose remain inaccessible and enigmatic. Though I am critical of the more packaged accounts of the "Johannine community," I do assume that a network of churches persisted behind the scenes and I value reconstructive work for its exploratory potential, as long as its limitations are emphatically acknowledged.

late-modernity, and (to go with the standard language) postmodernity. We all write within the confines of our social locations, and these confines may be as potentially illuminating as they are confining. The responsibility interpreters bear is to recognize these social locations. In the introductory remarks to his account of the Johannine community hypotheses, Kysar acknowledges that "contemporary biblical scholarship is deeply embedded in its culture and is, therefore, most often the result of a complex of influences, many of which are elusive."[2] The reflections below sketch the emergence of the sectarian hermeneutic with regard to these influences and their impact on Johannine studies. Again, many of these influences have been remarkably constructive, even if others have been misleading.

Rather than provide an exhaustive analysis of the pertinent historical and conceptual developments, I briefly identify below a number of key assumptions and movements that have embedded the sectarian hermeneutic so thoroughly within biblical scholarship.[3] A mere summary runs the risk of committing that which I hope to challenge—taking a complex set of ideas and oversimplifying them into a caricature that is then vilified would constitute an act of "othering." The secondary literature is overburdened with the construction of straw men who are then triumphantly conquered by the scholarly pen (or keypad). Caricatures are easy prey for the academic seeking a spot on our crowded playing fields. Alert to this temptation, I nonetheless offer a "sketch." My brush strokes here are broad in part because more exhaustive treatments have been penned.[4] The purpose here is to provide a condensed overview, not

---

[2]   Robert Kysar, "The Whence and Whither of the Johannine Community," in *Life in Abundance: Studies of John's Gospel in Tribute to Raymond E. Brown*, ed. John R. Donahue (Collegeville, Minn.: Liturgical Press, 2005), 65–81.

[3]   Kysar himself identifies four "originating events" that led to the Johannine community model, the first three pertaining to key figures: 1) Raymond Brown, 2) J. Louis Martyn, 3) Wayne Meeks, and 4) the Qumran discoveries ("Whence and Whither," 67–70). My own account below largely agrees with his assessment, though I cast the net a bit wider to macro-level trends.

[4]   Recent studies providing more detailed overviews noting what I call the "sectarian hermeneutic" include Richard Bauckham, "For Whom Were Gospels Written?" in *The Gospels for All Christians: Rethinking the Gospel*

a history of research, in order to discern the contingency of reading the Gospel and Epistles of John as sectarian texts. What must be resisted is an easy dismissal of the great legacy of Johannine scholarship, a field in which many giants have labored and into which I now stumble as a co-laborer arriving late in the day (to mix Gospel images). But our hermeneutical circles have to be tested regularly, and there are grounds to question the sectarian readings of this ancient literary corpus canonically attributed to "John." Again, this expression of early Christianity is most certainly distinctive—I make no attempt to show otherwise. My concern, rather, is to raise questions about the ingrained propensity for perfecting difference into agonistic extremes.

The Conflict Model of Christian Origins:
Diversity as an Adversity to Overcome

Threaded into the discipline of New Testament scholarship is a longstanding approach to Christian origins grounded in an Hegelian understanding of history in which developments arise out of dialectical antitheses (which, as noted earlier, some associate with today's discourse on "othering" in the humanities).[5] Dialectical reasoning has its advantages, and I informally weigh a range of alternatives in subsequent chapters and offer something of a synthesis at the end. As a model for historical inquiry, however, the Hegelian sense of progression through time has been recognized as problematic (especially when the progression seemed to find its fulfillment in Western culture). In the study of Christian origins, dialectical thinking in these terms has led to the interpretation of difference as inexorably leading to conflict and the assumption that *di*versity

---

Audiences, ed. Richard Bauckham (Grand Rapids: Eerdmans, 1998), 9–48; Kåro Sigvald Fuglseth, *Johannine Sectarianism in Perspective: A Sociological, Historical, and Comparative Analysis of Temple and Social Relationships in the Gospel of John, Philo and Qumran*, NovTSup 119 (Leiden: Brill, 2005); Edward W. Klink III, *The Sheep of the Fold: The Audience and Origin of the Gospel of John*, SNTSMS 141 (Cambridge: Cambridge University Press, 2007), 1–106; and David A. Lamb, *Text, Context, and the Johannine Community: A Sociolinguistic Analysis of the Johannine Writings*, LNTS 477 (London: T&T Clark, 2014), 1–28.

[5] See Oscar Cullmann's opening remarks in "A New Approach to the Interpretation of the Fourth Gospel—I," *ExpTim* 71, no. 1 (1959): 8–12.

is always an *ad*versity that powerbrokers sought to overcome. Ferdinand Christian Baur's dichotomization of Hellenistic and Jewish Christianity around the figures of Paul and Peter has erected much of the stage on which later New Testament exegesis has taken place.[6] Marcus Bockmuehl laments that his

> critical legacy continues to loom large in many key debating points regarding the nature of early Christianity: conflict versus consensus, legalism versus the "law-free" gospel, Jewish Christian particularism (of a supposedly narrow and introspective type) versus Pauline progressive Christian universalism, Protestantism versus Catholicism as the true heir of the apostolic gospel, and so forth.[7]

For Baur, John is the third "pillar-apostle" alongside Paul and Peter, a triumvirate of early Christian figures whose traditions were forged in a furnace of opposition and contradistinction.[8]

[6]   A seminal example of this approach is found in Ferdinand C. Baur, "Die Christuspartie in der korinthischen Gemeinde, der Gegensatz des petrinischen und paulinischen Christenthums in der ältesten Kirche, der Apostel Petrus in Rom," *TZT* 4 (1831): 61–206. For a discussion on Baur's treatment of Judaism and Paganism as antitheses that led to the synthesis of Christianity, see Anders Gerdmar, *Roots of Theological Anti-Semitism: German Biblical Interpretation and the Jews, from Herder and Semler to Kittel and Bultmann*, SJHC 20 (London: Brill, 2009), 97–120; idem, "Baur and the Creation of the Judaism-Hellenism Dichotomy," in *Ferdinand Christian Baur und die Geschichte des frühen Christentums*, ed. Martin Bauspieß, Christof Landmesser, and David Lincicum, WUNT 333 (Tübingen: Mohr Siebeck, 2014), 107–28. On the influence of Hegel on Baur, see Horton Harris, *The Tübingen School* (Oxford: Clarendon, 1975), 155–58, and Corneliu C. Simuţ, *F. C. Baur's Synthesis of Böhme and Hegel: Redefining Christian Theology as a Gnostic Philosophy of Religion*, PRWR 4 (Leiden: Brill, 2015), 231–61. Martin Hengel challenged this dichotomy in his (ET) *Judaism and Hellenism: Studies in Their Encounter in Palestine during the Early Hellenistic Period* (Philadelphia: Fortress, 1974 [1973]).

[7]   Markus Bockmuehl, *Simon Peter in Scripture and Memory: The New Testament Apostle in the Early Church* (Grand Rapids: Baker Academic, 2012), xv.

[8]   Ferdinand Christian Baur, *The Church History of the First Three Centuries*, trans. Allan Menzies, 2 vols., 3rd ed. (London: Williams and Norgate, 1878). See his section on "Johannine Christianity," 1:153–83. For Baur, John writes long after the "dialectical process" seen in Paul has resulted in the split between Christianity and Judaism (158).

Though conflict had an undeniable impact on Christian origins, New Testament scholarship is in many respects so beholden to the residual impulses of this history-of-religion paradigm that its assumptions may go undetected. Many would join Bockmuehl in hoping that "nineteenth-century polarities such as progress-through-conflict or structure-versus-freedom may give way to more nuanced accounts of unity and diversity in our understanding of the emergence of Christianity."[9] Though scholars today would quickly disavow many of the presuppositions of this dialectical approach (which would serve to vindicate and reinforce anti-Jewish sentiment in later decades),[10] the tendency to read difference as automatically combative remains in some corners a fixed anchor point in contemporary understandings of early Christianity.[11]

In a tour de force of enduring significance, Walter Bauer's *Orthodoxy and Heresy in Earliest Christianity* continues along related (though not parallel) lines.[12] For Bauer, "orthodoxy" is simply what catholic Christianity ascribed to that aligned with its own hard-won security in the second and third centuries. The radical diversity that thrived in the earliest generation of the

[9]   Bockmuehl, *Simon Peter*, xv–xvi.

[10]   See Jonathan Numada, "The Repetition of History? A Select Survey of Scholarly Understandings of Johannine Anti-Judaism from Baur until the End of the Weimar Republic," in *The Origins of John's Gospel*, ed. Stanley E. Porter and Hughson T. Ong, JOST 2 (Leiden: Brill, 2015), 261–84.

[11]   Though Judith Lieu notes that "the Christian movement of the second century and beyond has come to be understood within an overarching framework of 'diversity' rather than of a polarity between orthodoxy and heresy," the legacy of the diversity-as-adversity approach still has a foothold and dominates much of the secondary literature that serves as an entry point for students of John's Gospel. See Judith M. Lieu, "The Johannine Literature and the Canon," in *The Oxford Handbook of Johannine Studies*, ed. Judith M. Lieu and Martinus C. de Boer (Oxford: Oxford University Press, 2018), 396–415 (here 396).

[12]   Walter Bauer, *Orthodoxy and Heresy in Earliest Christianity*, ed. Robert A. Kraft and Gerhard Krodel, trans. the Philadelphia Seminar on Christian Origins (Philadelphia: Fortress, 1971 [1934]). Each section of this text has a different translator, and citations will include the name of the section translator in parentheses following the page number(s).

Christian movement was retrospectively judged on the basis of a Rome-centered authority that set the terms of orthodox and heretical. A battle of sorts was therefore underway, with the winner gaining the rights to set these terms. Bauer thus recounts the intellectual melees whose victors determined what was orthodox and what was not. Martial language abounds throughout this landmark work, featuring "ecclesiastical warriors on the battlefield"[13] whose hands would wield a stylus as though a sword: "The struggle between orthodox and heretics, insofar as it was fought in the literary arena, took the form of an effort to weaken the weaponry of the enemy as much as possible."[14]

The Bauer thesis has been challenged and modified by later generations of scholars.[15] For our purposes, though, it is worth taking a brief look at Bauer's reflections on the Johannine Epistles as an example of the rhetoric and assumptions of the conflict models that have set the (cynical) tone of discourse. Bauer's reading of John's Epistles is emblematic of the ongoing trend of overinterpreting the available evidence in the direction of conflict. On the departure of community members referred to in 1 John, Bauer writes, "We hear that it took place in such a way that the heretics left the community and made themselves independent so that they now viewed their orthodox fellow Christians with *hellish, fratricidal hatred* (*hollischem brudermörderischen Haß*): 'If they really had belonged to

13   Bauer, *Orthodoxy and Heresy* (trans. David Steinmetz), 142.
14   Bauer, *Orthodoxy and Heresy* (trans. Howard Bream and Robert L. Wilken), 160.
15   For a recent critique of Bauer's model and approach, see the detailed treatment in Christoph Markschies, *Christian Theology and Its Institutions: Prolegomena to a History of Early Christian Theology*, trans. Wayne Coppins, BMSEC (Waco, Tex.: Baylor University Press, 2015), 303–31. James D. G. Dunn, *Unity and Diversity in the New Testament: An Inquiry into the Character of Earliest Christianity*, 3rd ed. (London: SCM Press, 2010 [1997]), 1–8; Thomas A. Robinson, *The Bauer Thesis Examined: The Geography of Heresy in the Early Christian Church* (Lewiston, N.Y.: Edwin Mellen Press, 1988); Andreas J. Köstenberger and Michael J. Kruger, *The Heresy of Orthodoxy: How Contemporary Culture's Fascinations with Diversity Has Reshaped Our Understanding of Early Christianity* (Wheaton, Ill.: Crossway, 2010); and the essays in *Orthodoxy and Heresy in Early Christian Contexts: Reconsidering the Bauer Thesis*, ed. Paul A. Hartog (Eugene, Ore.: Pickwick, 2015).

our group, they would have remained with us' (2.19)."[16] To further illustrate the harsh Johannine intolerance of dissent, Bauer draws attention to

> the *anxious* (*angstvolle*) instruction in 2 John, which originated in similar conditions [to 1 John], that heretics should not be received into one's house, nor even be greeted (10 f.). Only by *strictest separation* (*strengster Absperrung*) from the heretics can salvation be expected; orthodoxy here appears to have been pushed completely onto the defensive, and to be *severely restricted* (*schwer gehemmt*) in its development. And perhaps we do more justice to the actual historical situation if we suppose that it was not the heretics who withdrew, but rather the orthodox who had retreated in order to preserve what could be protected from entanglement with "the world."[17]

Having elevated "history" as his chief aim and interpretative commitment,[18] Bauer was distrustful of the texts that came to be regarded as "orthodox," and thus fashioned historical contexts more compatible with his own bias against orthodox biases. In the passage above, he assumes that the so-called orthodox left the so-called heretics, not the other way around, as the Elder records it. And he

[16]   Bauer, *Orthodoxy and Heresy*, 92 (trans. Gerhard Krodel, emphases added). The German text is from Walter Bauer, *Rechtgläubigkeit und Ketzerei im ältesten Christentum*. 2. Auflage, BHT 10 (Tübingen: Mohr Siebeck, 1963 [1934]). Similarly, he writes in *Das Johannesevangelium* that "John reacts to the antipathy of the world outside with hot hatred. . . ." See Walter Bauer, *Das Johannesevangelium*, HNT 6/3 (Tübingen: J. C. B. Mohr, 1933 [1925]) (cited in Martin Hengel, *The Johannine Question*, trans. John Bowden [London: SCM Press, 1989], 173–74, n. 79).

[17]   Bauer, *Orthodoxy and Heresy*, 92 (trans. Gerhard Krodel, emphases added).

[18]   In his "*scientific approach* to history" (emphases original), Bauer resists evaluations grounded in later canonical or doctrinal positions (Bauer, *Orthodoxy and Heresy*, xxii [trans. Robert A. Kraft]). "Further, historical thinking that is worthy of this name refuses to employ here the correlatives 'true' and 'untrue,' 'bad' and 'good.' It is not easily convinced of the moral inferiority attributed to the heretics" (Bauer, *Orthodoxy and Heresy*, xxiv [trans. Kraft]). It is not a stretch to observe that his attempt to rebalance the scales in an idealized historical purism actually tipped the scales in the direction of doubting the claims of the orthodox and using qualifiers that certainly implied "untrue" and "bad."

situates 2 John in the same pugilistic scenario out of which 1 John arose. What is important to note here is the tendency to exaggerate the intensity of the conflict: there must have been frustration and pain over the exodus of certain group members, but the nurturing of "hellish, fratricidal hatred" can hardly be read out of the line Bauer cites (seemingly in support): "If they really had belonged to our group, they would have remained with us." And is the Elder truly "anxious" in 2 John? Similarly, is the best understanding of the conflict between the Elder and Diotrephes (which Bauer goes on to discuss) one in which the former is usurping the latter, reversing the claims in 3 John?[19]

Bauer's refusal to allow an uncritical ecclesiastical hermeneutic to set the terms of inquiry is commendable in many respects; yet reactions are at times overreactions. Additionally, the model of history he helped pioneer does not merely take the voices of early Christian orthodoxy with a grain of salt. Those voices, rather, are often rendered shrill, quivering with defensive anger, and thus easily dismissed by a later generation of scholars. Differences between early Christian groups are accented and, as in the very brief example above, the polemical language exaggerated.

John's Questionable Reception in the Second Century: Obscurity and Misappropriation as Signs of Sectarianism

Bauer points to a longstanding mood of ambivalence and at times antipathy toward the Fourth Gospel that seems to have persisted in second-century Rome, the geographical seat of ecclesiastical power (at least in the western part of the Empire).[20] Many historians of early Christianity would concur with the general idea that, during the second century, John's favor among Montanists and Valentinians tainted the Gospel's reputation and impeded its acceptance in the Roman West (until it was salvaged by Irenaeus from gnostic circles and used against them).[21] The sectarian hermeneutic

---

[19]   Bauer, *Orthodoxy and Heresy*, 93 (trans. Krodel).

[20]   Voiced most acutely by Gaius. See Bauer's discussion in *Orthodoxy and Heresy*, 206–12 (trans. Paul J. Achtemeier).

[21]   Bauer's ideas about John became more widely promoted in English-speaking scholarship through J. N. Sanders' brief monograph, *The Fourth*

in Johannine studies is surely influenced by this account of John's apprehensive uptake in the second century. The question lingers—is John a Gospel of mere provincial appeal (e.g., Asia), or the sort of text that holds special fascination primarily for fringe groups (e.g., Montanists and gnostics), and which could therefore only enter the mainstream by serving the utilitarian purpose of beating heretics at their own game?

The narrative of John's obscurity and heterodox appropriation in the second century has been rigorously challenged.[22] Though there is enough evidence to problematize any blanket conclusions, Bauer's observations nevertheless hold the day, and perhaps with good reason.[23] Rather than offering a detailed alternative account that produces a string of second-century texts citing or alluding to John, I simply raise a few questions about reception history: If a Christian composition is deemed authoritative and sacred by its use within the universal church, how much time should be allotted for that process of acceptance to become solidified? And should not some accommodation be made if a particular text needs more time than others because of its association with suspect interpretations? As Tatian, Irenaeus, and the compilers of the Muratorian Canon attest, John's Gospel belonged alongside Matthew, Mark, and Luke. Should John be viewed as a marginal work because its

---

Gospel in the Early Church: Its Origin & Influence on Christian Theology up to Irenaeus (Cambridge: Cambridge University Press, 1943).

[22] Significant studies include Charles E. Hill, The Johannine Corpus in the Early Church (Oxford: Oxford University Press, 2004); idem, "'The Orthodox Gospel': The Reception of John in the Great Church prior to Irenaeus," in The Legacy of John: Second-Century Reception of the Fourth Gospel, ed. Tuomas Rasimus, NovTSup 132 (Leiden: Brill, 2009), 233–300; Martin Hengel, Johannine Question, 1–23; Titus Nagel, Die Rezeption des Johannesevangeliums im 2. Jahrhundert: Studien zur vorirenäischen Aneignung und Auslegung des vierten Evangeliums in christlicher und christlich-gnostischer Literatur, ABG 2 (Leipzig: Evangelische Verlagsanstalt, 2000). For a modest proposal that Ignatius' ecclesial model is compatible with Johannine theology, see Andrew J. Byers, "Johannine Bishops? The Fourth Evangelist, John the Elder, and the Episcopal Ecclesiology of Ignatius of Antioch," NovT 60 (2018): 121–39.

[23] Francis Watson makes the case (which affirms Bauer) that Gaius of Rome rejected John's Gospel. See his Gospel Writing: A Canonical Perspective (Grand Rapids: Eerdmans, 2013), 473–93.

enthusiastic embrace in the West was temporarily slowed due to its diversity of readers? Ironically, Bauer's impressive study enjoyed a positive reception when it was published in 1934, but only in its own provincial milieu within continental higher criticism.[24] It was not until its publication in English almost forty years later that it became a work of enduring and widespread significance. The point: an initial span of obscurity is not a straightforward measure of a composition's worth any more than instant mass appeal is sign of a text's theological integrity. Relatedly, the appropriation of a text by readers outside the standard domains need not disqualify a work's validity and significance. Irenaeus did not find in John a Gospel that could be harmonized with Matthew, Mark, and Luke. It was serviceable in the diversity with which it enriched the plural Gospel witness to Jesus and broadened the horizons of orthodox Christology. Obscurity and heterodox appropriation need not brand John's Gospel as a backwards text from the Mediterranean backwaters easily dismissed as "sectarian."

When Historical Reconstructions Met Sociological Approaches: The Birth of a Community that Became a Sect

The "sectarian hermeneutic" influencing today's academic interpretation of John and his Epistles was born when "the Johannine community" met social historians and those working within the social-scientific paradigm. The *religionsgeschichtliche* conflict model and the related suspicions raised by the Fourth Gospel's amenability among heterodox groups were part of the gestation process. But when Louis Martyn, Raymond Brown, and others offered the world of biblical scholarship a believable profile of a social group behind the Johannine literature (with C. H. Dodd's pioneering work lingering in the background),[25] it was only a brief matter of time before

---

[24]   See appendix 2 ("The Reception of the Book"), revised and augmented by Robert A. Kraft in Bauer, *Orthodoxy and Heresy*, 286–316.
[25]   J. Louis Martyn, *History and Theology in the Fourth Gospel*, 3rd ed. (Louisville: Westminster John Knox, 2003); and Raymond E. Brown, *The Community of the Beloved Disciple: The Life, Loves, and Hates of an Individual Church in New Testament Times* (New York: Paulist Press, 1979), 158. C. H. Dodd's work on identifying a particular Johannine tradition served as a precursor to the enterprise. See especially C. H. Dodd, *Historical*

New Testament scholars would open the exciting and relatively new methodological toolbox of the social sciences.

Shaped by the values and disciplines emerging out of nineteenth-century Germany, the holy grail for many academic exegetes became the history behind the text.[26] Over time, as quests for the historical Jesus disillusioned their many inquisitors,[27] attention turned from the *Jesus* behind the text to the *communities* behind the text.[28] Mirror-reading the Gospels—with hopeful glimpses into the underlying traditions granted by form and redaction criticism—could furnish that most precious of historicist commodities: a *Sitz im Leben*.[29] Thus

---

Tradition in the Fourth Gospel (Cambridge: Cambridge University Press, 1963). See the discussions on Dodd's contribution to the discernment of historical realities behind the text in David K. Rensberger, *Johannine Faith and the Liberating Community* (Philadelphia: Westminster, 1988), 20–21, and in Tom Thatcher, "The Semiotics of History: C. H. Dodd on the Origins and Character of the Fourth Gospel," in *Engaging with C. H. Dodd on the Gospel of John: Sixty Years of Tradition and Interpretation*, ed. Tom Thatcher and Catrin H. Williams (Cambridge: Cambridge University Press, 2013), 1–28.

[26] See the helpful account of these developments by Johannes Zachhuber, "The Historical Turn," in *The Oxford Handbook of Nineteenth-Century Christian Thought*, ed. Joel D. S. Rasmussen, Judith Wolfe, and Johannes Zachhuber (Oxford: Oxford University Press, 2017), 53–71.

[27] See the sobering and yet moving account of this in Dale C. Allison, *The Historical Christ and the Theological Jesus* (Grand Rapids: Eerdmans, 2009).

[28] On this phenomenon in Gospel studies, see Francis Watson, "Toward a Literal Reading of the Gospels," in *The Gospels for All Christians: Rethinking the Gospel Audiences*, ed. Richard Bauckham (Grand Rapids: 1998), 195–217.

[29] The phrase *Sitz im Leben* was introduced into New Testament studies by Hermann Gunkel. For a recent discussion on Gunkel's legacy on contemporary uses (and misuses) of the phrase, see Samuel Byrskog, "A Century with the *Sitz im Leben*: From Form-Critical Setting to Gospel Community and Beyond," *ZNW* 98 (2001): 1–27. As Byrskog points out, the original idea of a *Sitz im Leben* involves the "formation and history of certain literary types and forms," and only later did it become a designation for the historical Gospel communities ("*Sitz im Leben*," 8). Classic works employing a form-critical analysis of the Gospels (with focus primarily directed to the Synoptics) are Karl Schmidt, *Der Rahmen der Geschichte Jesu* (Berlin: Trowittzsch & Sohn, 1919); Martin Dibelius, *Die Formgeschichte der synoptischen des Evangeliums* (Tübingen: J. C. B. Mohr, 1919), ET: *From Tradition to Gospel*, trans. Bertram Lee Woolf

began an immensely fecund era in biblical scholarship.[30] Though some grasped it with greater confidence in the historical task than others, the grail could now be held within the academic fingertips as the Matthean, Markan, Lukan, and Johannine communities were birthed out of the historical-critical imagination. Now that contexts were on hand, it was deemed that these texts could be read with greater clarity. This development unmistakably yielded insights, and the reconstructive historical work behind the prolific span of publications was not entirely fanciful. In fact, these conjectural reconstructions arose from a discipline sharpened and resourced by the discovery of new manuscripts and by the archaeological unlocking of dust-strewn secrets. But no reconstruction was historically verifiable, and it is not disrespectful of these august endeavors to note that a different arc was now added to the hermeneutical circle as contexts were constructed from texts by which those same texts were reread.

With specific Gospel communities now identified, comparative work could be done. Naturally, after unearthing an ancient historical community, the next historiographical step was to study it vis-à-vis other ancient social groups. Josephus' accounts of three αἱρέσεις—the schools or parties (often translated as "sects") of the Pharisees, Sadducees, and Essenes—offered opportunities for

---

(London: James Clarke, 1971); and Rudolf Bultmann, *Die Geschichte der synoptischen Tradition* (Göttingen: Vandenhoeck & Ruprecht, 1921), ET: *The History of the Synoptic Tradition*, trans. John Marsh, rev. ed. (Oxford: Blackwell, 1972). Pioneering redaction-critical works include Günther Bornkamm, Gerhard Barth, and Heinz Joachim Held, *Tradition and Interpretation in Matthew*, trans. Percy Scott, 2nd and enlarged ed. (London: SCM Press, 1982); Hans Conzelmann, *The Theology of St. Luke*, trans. Geoffrey Buswell (New York: Harper & Brothers, 1960); and Willi Marxsen, *Mark the Evangelist: Studies on the Redactional History of the Gospel*, trans. James Boyce, Donald Juel, and William Poehlmann (Nashville: Abingdon, 1969). On their works and influence, see the discussion in Byrskog, "*Sitz im Leben*," 10–11.

[30] After writing this chapter, I found the helpful articles by Wally Cirafesi to which the reader is directed for more details on the history of scholarship's construction of Johannine histories: Wally W. Cirafesi, "The Johannine Community Hypothesis (1868–Present): Past and Present Approaches and a New Way Forward," *CurBR* 12 (2014): 173–93; idem, "The 'Johannine Community' in (More) Current Research: A Critical Appraisal of Recent Methods and Models," *Neot* 48 (2014): 341–64.

drawing parallels or noting contrasts.[31] In Johannine studies, focus
was placed primarily on the Essenes. Since they are described not
only in terms of their ideas but also in terms of their collective lives
in local community contexts, this social group provided much
promise in the program of understanding the Johannine community.[32] From the accounts given by Josephus and Philo, the Essenes
seemed widely integrated within the cultural milieu of ancient Palestine. Local instantiations were networked with others throughout the region. Yet—oddly, in my view—it is not this networked
and integrated expression of Essene communal life that informed
the wider comparative study with John. Crucially, *it is the quasi-
monastic life of those Essenes centered at Qumran that attracted the
most attention.* Reading the Fourth Gospel alongside the Qumran
texts has helpfully allowed scholars to confirm that John was a Jewish writer; an arguably less helpful result of this comparative analysis is that the insular Qumran community seems to have become
a social model whose contours were implicitly mapped onto the
scholarly construct of the "Johannine community."[33]

[31] Josephus, *Ant.* 13.171–172; *J.W.* 2.119–164. As Wayne Meeks
points out, the term αἵρεσις is used by Luke to refer to the Sadducees, Pharisees, and the early Christian group (Acts 5:17; 15:5; 26:5; 24:5, 14; 28:22).
See his discussion on the term in Wayne A. Meeks, "Breaking Away: Three
New Testament Pictures of Christianity's Separation from the Jewish Communities," in *"To See Ourselves as Others See Us": Christians, Jews, "Others"
in Late Antiquity,* ed. Jacob Neusner and Ernest S. Frerichs (Chico, Calif.:
Scholars Press, 1985), 93–115 (here 93–94). The term is used negatively in
1 Cor 11:19; Gal 5:20; 2 Pet 2:1.
[32] Philo and Josephus both describe the Essenes as living in villages
and towns throughout Judea—Josephus, *J.W.* 2.124–127; Philo, *Hypoth.*
11.1; *Prob.* 76. It is the more sectarian Qumran community that scholars
tend to see as a mirror of the Johannine community. See, e.g., Philip F.
Esler's essay "Introverted Sectarianism at Qumran and in the Johannine
Community," in his *The First Christians in Their Social Worlds: Social-
Scientific Approaches to New Testament Interpretation* (London: Routledge,
1994), 70–91.
[33] A recent example of this approach is Stephen E. Witmer,
"Approaches to Scripture in the Fourth Gospel and the Qumran Pesharim,"
NovT 48 (2006): 313–28. A helpful volume on this line research is Mary
L. Coloe and Tom Thatcher, eds., *John, Qumran, and the Dead Sea Scrolls:
Sixty Years of Discovery and Debate,* SBLEJL 32 (Atlanta: SBL Press, 2011);

Thanks particularly to Martyn and Brown, Johannine scholars who felt long left on the margins of the historical Jesus quests finally had a history to work with. With an identifiable "Johannine community" in place, it was simply a matter of time before the models arising in sociology and cultural anthropology would be plied by interpreters of John's Gospel and Epistles.[34] Since the community was envisaged as similar to Qumran's and portrayed as deviant in some way from a larger social entity (generally understood in the reconstructions as a wider Jewish milieu in the late first century), historians brought into Johannine scholarship sociology's understanding of *sects*. Though the trajectories had been previously established by Max Weber, Ernst Troeltsch, and others,[35] it

---

but see Richard Bauckham's cogent arguments against drawing parallels between the Johannine literature and the Qumran texts in "The Qumran Community and the Gospel of John," in his *The Testimony of the Beloved Disciple: Narrative, History, and Theology in the Gospel of John* (Grand Rapids: Baker Academic, 2007), 125–36.

[34]   Though my focus is on Martyn and Brown due to their comparative influence in shaping the conversations, several other writers produced reconstructed models of Johannine Christianity at around the same time. See, e.g, Oscar Cullmann, *The Johannine Circle: Its Place in Judaism, Among the Disciples of Jesus and in Early Christianity; A Study in the Origin of John's Gospel*, trans. John Bowden (London: SCM Press, 1976 [1975]); R. Alan Culpepper, *The Johannine School: An Evaluation of the Johannine School Hypothesis Based on an Investigation of the Nature of Ancient Schools* (Missoula, Mont.: Scholars Press, 1975); Klaus Wengst, *Bedrängte Gemeinde und verherrlichter Christus: Der historische Ort des Johannesevangeliums als Schlüssel zu seiner Interpretation*, 2nd ed., Biblisch-Theologische Studien 5 (Neukirchen-Vluyn: Neukirchener, 1983).

[35]   Max Weber and Ernst Troeltsch pioneered sociological approaches to religious groups, with "church" and "sect" becoming antithetical nodes within an emerging paradigm. For Weber, see the short, translated essay "'Churches' and 'Sects' in North America: An Ecclesiastical and Sociopolitical Sketch" in Max Weber, *The Protestant Work Ethic and the "Spirit" of Capitalism and Other Writings*, trans. Peter Baehr and Gordon C. Wells (New York: Penguin, 2002), 203–220; on Troeltsch, see his *Die Soziallehren der christlichen Kirchen und Gruppen*; ET: *The Social Teaching of the Christian Churches*, 2 vols., Library of Theological Ethics (Louisville: Westminster John Knox Press, 2009/2010 [1931, 1911]); a helpful sketch of twentieth-century developments can be found in Richard H. Roberts, "Theology and the Social Sciences," in *The Modern Theologians: An*

is the wedding of sociological and very soon afterwards social-scientific criticism to the scholarly exercise of reconstructing the Johannine community that has locked into place the "sectarian hermeneutic," a default lens for understanding the Gospels and letters of John.

It seems that Wayne Meeks made the initial move.[36] Though Raymond Brown resisted the language of "sect" in his portraiture of the Johannine community,[37] Meeks' 1972 article seems to have standardized the phrase "Johannine sectarianism" in scholarly idiom.[38] His focus was on the "uniqueness of the Fourth Gospel." Concentrating on John's mythical language, particularly the descent-ascent motif, Meeks criticized prior studies for falling short in the interpretative task and suggested "we may find a clue to the proper understanding" of John's awkward language "in the attempt of some contemporary anthropologists to get at the function of myths in the societies that create them."[39] His use of sociological approaches assumed a Johannine community. It also assumed a very particular profile for that community:

Introduction to Christian Theology in the Twentieth Century, ed. David F. Ford, 2nd ed. (Oxford: Blackwell, 1997), 704–19. It is also worth noting once more the influence of Bryan R. Wilson's *Magic and the Millennium: A Sociological Study of Religious Movements of Protest among Tribal and Third-World People* (New York: Harper & Row, 1973).

[36]   Wayne A. Meeks makes clear in "The Man from Heaven in Johannine Sectarianism," *JBL* 91, no. 1 (1972): 44–72 (here 194) that he is relying not on the standard idea of "sect" found in the sociology of religion. He is more interested in the sociology of knowledge and the insights offered by Peter Berger and Thomas Luckmann, *The Social Construction of Reality: A Treatise in the Sociology of Knowledge* (New York: Doubleday, 1967). For a discussion on this approach, see Ruth Sheridan, "Johannine Sectarianism: A Category Now Defunct?" in *The Origins of John's Gospel*, ed. Stanley E. Porter and Hughson T. Ong, vol. 2 of *Johannine Studies*, ed. Stanley E. Porter (Leiden: Brill, 2015), 142–66 (esp. 161–63). For an incisive overview of Meeks' article, particularly on its discussions of sociolinguistics, see Lamb, *Text, Context, and the Johannine Community*, 104–10.

[37]   Brown, *Community of the Beloved Disciple*, 7, 14–17; and "'Other Sheep Not of the This Fold': The Johannine Perspective on Christian Diversity the Late First Century," *JBL* 97, no. 1 (1978): 5–22.

[38]   Meeks, "Man from Heaven."

[39]   Meeks, "Man from Heaven," 48.

The group had to distinguish itself over against the sect of John the Baptist and even more passionately over against a rather strong Jewish community, with which highly ambivalent relationships had existed. It suffered defections, conflicts of leadership, schisms. I shall argue that one function of the "symbolic universe" communicated in this remarkable body of literature was to make sense of all these aspects of the group's history.[40]

The reference to "defections, conflicts of leadership, schisms" betrays the lasting impact of dialectical models that took any possible reference to behind-the-scenes tension in John and inflated them to their fullest potential. With historical reconstructions of the Johannine community readily on hand, Meeks' approach was not an unnatural one to make. And whereas the arrival on the scene of Jesus as "the Stranger *par excellence*"[41] might be interpreted as a means of divine outreach that establishes a hospitable community open to the world and to the other, the ascent/descent of the Stranger actually serves only to further estrange the few who embrace him:

> Many well-known commentaries, particularly those in English, treat the descent/ascent motif in John, if they discuss it at all, as a symbol of unity. It is supposed to represent the union of heaven and earth, the spiritual and the physical, eternity and history, God and man. Our analysis of the function of this motif and its related components within the literary structure of the Gospel suggests an interpretation diametrically opposed: in every instance the motif points to contrast, foreignness, division, judgment. Only within that dominant structure of estrangement and distance is developed the counterpoint of unity—between God and Christ, between God, Christ, and the small group of the faithful.[42]

For Meeks, John could in no way have been a "missionary tract, for we may imagine that only a very rare outsider would get past the barrier of its closed metaphorical system. It is a book for

---

[40] Meeks, "Man from Heaven," 49–50.
[41] Meeks, "Man from Heaven," 50.
[42] Meeks, "Man from Heaven," 66–67.

insiders" serving "to provide a reinforcement for the community's social identity, which appears to have been largely negative. It provided a symbolic universe which gave religious legitimacy, a theodicy, to the group's actual isolation from the larger society."[43] Though many interpreters have noted that John's symbolic diction would have had considerable purchase in both Jewish and Greco-Roman contexts,[44] Meeks reads it as the obtuse idiom of an insider language.

Though something of a debate persists between social historians like Meeks and those employing the more formal models of social-scientific criticism,[45] Bruce Malina's preference for "antisociety" over "sect" still casts John in a sectarian mold (even if not in a technical sense). In the commentary he has written with Richard Rohrbaugh, the Johannine group speaks in the

[43]   Meeks, "Man from Heaven," 70.

[44]   See C. H. Dodd, *The Interpretation of the Fourth Gospel* (Cambridge: Cambridge University Press, 1953); and more recently Stephen C. Barton, "Can We Identify the Gospel Audiences?" in *The Gospels for All Christians: Rethinking the Gospel Audiences*, ed. Richard Bauckham (Grand Rapids: Eerdmans, 1998), 192; Barton, "Early Christianity and the Sociology of the Sect," in *The Open Text: New Directions for Biblical Studies?* ed. Francis Watson (London: SCM Press, 1993), 140–62 (esp. 148); John C. Painter, "Johannine Symbols: A Case Study in Epistemology," *JTSA* 27 (1979): 26–41; Alexander Jensen, *John's Gospel as Witness: The Development of the Early Christian Language of Faith* (Aldershot: Ashgate, 2004); Carlos Raúl Sosa Siliezar, *Savior of the World: A Theology of the Universal Gospel* (Waco, Tex.: Baylor University Press, 2019), 8; and Lamb, *Text, Context, and the Johannine Community*.

[45]   Philip A. Harland helpfully distinguishes between NT scholars who have taken a more formal approach in applying the available models ("social scientists") and those who take more eclectic, selective approaches ("social historians"). See his *Dynamics of Identity in the World of the Early Christians: Associations, Judeans, and Cultural Minorities* (London: T&T Clark, 2009), 4–5. The latter have been (sometimes severely) criticized by the former. For a defense of the more *ad hoc* application of social-scientific ideas and methods to New Testament studies, see David G. Horrell, "Whither Social-Scientific Approaches to New Testament Interpretation? Reflections on Contested Methodologies and the Future," in *After the First Urban Christians: The Social-Scientific Study of Pauline Christianity Twenty-Five Years Later*, ed. Todd D. Still and David G. Horrell (London: T&T Clark, 2009), 6–20.

"antilanguage"[46] of this antisociety and finds its modern parallels in "deviants" such as "criminals, sinners, unbelievers, apostates, prisoners, or mental patients," as well as "prison inmates and members of street gangs, the drug culture, the underworld, new religious cults, and underground political groups."[47] The Gospel and Epistles of John certainly envision a mode of life different from the surrounding social contexts. Whatever "Johannine Christianity" is, it certainly hopes to advance a counterintuitive message of cosmic import. Like other early Christian voices, John's is one from the margins. The question is whether or not that voice was hospitable, outward-oriented, and missional, or if it was instead suspicious, inward-focused, and self-enclosed. Though David Lamb points out that an "antilanguage" need not correspond to an antisociety in the current field of sociolinguistics,[48] the radicalizing of this hypothetical community through social-scientific methodologies into a deviant group (whether an "antisociety" or a "sect") has taken root.[49]

---

[46] Bruce J. Malina, *The Gospel of John in Sociolinguistic Perspective*, 48th Colloquy of the Center for Hermeneutical Studies (Berkley, Calif.: Center for Hermeneutical Studies, 1985); "John's: The Maverick Christian Group: The Evidence of Sociolinguistics," *BThB* 24 (1994): 167–82. Malina draws on Michael A. K. Halliday's concept of antilanguage. See Halliday's *Language as Social Semiotic: The Social Interpretation of Meaning* (London: Arnold, 1978). Again, see Lamb's overview and assessment of Malina's claims in *Text, Context, and the Johannine Community*, 113–22.

[47] Bruce J. Malina and Richard L. Rohrbauch, *Social-Science Commentary on the Gospel of John* (Minneapolis: Fortress, 1998), 9–10.

[48] According to Lamb, Halliday's idea of "antilanguage" "has not been widely adopted in the field of sociolinguistics." Once Malina brought the concept into Johannine studies, however, it has persisted. See Lamb, *Text, Context, and the Johannine Community*, 115–16.

[49] After Meeks' article, Robin Scruggs wrote an influential piece arguing that all early Christian groups were sectarian; see Robin Scruggs, "The Earliest Christian Communities as Sectarian Movement," in *Christianity, Judaism and Other Greco-Roman Cults: Studies for Morton Smith at Sixty*, ed. Jacob Neusner, SJLA 12 (Leiden: Brill, 1975), 2:1–23. As a scarce sampling of scholarship viewing the Johannine literature as sectarian, see (in addition to sources already cited in this chapter) Fernando F. Segovia, "The Love and Hatred of Jesus and Johannine Sectarianism," *CBQ* 43, no. 2 (1981): 258–72; Jerome H. Neyrey, *An Ideology of Revolt: John's Christology in Social-Science Perspective* (Philadelphia:

There is a manifest pattern in the interpretive logic. John's Gospel is recognized as unique.[50] That uniqueness is then historicized into the construct of a unique community. Given John's polemics and perceived dualism, that unique community is then understood as defensive and antagonistic. Its creative use of language becomes sectarian rhetoric or an antilanguage. Difference persists, yet in the form of conflict. Johannine *diversity* within early Judaism and early Christianity thus becomes Johannine *enmity* towards them both. And since the humanities are well equipped to analyze rogue social groups through the sociology of the sect or through the social-scientific study of deviance, the "anti-" nature of Johannine Christianity becomes reinforced across multiple fields of study.

Historical reconstructions, the sociology of religion, and social-scientific approaches are bearing much exegetical fruit, and I will be drawing on their insights in the following chapters. The first approach may be easily criticized by later generations of scholars skeptical of reconstructive work and more committed to reader-oriented or narrative-critical readings uninterested in potential historical realities amorphously attached to literary strata.[51] Both Brown and Martyn, however, were humble about their bold visions of Johannine history. Brown pointed out that "my reconstruction claims at most probability; and if sixty percent of my detective work is accepted, I shall be happy indeed."[52] With similar restraint, Martyn suggested "it would be a valuable practice for the historian to

---

Fortress, 1988); Rensberger, *Johannine Faith*; "Sectarianism and Theological Interpretation in John," in *"What Is John?"* vol. 2: *Literary and Social Readings of the Fourth Gospel*, ed. Fernando F. Segovia, SBLSymS 7 (Atlanta: SBL Press, 1998), 139–56; Joan Cecilia Campbell, *Kinship Relations in the Gospel of John*, CBQMS 42 (Washington, D.C.: Catholic Biblical Association of America, 2007). For interesting challenges that retain an understanding of Johannine uniqueness but cut a different path, see Fuglseth, *Johannine Sectarianism* and Raimo Hakola, *Reconsidering Johannine Christianity: A Social Identity Approach*, BibleWorld (London: Routledge, 2015).

[50]   "The uniqueness of the Fourth Gospel in early Christian literature . . ." is how Meeks opens "Man from Heaven," 44.

[51]   Ruth Sheridan, "Identity, Alterity, and the Gospel of John," *BibInt* 22 (2014): 188–209 (here 203).

[52]   Brown, *Community of the Beloved Disciple*, 7.

rise each morning saying to himself, three times and slowly with emphasis, 'I do not know.'"[53] I accept a less precise, general version of the Martyn-Brown account of the Fourth Gospel's *Sitz im Leben*, though I will refer more to a "Johannine network" than a "Johannine community." I am not convinced that the language of being put out of the synagogue (ἀποσυνάγωγος) in John 9:22, 12:42, and 16:2 affords a direct glimpse into the social history, but I think it provisions the reader with a sense of the pathos out of which the Johannine idea of "othering" emerges. Along with embracing certain elements of the history-of-the-community approach, I am also keen to learn from social historians. I remember the thrill of reading Wayne Meeks' *The Firt Urban Christians* for the first time and I regularly incorporate sociological insights in my seminary teaching.[54] As for the social-scientific angles, my reading of John's portrayal of "the Jews" finds parallels in an essay by Philip Esler, a leading figure in that methodological orientation to biblical texts. Though my own hermeneutical commitments align more closely with what has come to be known as theological interpretation, I am pleased to coordinate the disciplines of theology and the social sciences in my readings of the New Testament.[55] It is only responsible to acknowledge, however, the limitations of both mirror-reading and of New Testament scholarship's application of the methodological resources from relevant fields.

Several scholars have leveled cautionary or even incisive critiques of the historical, sociological, and social-scientific studies leading to a sectarian reading of the Gospels.[56] On this point, Francis Moloney writes,

[53] Martyn, *History and Theology in the Fourth Gospel*, 146.

[54] Wayne A. Meeks, *The First Urban Christians: The Social World of the Apostle Paul*, 2nd ed. (New Haven, Conn.: Yale University Press, 2003 [1983]).

[55] Though I am largely sympathetic with John Milbank's dichotomizing of the two disciplines, I tend toward a more eclectic appropriation from varying angles. See John Milbank, *Theology and Social Theory: Beyond Secular Reasoning*, 2nd ed. (Oxford: Blackwell, 2006 [1990]).

[56] E.g., see Timothy J. M. Ling, *The Judaean Poor in the Fourth Gospel*, SNTSMS 136 (Cambridge: Cambridge University Press, 2009) (though Ling utilizes social-scientific approaches to challenge sectarian readings); Luke T. Johnson, "On Finding the Lukan Community: A Cautious Cautionary Essay," in *Society for Biblical Literature 1979 Seminar Papers*, ed.

There is a sense of arrogance in the claim that for two thousand years the Gospel of John has enjoyed favor and had influence because it has been mistreated.... At last, it appears, with the arrival of a social science reading of the text, true light has dawned.[57]

Similarly, Eyal Regev has lodged a stinging critique of the way many New Testament scholars have worked with the sociology of the sect in the study of Christian origins. The claim that early Christian groups, including the so-called Johannine community, were sectarians is often premised on a misunderstanding of the sociological definition of "sect" or on a selective or misapplied use of the models.[58] In one of the most comprehensive sociological studies of Johannine Christiantity, Kåro Fuglseth concludes that the Gospel of John simply does not evidence a "sect."[59] His terminological preference for "cult" accords well with the work of prominent sociologists Rodney Stark and William Bainbridge, but the degree to which their categories suffice for early Christian group identity is not without its flaws.[60] It also seems important to note that the social-scientific models applied to the (hypothetically reconstructed) Gospel communities have largely emerged out of modern-day treatments of actual social groups whose languages can be heard, ideas

---

Paul J. Achtemeier (Missoula, Mont.: Scholars Press, 1979), 87–100; Stanley K. Stowers, "The Social Sciences and the Study of Early Christianity," *Approaches to Ancient Judaism: Theory and Practice*, ed. W. S. Green, vol. 5 (Missoula, Mont.: Scholars Press, 1985), 5:149–81; Richard Bauckham, ed., *The Gospels for All Christians: Rethinking the Gospel Audiences* (Grand Rapids: Eerdmans, 1998); Hugo Méndez, "Did the Johannine Community Exist?" *JSNT* 42, no. 3 (2020): 350–74.

[57] Francis J. Moloney, *Love in the Gospel of John: An Exegetical, Theological, and Literary Study* (Grand Rapids: Baker Academic, 2013), 210, n. 45 (cited in Christopher W. Skinner, "Introduction: [How] Can We Talk About Johannine Ethics? Looking Back and Moving Forward," in *Johannine Ethics: The Moral World of the Gospel and Epistles of John*, ed. Christopher W. Skinner and Sherri Brown [Minneapolis: Fortress, 2017], xvii–xxxvi [here xxix, n. 43]).

[58] Eyal Regev, "Were the Early Christians Sectarians?" *JBL* 130, no. 4 (2011): 771–93.

[59] Fuglseth, *Johannine Sectarianism*.

[60] See the critique by Sheridan, "Johannine Sectarianism." For Stark and Bainbridge, see Rodney Stark and William S. Bainbridge, *A Theory of Religion* (New Brunswick, N.J.: Rutgers University Press, 1996 [1987]).

discussed, and practices observed. A glaring methodological challenge in applying these models to early Christians affiliated with the Gospel narratives is that we have access only to their texts (which perhaps explains the impulse to focus on John's allegedly sectarian *language*).[61] It is true that these ancient narratives speak of practices and promote a vision for group identity, but in Gospel studies, any social-scientific methodology must be applied to a *reconstructed* group, not to a live collective subject. A Gospel community is thus an imagined entity for the sake of analysis; since analytical work is tidier with a subject group that is well-defined with distinct boundaries, the models are more applicable if the reconstructed Gospel communities are envisaged as "enclosed, particular, and even 'sectarian.'"[62]

Some New Testament texts certainly lend themselves to a more straightforward process of reconstructing context (e.g., 1 and 2 Cor). Less conducive for such an enterprise is narrative material—though stories are powerful means of promoting visions for group identity,[63] excavating through the prose to access their provenance with verifiable accuracy is ultimately impossible. Among the canonical Gospels, however, one comes with an epistolary database. Luke may have produced a second volume, but John is the only evangelist whose Jesus-story is accompanied within the canon with letters bearing his name. Though the relationship between the Johannine Epistles and Gospel is regularly debated, their shared namesake invites, perhaps even demands, the work of historical reconstruction though some (cautious)

[61]   Though Bruce Malina aptly notes that many of the social-scientific approaches applied in New Testament study have been tested on more germane agricultural and peasant contexts. See Bruce J. Malina, "Rhetorical Criticism and Social-Scientific Criticism: Why Won't Romanticism Leave Us Alone?" in *The Social World of the New Testament: Insights and Models*, ed. Jerome H. Neyrey and Eric C. Stewart (Peabody, Mass.: Hendrickson, 2008), 5–21 (esp. 7–8).

[62]   Klink, *Sheep of the Fold*, 54.

[63]   Coleman A. Baker, "A Narrative-Identity Model for Biblical Interpretation: The Role of Memory and Narrative in Social Identity Formation," in *T&T Clark Handbook to Social Identity in the New Testament*, ed. J. Brian Tucker and Coleman A. Baker (London: T&T Clark, 2014), 105–18.

form of mirror-reading (though Judith Lieu would remind us that 1 John, "more than any other NT letter, lacks any explicit identifiers"[64]). In defending the use of social-scientific methods in New Testament studies, Esler helpfully notes that "no ontological status is accorded to the models; they are seen merely as heuristic tools."[65] While acknowledging that these models are infused with modernist presuppositions, he contends that these are "essential if we are to address cultural experience different from our own in terms we can comprehend."[66]

Esler's points are well made, and I am much less negative than some on the use of sociological and social-scientific studies in Gospel research. Even so, the sectarian hermeneutic their tools and perceptions have helped prop up dominates the field inordinately, and thus deserves more rigorous scrutiny.

Summary and Prospect

I have offered a sweeping account of how John is viewed as an ancient voice consciously promoting an "us" and a "them." That account began with the dialectical approach to history that too readily translates diversity into an adversity to be overcome, thus constructing the frames of Gospel reading with the idea that difference inherently leads to conflict. With the historical turn that rightly longed for a provenance behind each ancient text, scholars eventually pried and prodded the canonical Gospels until they yielded something of a history, or at least a history of the (undoubtedly erudite) scholarly imagination. With the Gospel "communities" accessed through these reconstructions, models from the social sciences could then be applied. Since these Gospel communities were envisioned as distinct groups intent on self-preservation, the methodologies most often applied were those that dealt with sects. Though the term "sect" certainly bears investigative promise

---

[64]   Judith M. Lieu, "Us or You? Persuasion and Identity in 1 John," *JBL* 127, no. 4 (2008): 805–19 (here 805).

[65]   Philip F. Esler, "Introduction: Models, Context, and Kerygma in New Testament Interpretation," in *Modelling Early Christianity: Social-Scientific Studies of the New Testament in Its Context*, ed. Philip F. Esler (London: Routledge, 1995), 1–20 (here 7).

[66]   Esler, "Introduction," 7.

in classifying socio-historical realities underlying the Johannine literature, it unavoidably conjures "some kind of deviant, separatist or segregated group, often with negative connotations."[67] We must employ the language of our own day in studying early Christian groups, and John certainly pictures a community that is distinguished from "the world" and those "others" aligned with it. But the "negative connotations" of the language employed undermine and obscure the Johannine vision of a missional otherness and a participatory—and thus inclusive—ecclesiology.

To clarify, my concern is not with historical reconstructions or the social sciences per se. What I seek to challenge is the interpretative frame, the "sectarian hermeneutic," that has arisen from their applications and reads Johannine Christianity as antagonistic, socially insular, and ideologically hermetic. The task now turns from identifying hermeneutical trends contributing to this reading frame to the work of challenging their axiomatic power through exegesis. Can a close reading of John's treatment of "others" yield alternative interpretations?

[67] Fuglseth, *Johannine Sectarianism*, 45.

2

John and Other Jews

Competing Visions of "Israel"

John's initial presentation of Christology is abstract. In his Prologue's opening, the introductory terminology of "Logos," "God," "Life," and "Light" obtains a breadth of potential meanings. The cost borne for such widespread appeal is ambiguity. As ink spills from the Johannine pen, however, these inscrutable categorizations accrue specificity with the provision of further details. All christological abstraction ends in 1:11-14 when the "true light" enters a specific territorial domain ("his own place [τὰ ἴδια]") and a particular social context ("his own people [οἱ ἴδιοι]"). This Logos inhabits both spheres as an embodied personage: Jesus Christ. As the narrative soon makes explicit, this region and this people are *Jewish*. And when the Logos becomes flesh, it is *Jewish* flesh.

So why does Jesus, the Word made Jewish flesh, call "the Jews" the offspring of the devil?[1]

---

[1]   This chapter is a modified and expanded version of my paper "Theosis and 'the Jews': Divine and Ethnic Identity in the Fourth Gospel," delivered as the Tyndale Fellowship Conference New Testament Lecture at Tyndale House, Cambridge (June 27, 2018). I am grateful to Ian Paul for extending the invitation, and to Dirk Jongkind for allowing me to publish this chapter here.

Post-*Shoah* Johannine scholarship has struggled to come to exegetical grips with a Christian canonical text in which Jews are referred to as the children of personified evil.[2] The Fourth Gospel has served as a textual trove from which patristic theologians formulated Trinitarian creeds, and from which Christendom preachers proclaimed salvation from European pulpits, yet also a source from which Nazi propagandists promoted a campaign of genocide.[3] Arguably the most important christological work from early Christianity, John's Gospel is a civilization-shaping text. Its portrayal of "the Jews" has been understood, however, as a vilification of an ethnic group in such a way that some elements of Western civilization have been shaped and reshaped by this text in certain respects that are regrettable and even appalling. As noted, John's questionable reception began early, falling into the hermeneutical hands of Valentinian gnostics and Montanists not long after it was penned. Perhaps it should come as no surprise that this beloved Gospel has been embraced in recent times by even more dangerous interpretive communities, featuring in the propaganda of the Third Reich in the twentieth century and on neo-Nazi websites in the twenty-first century.[4]

---

[2]   I appreciate Ruth Sheridan's approach in resisting to draw "a straight line through history from the Gospel of John to the Shoah (the 'Holocaust')" but aiming rather "to illustrate the important connections among literature, empathy, the psyche, and ideology in creating and sustaining a vision of the 'other' in cultural history." From Ruth Sheridan, "Identity, Alterity, and the Gospel of John," *BibInt* 22 (2014): 188–209 (here 208).

[3]   See Anders Gerdmar, *Roots of Theological Anti-Semitism: German Biblical Interpretation and the Jews, from Herder and Semler to Kittel and Bultmann*, SJHC 20 (London: Brill, 2009), 391–95, 556–59; Susannah Heschel provides an overview of the dejudaizing of Jesus in German theology in *The Aryan Jesus: Christian Theologians and the Bible in Nazi Germany* (Princeton: Princeton University Press, 2008); see also the brief discussions of John's legacy of anti-Jewish interpretation in Tobias Nicklas, "Creating the Other: The 'Jews' in the Gospel of John: Past and Future Lines of Scholarship," in *Perceiving the Other in Ancient Judaism and Early Christianity*, ed. Michal Bar-Asher Siegal, Wolfgang Grünstädl, and Matthew Thiessen, WUNT 1/394 (Tübingen: Mohr Siebeck, 2017), 49–66.

[4]   Amy-Jill Levine, "Reflections on Reflections: Jesus, Judaism, and Jewish-Christian Relations," *SCJR* 8 (2013): 1–13 (here 11).

The accusation in John 8:44, "you are of [your] father, the devil," is not leveled against Jewish interlocutors by some dismissible minor character but by Jesus, the story's protagonist, a divine figure within the Trinitarian divine identity this Gospel prompted later readers to formulate, and as such the object of Christian worship. The welcome rise in Jewish scholarship on the New Testament and the sobering effects of retrospective reflection on the horrors of Nazi Europe have, rightfully, placed the Fourth Evangelist's depiction of "the Jews" at center stage in scholarly dialogue.

Does John so negatively "other" the ethnic group of the Jews that the darkest chapters of his Gospel's reception history are actually faithful to the text?

Seeking to Resolve the "Virtually Irresolvable Question"

I side with the majority of Johannine scholars who view the Fourth Gospel as a Jewish text that has emerged from some inter-Jewish conflict.[5] If an act of binary othering is underway, it is within the confines of shared ethnic boundaries. Tom Thatcher refers to this Jewish evangelist's composition of an early Jewish text as a "paradox" since "the Fourth Gospel seems to be at once both *the most Jewish* and *the most anti-Jewish* of the gospels."[6] At the heart of the divisive and at times incendiary exegetical enterprise of exploring John's use of the designation Ἰουδαῖοι is a question raised by Martinus C. de Boer and identified as a "virtually irresolvable question" by the editors of the influential volume *Anti-Judaism and the Fourth Gospel*. If John is a Jewish writer producing a self-consciously Jewish text, the "irresolvable question" is this: Why is it that, in "an inner-Jewish conflict, one side (the Fourth Evangelist) calls the other

---

[5]   Hence the chapter title, "John and Other Jews."
[6]   Tom Thatcher, "John and the Jews: Recent Research and Future Questions," in *John and Judaism: A Contested Relationship in Context*, ed. R. Alan Culpepper and Paul N. Anderson, RBS 87 (Atlanta: SBL Press, 2017), 3–38 (here 6; emphases original). The same provocative statement has been made by C. K. Barrett, *The Gospel of John and Judaism*, trans. D. Moody Smith (Philadelphia: Fortress, 1975 [1970]), 71, and by Wayne A. Meeks, "'Am I a Jew?' Johannine Christianity and Judaism," in *Christianity, Judaism and other Greco-Roman Cults: Studies for Morton Smith at Sixty*, ed. J. Neusner (Leiden: Brill, 1975), 172.

side (the opponents of the Johannine community) 'the Jews'"?[7] As de Boer himself phrases it, "Why does John refer to those who are hostile to Jesus and his disciples as 'the Jews,' with the potentially misleading implication that Jesus himself and his (initial) disciples, as well as the Gospel's writer(s) and original, intended readers, were not themselves Jews?"[8]

I address this "virtually irresolvable question" by proposing that John's polemical references to οἱ Ἰουδαῖοι are part of a rhetorical program to delegitimate not Jewish ethnicity, *but any attempt to employ ethnic particulars as a soteriological advantage or an ecclesiological prerequisite.* The Fourth Evangelist de-ethnicizes salvation and deracializes group identity by envisioning the people of God as divine "children" who are generated "from above." As already acknowledged, negative alterity most certainly features in Johannine thought. But if John's polemic against οἱ Ἰουδαῖοι is a program of othering, it is also part of a larger program of *de*-othering in which he seeks to dissolve the wall erected by an ethnic boundary line, not for the purpose of denigrating ethnic identity but in order to make the identity of Johannine "Israel" more inclusive by elevating divine kinship over ancestral lineage. Rather than a universalistic Christianity pitted against a particularistic Judaism, John represents an inter-Jewish debate about the parameters of God's people. *As a negative construct,* the Ἰουδαῖοι are (for the most part) leadership figures who would limit Israel to Ἰουδαῖοι, a social

---

[7] Reimund Bieringer, Didier Pollefeyt, and Frederique Vandecasteele-Vanneuville, "Wrestling with Johannine Anti-Judaism: A Hermeneutical Framework for the Analysis of the Current Debate," in *Anti-Judaism and the Fourth Gospel*, ed. Reimund Bieringer, Didier Pollefeyt, and Frederique Vandecasteele-Vanneuville (Louisville: Westminster John Knox, 2001), 3–37 (here 22–23). Robert Kysar expresses the same sentiment: "Indeed, the meaning of the expression 'the Jews' continues to puzzle scholars and seems finally irresolvable." See Robert Kysar, "The Whence and Whither of the Johannine Community," in *Life in Abundance: Studies of John's Gospel in Tribute to Raymond E. Brown,* ed. John R. Donahue (Collegeville, Minn.: Liturgical Press, 2005), 65–81 (here 71).

[8] Martinus C. de Boer, "The Depiction of 'the Jews' in John's Gospel: Matters of Behavior and Identity," in *Anti-Judaism and the Fourth Gospel*, 141–57 (here 149). On this point, see also Thatcher, "John and the Jews," 11–12.

identity that the Jewish evangelist finds too limiting. John's polemi-cal sights are arrayed not against an ethnicity, nor Jewishness per se, but against a line of thinking that premises covenant membership on an ethnic Jewishness rigidly defined by bloodline or descent. John thus uses the negative label "the Jews" for those within his nar-rative who imply that salvation is not just *of* the Jews but strictly *for* the Jews. And importantly, John's approach here may be recognized as explicitly "Jewish" just as it may be retrospectively "Christian."

To set the groundwork for discussing these claims and obser-vations in detail, I will first recount contemporary approaches to understanding this Gospel's anti-Semitism and anti-Judaism, lead-ing into a concise discussion on contemporary ideas of Jewish eth-nic identity in antiquity.

Approaches to Resolving or Explaining Johannine Anti-Semitism and Anti-Judaism

Any serious attempt to offer an exegetical rereading of John's por-trayal of "the Jews" must give some account as to how it is situated within the current scholarly dialogue.[9] There are essentially two influential approaches of explaining (or explaining away, as some would suggest) John's apparent anti-Semitism and anti-Judaism,[10]

---

[9]   For a recent overview of the discussion see the chapter "'The Jews' in the Gospel of John and the 'Parting of the Ways,'" in Jörg Frey, *The Glory of the Crucified One: Christology and Theology in the Gospel of John*, BMSEC (Waco, Tex.: Baylor University Press, 2018), 39–72. Paul Ander-son discusses six approaches to the issue of John's alleged anti-Judaism in Paul N. Anderson, "Anti-Semitism and Religious Violence as Flawed Inter-pretations of the Gospel of John," in Culpepper and Anderson, *John and Judaism*, 265–311 (here 267–73).

[10]   The terms "anti-Semitism" and "anti-Judaism" have been sharply debated, with the former generally expressing hostility toward Jewish eth-nicity and the latter generally referring to hostility toward Jewish religious beliefs and practices. A helpful overview of the nuances can be found in Terence L. Donaldson, *Jews and Anti-Judaism in the New Testament: Deci-sion Points and Divergent Interpretations* (Waco, Tex.: Baylor University Press, 2010), 12–20. Note also Richard Hays' remarks, that "in no case do the New Testament texts show any evidence of racially motivated 'anti-Semitism.' To speak of 'anti-Semitism' in the New Testament is an anachro-nistic misnomer. The issues are entirely religious and confessional, hinging upon the acceptance of Jesus as Messiah and upon questions of observance

each of which opens a hermeneutical Pandora's box containing an unmanageable mass of secondary literature. The first is to limit the referent of "the Jews" to a specific target group among other Jews. The second (often paired with the first) is to reconstruct an inner Jewish conflict as the Gospel's historical context. I discuss each of these approaches briefly to provide an overview of scholarly engagements with this exegetical conundrum, among the most controversial in contemporary New Testament scholarship.

Limiting the Semantic Range of οἱ Ἰουδαῖοι

The term Ἰουδαῖος occurs roughly seventy times in John. Jewish scholar Adele Reinhartz memorably writes that in her initial forays into the Fourth Gospel, each of these references "felt like a slap in the face."[11] Yet, as Reinhartz has acknowledged, Ἰουδαῖος is not always freighted with hostility.[12] The term's puzzling semantic fluidity has left open enough exegetical space for scholars to render John's οἱ Ἰουδαῖοι in at least four ways: "the Jews," (without inverted commas), "'the Jews'" (within inverted commas), "the Judaeans," and "the Jewish authorities."

The first option—the Jews, without inverted commas—is obviously the most straightforward translation of οἱ Ἰουδαῖοι, but the complete lack of any definitional qualification bears the hermeneutical implication of an ongoing and contemporary application of the text's polemics, since οἱ Ἰουδαῖοι could well mean all Jews of any era, modern or ancient. While nobly resisting any attempt to indemnify the Fourth Evangelist through editing or sanitizing anti-Jewish sentiments that may be inherent to the text, the exegetical risk taken with this translation option is the prospect of giving canonical support for anti-Jewish readings in contexts quite different from John's own, a risk many interpreters are willing to take in order to avoid possible collusion with a racist or anti-ethnic agenda

---

of the Law." See Richard B. Hays, *The Moral Vision of the New Testament: Community, Cross, New Creation: A Contemporary Introduction to New Testament Ethics* (New York: HarperCollins, 1996), 429.

[11] Adele Reinhartz, *Befriending the Beloved Disciple: A Jewish Reading of the Gospel of John* (London: Continuum, 2001), 13.

[12] Adele Reinhartz, *Cast Out of the Covenant: Jews and Anti-Judaism in the Gospel of John* (Lanham, Md.: Fortress, 2018), 67–80.

that would seek to cover up John's impropriety. The placement of 'the Jews' within inverted commas—a second option—signals some need for qualification, yet risks overdetermination, possibly particularizing the text's polemics too narrowly. The third translation option, "the Judeans," assigns a geographical connotation to the term, limiting the Ἰουδαῖοι to an isolated subgroup of Jews centered in the powerbase of Judea, and especially in Jerusalem.[13] This translation is feasible for most instances of οἱ Ἰουδαῖοι in John, but, alas, not for all (see 4:9, 22b; 6:41, 52; 18:35).[14] As Jörg Frey concludes, "the attempt of a politically correct 'disentangling' of 'Judeans' as an object of the Johannine polemic from the religious fellowship of the 'Jews' is not viable for the interpretation of the Gospel of John."[15] A fourth and related option, "the Jewish authorities," acknowledges the predominant contextual sense of οἱ Ἰουδαῖοι (especially in its negative usage), but, along with "the Judeans," proves too restrictive on John's perplexing fluidity—the phrase οἱ Ἰουδαῖοι simply does not refer to antagonistic Jewish leaders on every occasion.[16]

There is nothing straightforward in deciding between these translation choices. Many Jewish scholars understandably balk at the option of "Judeans" since, as Amy-Jill Levine puts it, it would

[13]   John Barclay has recently argued that "Judaean" and "Jew" are so closely related that they should be viewed as roughly interchangeable. See John M. G. Barclay, "Ἰουδαῖος: Ethnicity and Translation," in *Ethnicity, Race, Religion: Identities and Ideologies in Early Jewish and Christian Texts, and in Modern Biblical Interpretation*, ed. Katherine M. Hockey and David G. Horrell (London: T&T Clark, 2018), 46–58.

[14]   The literature is expansive. Some view the Ἰουδαῖοι as synonymous with the powerful elite (e.g., Urban C. von Wahlde, "The Johannine 'Jews': A Critical Survey," *NTS* 28 [1982]: 33–60) or as a smaller unit among them (Cornelis Bennema, "The Identity and Composition of Οἱ Ἰουδαιοι in the Gospel of John," *TynBul* 60, no. 2 [2009]: 239–63). Other important studies include Malcolm Lowe, "Who Were the Ἰουδαῖοι?" *NovT* 18 (1976): 101–30, and the detailed response from John Ashton, "The Identity and Function of the Ἰουδαῖοι in the Fourth Gospel," *NovT* 27 (1985): 40–75. For a recent and thorough account of how the term is used in John, see Anderson, "Anti-Semitism," 285–95.

[15]   Frey, *Glory of the Crucified One*, 44.

[16]   Urban C. von Wahlde attributes the wider connotation of Ἰουδαῖοι in John 6:41 and 6:52 to later redaction. See Urban C. von Wahlde, "The Jews in the Gospel of John: Fifteen Years of Research [1983–1998]," *EThL* 76 (2000): 30–55 (here 41).

create a "*judenrein* text, a text purified of Jews." And since Jesus is a *Galilean*, he would no longer be a Ἰουδαῖος.[17] Similarly, Reinhartz warns that wrapping "the Jews" in inverted commas, thus limiting the scope of the Gospel's polemical target by suggesting a particular group of Jews or a particular understanding of the term, may be an attempt "to defuse the Gospel's anti-Judaism" in an effort (even if inadvert) "to whitewash" John and "absolve it of responsibility for the anti-Jewish emotions and attitudes it conveys."[18] With these arguments at the forefront of my thinking, I am nonetheless following recent arguments by Ruth Sheridan[19] and translating οἱ Ἰουδαῖοι as "the Jews" (within quotation marks) on the grounds that the term's use within the Gospel is dependent on immediate contexts and also bears rhetorical functions, even if those contexts and functions are not manifestly clear to modern readers. Some textual qualification of the particularities of historical and narrative settings alongside John's rhetorical aims is necessary for a composition regarded by many as sacred Scripture and regularly mined for devotional meaning and practical application in quite different contexts today.[20]

Ancient writers did not have at their disposal an arsenal of punctuation marks (like inverted commas), but John signals the need to qualify his generalized characters and character groups. As discussed presently, the broad labels in John 1:1-18 for Christology, theology, and anthropology acquire clarification throughout the Prologue. Further christological specifications of Jesus' identity are supplied through titles attributed to him by John the Baptist and the disciples in the Johannine call narrative. The Prologue's generic language of "children of God" also gains further specificity as the narrative unfolds. In the Epistles, the author deploys generic labels that can be either positive ("beloved," "children," "friends") or negative

[17] Levine, "Reflections on Reflections," 11.

[18] Adele Reinhartz, "'Jews' and Jews in the Fourth Gospel," in Bieringer, Pollefeyt, and Vandecasteele-Vanneuville, *Anti-Judaism and the Fourth Gospel*, 213–27 (here 227).

[19] Ruth Sheridan, "Issues in the Translation of οἱ Ἰουδαῖοι in the Fourth Gospel," *JBL* 132, no. 3 (2013): 671–95.

[20] To clarify, when I cite Scripture passages that speak of "the Jews," and when I am not speaking of John's distinctive use of the phrase, I will leave off the quotation marks.

("antichrists," "deceiver"). These are not simply caricatures, however. The Elder can speak of *Diotrephes* as a specific figure and asks *Gaius* to greet the friends "by name" (3 John 15), just as Jesus might call "by name" (10:3) the *sheep* constituting his generic "flock." The "John" behind this literary collection regularly works with broad labels implying a range of meanings that immediately or eventually acquire qualification in the narrative sequence or within the epistolary details (and many of these meanings and details surely would have been common knowledge requiring no further specification). The broad appellation "the Jews" is no different. It serves as a generic title but designates a character group that cannot be understood generically.[21] John inducts his readers into his narrative by providing a couple of early translations and he even begins numbering the signs for us. Likewise, he gives us a clear sense as to the identity of the Ἰουδαῖοι. As soon as they are introduced into the narrative (1:19), the broad label undergoes qualification—these are Jews "out of Jerusalem (ἐξ Ἱεροσολύμων)" (1:19) and soon afterward made synonymous with the Pharisees (1:24). By introducing the character group in this fashion, the Gospel writer indicates that whenever the label appears, *it is not to be understood as unqualified and thus taken at face value.* Most negative instances clearly entail Jewish authorities opposed to Jesus (and the Johannine ecclesial vision). For rhetorical reasons, however, John prefers to keep the general title, which permits a strategic interplay between ambiguity and clarity. Yet he expects enough hermeneutical savvy from his readers and auditors to pick up on the qualifications supplied or withheld. Hence my choice for inverted commas.[22]

[21]   Judith Lieu points out that, as nuanced as the label Ἰουδαῖοι may be, it "blankets" its comprised characters and "effects a degree of homogenizing." I am here pointing out that the blanketing term is strategically qualified at certain points in the narrative, just as John strategically leaves the term ambiguous at other points (which will be discussed more in chapter 5). For Lieu's quote, see Judith M. Lieu, *Christian Identity in the Jewish and Graeco-Roman World* (Oxford: Oxford University Press, 2004), 289.

[22]   Similar points are made by Wendy North who observes that, as a communicator, John readily provides means by which his readers would understand the referent of "the Jews." See Wendy E. S. North, "'The Jews' in John's Gospel: Observations and Inferences," in *Judaism, Jewish Identities and the Gospel Tradition: Essays in Honour of Maurice Casey*, ed. James Crossley (London: Equinox, 2010), 207–26.

Envisioning an Inter-Jewish Conflict as the Gospel's Historical Context

Those who see John as anti-Jewish note that the sting of his harsh rhetoric toward "the Jews" has been hermeneutically mitigated for many scholars through mirror reading and the resultant historical reconstructions discussed in the previous chapter. If it can be shown that the Johannine community suffered a painful expulsion from the Jewish synagogue, as prominent interpreters like J. Louis Martyn and Raymond Brown have argued,[23] then the caustic use of οἱ Ἰουδαῖοι becomes not justifiable but at least understandable—if the conflict is *inter*-Jewish then surely it is not so blatantly *anti*-Jewish.[24] Hypothetical formulations of a sectarian context, drawn largely from John 9, seem to have occasioned many exegetical sighs of relief for scholars who are uncomfortable with canonized vehemence against a particular ethnic group that has undeniably endured ostracism—and much worse—by readers of this Gospel throughout the centuries.[25] Regardless of whether or not a sup-

[23]   J. Louis Martyn, *History and Theology in the Fourth Gospel*, 3rd ed. (Louisville: Westminster John Knox, 2003); Raymond E. Brown, *The Community of the Beloved Disciple: The Life, Loves, and Hates of an Individual Church in New Testament Times* (New York: Paulist Press, 1979).

[24]   A number of studies have sought to demonstrate that the sort of harshness seen in John was a standard feature of ancient polemical discourse. See, e.g., Graham. N. Stanton, "Aspects of Early Christian-Jewish Polemic and Apologetic," *NTS* 31 (1985): 377–92; Stephen Motyer, *Your Father the Devil? A New Approach to John and 'the Jews,'* Paternoster Biblical Monographs (Milton Keynes: Paternoster, 1997); Luke T. Johnson, "The New Testament's Anti-Jewish Slander and the Conventions of Ancient Polemic," *JBL* 108 (1989): 419–41.

[25]   Adele Reinhartz has energetically worked to undermine the Martyn-Brown hypothesis, in part because its depiction of the Johannine community as oppressed by fellow Jews "lets the gospel off the hook for its anti-Jewish expressions." See Adele Reinhartz, "The Johannine Community and Its Jewish Neighbors: A Reappraisal," in *"What Is John?"* vol. 2: *Literary and Social Readings of the Fourth Gospel*, ed. Fernando Segovia, SBLSymS 3 (Atlanta: Scholars Press, 1998), 111–38. She has offered a sensible reading of John 11 (and 12:11) that weakens claims made on the Martyn-Brown readings of John 9, raising the prospect that the Johannine Christians voluntarily withdrew from "the Jews" (what Reinhartz refers to as the "propulsion theory") rather than the latter forcibly ejecting the former (the "expulsion theory"). See Reinhartz, *Cast Out of the Covenant*, 131–57. Similar arguments are put forward by Reuven Kimelman, "*Birkat Ha-Minim* and the Lack of Evidence

posed Jewish background eases the conscience of Christian readers, the claim that the pain of an intramural conflict is at least partially inscribed within John's pages is historically compelling. I do not presume access to the particulars; nor do I presume that John's polemics are justified merely because they occur within an inter-Jewish controversy. I do, however, believe that John's rhetoric must be read within some form of debate between Jews and Johannine Jewish Christians over the identity of Israel and its Messiah.

Jewish Ethnicity in Antiquity and in John's Gospel: Particularism vs. Universalism?

Before presenting the exegetical arguments for my own proposal—that John's othering of "the Jews" is actually part of a program of de-othering that eliminates ethnicity as soteriological criterion—I acknowledge the importance of situating any claim that John is not anti-Jewish or anti-Semitic within the wider discussion of how Jewish ethnicity was understood in antiquity. Several recent studies have shown that today's conceptual language of "race," "ethnicity," and "religion" are constructs more modern than ancient.[26] Even so, some

for an Anti-Christian Prayer in Late Antiquity," in *Aspects of Judaism in the Greco-Roman World*, ed. E. P. Sanders, Albert I. Baumgarten, and Alan Mendelson, vol. 2 of *Jewish and Christian Self-Definition* (Philadelphia: Fortress, 1981), 226–44; Steven T. Katz, "Issues in the Separation of Judaism and Christianity after 70 CE: A Reconsideration," *JBL* 103 (1984): 43–76; and Raimo Hakola, *Identity Matters: John, the Jews and Jewishness*, NovT-Sup 118 (Leiden: Brill, 2005). Joel Marcus, however, has rebutted the dismissals of Martyn's claims that John's Jewish believers were threatened by the *Birkat Ha-Minim*. See Joel Marcus, *"Birkat Ha-Minim* Revisited," *NTS* 55, no. 4 (2009): 523–51. The sharp alternatives between Martyn/Brown and Reinhartz (et al.) are brought together in Francis Watson's suggestion that both groups would have likely affirmed "that being a Jew is incompatible with being a follower of Jesus the Messiah." On this reading, "expulsion or separation takes place because *both* parties agree that it should." See Francis Watson, *Gospel Writing: A Canonical Perspective* (Grand Rapids: Eerdmans, 2013), 329–30 (emphases original).

[26] Like Erich Gruen, "ethnicity" is a term I am using "loosely, unfettered by a precise denotation." See Erich S. Gruen, *Ethnicity in the Ancient World—Did it Matter?* (Berlin: De Gruyter, 2020), 4. See also the introductory chapter in Denise Kimber Buell, *Why This New Race: Ethnic Reasoning in Early Christianity* (New York: Columbia University Press, 2005), 1–34, and in David G. Horrell's introduction to Hockey and Horrell, *Ethnicity,*

account must be given to describe the varying ways group identity was understood and expressed by Ἰουδαῖοι in the ancient world.²⁷

Since I am arguing that John challenges a form of what is often referred to as "Jewish particularism," I acknowledge here that longstanding misperceptions and hazardous influences have underwritten similar claims. I criticized in the previous chapter a Hegelian approach to history in which Baur pitted Jewish Christianity against Gentile Christianity and found their resolve in the synthesis of an early catholicism; yet the idea of Jewish exclusiveness vs. Christian inclusiveness is a longstanding trope potentially linked to that dialectical model. David Horrell has recently provided a magisterial study of what he calls a "structural dichotomy" uncomfortably parallel with prior history-of-religion models.²⁸ Comparing an alleged Jewish particularism with a more positively portrayed Christian universalism inadvertently denigrates Judaism. Horrell notes that "Judaism constitutes the 'other' to which early Christian inclusivism is contrasted"²⁹ and quotes Denise Kimber Buell's observation that "definitions of Christianity's racially inclusive ideal will perpetuate a racially loaded form of anti-Judaism if the implied point of contrast to Christianity's inclusiveness is Jewishness."³⁰ These sober judg-

---

Race, Religion, 1–20 (here 6–7). Important works cited by Horrell that also discuss race/ethnicity as modern constructs include Wilfred Cantwell Smith, *The Meaning and End of Religion* (Minneapolis: Fortress, 1991 [1962]); Brent Nongbri, *Before Religion: A History of a Modern Concept* (New Haven, Conn.: Yale University Press, 2013); and Jonathan Z. Smith, "Religion, Religions, Religious," in *Critical Terms for Religious Studies*, ed. Mark C. Taylor (Chicago: University of Chicago Press, 1998), 269–84.

²⁷   See the "prismatic approach" undertaken by Buell, *Why This New Race*, in which she collectively takes into account how our contemporary contexts shape our historical analyses alongside ideas about race, ethnicity, and religion in both recent and ancient history (33–34).

²⁸   Horrell, *Ethnicity and Inclusion: Religion, Race, and Whiteness in Constructions of Jewish and Christian Identities* (Grand Rapids: Eerdmans, 2020).

²⁹   Horrell, *Ethnicity and Inclusion*, 333.

³⁰   From Buell, *Why This New Race*, 12 (cited in Horrell, *Ethnicity and Inclusion*, 333). See also Denise Kimber Buell, "Early Christian Universalism and Modern Forms of Racism," in *The Origins of Racism in the West*, ed. Miriam Eliav-Feldon, Benjamin Isaac, and Joseph Ziegler (Cambridge: Cambridge University Press, 2009), 109–31.

ments stand as a caution against oversimplifications. And indeed, John's Gospel cannot be comfortably molded into the dichotomy of Jewish particularism vs. Christian universalism. What we find, rather, are different *Jewish* ways of construing "Israel." And John's version—identified as "Christian" in retrospect—entails specific confessional demands that undeniably promote particularism of a different sort, just as the model he critiques offers inclusion of a different sort.[31]

The type of ethnic particularism I believe John maligns is likely more rigid than conventional modes of invitation, belonging, and exclusion operative in the wider perspectives and practices of early Judaism. John Barclay has recently made the case that ancient Jewish concepts of ethnicity were on the whole more "polythetic" than "monothetic" during the Hellenistic era.[32] A monothetic construct of ethnicity requires one definitive feature for ethnic inclusion, such as immutable genetic descent. In a polythetic construct, ethnic identity is less fixed and more fluid, potentially determined by a range of common features, none of which serves exclusively as prerequisite. Arguing that the latter is more representative of ancient Jewish ideas on ethnicity, Barclay produces a polythetic "inventory" of ethnic "connotations" drawn from his reading of *Contra Apionem* by Josephus:

1. Descent and shared ancestry

2. A common territory

3. A shared language

4. A commonly embraced set of sacred texts

5. A shared allegiance to a temple

---

[31] John Barclay, for instance, has observed that "Paul's prescription for the Church's identity by no means abolishes particularism: it simply erects, in place of an ethnic particularism, an ecclesial particularism defined by faith in Christ." See John M. G. Barclay, "Universalism and Particularism: Twin Components of Both Judaism and Early Christianity," in *A Vision for the Church: Studies in Early Christian Ecclesiology in Honour of J. P. M. Sweet*, ed. Marcus Bockmuehl and Michael B. Thompson (Edinburgh: T&T Clark, 1997), 207–24 (here 215).

[32] Barclay, "Ἰουδαῖος," 49.

6. A shared set of religious customs and practices (which
   Barclay labels as "constitution")[33]

The presence of some or all of these, in varying permutations, could
be recognized as grounds for a common Jewish ethnicity.
The Fourth Evangelist belongs within the broad stream of envisioning Jewish identity in mutable terms. More specifically, he writes
as one of several other Christ-confessing Jewish writers who press
against perceived ethnic strictures in their vision of the christologically
reimagined people of God. The narrative aside that "Ἰουδαῖοι have no
dealings with Samaritans" (4:9) and the insinuated labeling of Nicodemus as a Galilean (intended by the Jewish leaders as an insult) are off-
hand remarks indicating that John is engaging a monothetic construal
of covenant identity. Though he would not have had Barclay's heuristic
taxonomy of ancient Jewish ethnic identity pinned to his writing desk,
John is nonetheless conscious of all six of these items and *strategically
challenges their exclusionary potential*. Though almost certainly a Jew,
he obviates *descent and shared ancestry* as an appropriate category for
understanding the social construct of the "children of God" when he
portrays Jesus accepting the claim of the Ἰουδαῖοι in John 8 that they
are Abraham's biological descendants while nonetheless questioning their covenant status. As the Jewish leaders observe at the end of
John 11, the ministry of Jesus places their sense of shared *territorial
place* under the threat of a potential Roman eviction; moreover, his
concern for other sheep not of this fold suggests a broader territorial
mission. Jesus similarly dismisses the cultic relevance of *geography*

---

[33] Barclay, "Ἰουδαῖος," 48. Barclay acknowledges some degree of
overlap with this list and the well-known features of "ethnicity" provided
by John Hutchinson and Anthony D. Smith: 1) a common proper name;
2) a myth of a common ancestry; 3) shared historical memories; 4) one
or more elements of a common culture; 5) a link with a homeland; and
6) a sense of solidarity with some portion of the wider group population.
See John Hutchinson and Anthony D. Smith, introduction to *Ethnicity*,
ed. John Hutchinson and Anthony D. Smith, Oxford Readers (Oxford:
Oxford University Press, 1996), 6–7. A recent, and more simplified, model
of racial/ethnic identity applied directly to John's Gospel is offered by
Andrew Benko in the form of 1) common ancestry, 2) common homeland,
and 3) common distinctive culture. See his discussion in Andrew Benko,
Race in John's Gospel: Toward an Ethnos-*Conscious Approach* (Lanham,
Md.: Fortress, 2019), 20–22.

when he tells the Samaritan woman that true worship is in Spirit and in truth, not based on one or another mountain summit. In terms of *shared language* as a ground for common identity, the trilingual titulus on the cross along with the evangelist's translations of "Rabbi" into διδάσκαλος and "Messiah" into Χριστός all hint toward an anticipated Gospel readership—and thus prospective social membership—of broader ethnic variety. Though the Johannine Jesus affirms the revelatory significance of the Jewish *scriptures*, he creates an inner-ethnic tension by calling the Torah "your law" when addressing his fellow Ἰουδαῖοι in 8:17 and 10:34. The spatial role of the *temple* as the material focal point of the divine presence on earth is replaced by Jesus' body according to John 2, and a number of *constitutional* elements of Jewish religious life (such as feasts and purification rites) are re-signified christologically for a wider appeal.[34]

Is John, therefore, nullifying Jewish ethnicity in his systematic subversion of the categories that seem to underlie a Jewish sense of social identity? My answer is no. His project consists of two parts: 1) John *undermines* the exclusivity of common descent, a shared language, and cultic territory yet 2) *reenvisions* (and thus still champions) the meaning and significance of the temple, the sacred scriptures, and the religious practices and rites. These complex tasks of simultaneously undermining and reenvisioning seem so grounded within the existing ethnoreligious tradition that they appear to me not as acts of cultural appropriation (as claimed by Adele Reinhartz[35]) but as a form of internal cultural critique and reform (even if premised on controversial claims about Jesus).

But why, to restate the "irresolvable" question, *would a Jewish text present Jewish characters who negatively label other Jews as "the Jews"?*

An Overview of the Argument: Divine vs. Ethnic Identity in Johannine Soteriology and Ecclesiology

Though I do not assume that it will take away the sting experienced by many Jewish readers of John, nor do I endorse a contemporary embrace of John's polemical language couched in terms recognizable

---

[34]   Of all the Jewish identity markers found in John, Raimo Hakola has observed that food regulations are curiously lacking. Hakola, *Identity Matters*, 31.

[35]   Reinhartz, *Cast Out of the Covenant*, 51–66.

as "ethnic" today, I restate here the explanation I offer to our irresolvable question, one that has resonance with important studies by Philip Esler and Stewart Penwell:[36] *John's polemical use of "the Jews" is not intended to attack or undermine Jewish social identity as an ethnicity; the rhetorical purpose, rather, is to call his readers, Jewish and non-Jewish, into a social identity that is divinely generated, not ethnically determined.* Though John certainly portrays a potentially exclusive soteriology premised on Christ-belief, he is challenging a differently exclusive soteriology premised on ethnicity. Whereas most early Jews held to a more "polythetic" view of ethnic identity as Barclay has argued and as Erich Gruen has recently affirmed,[37] the Fourth Evangelist seems to be challenging a more rigidly "monothetic" approach reliant on Abrahamic descent or biological heritage, likely promoted by key leaders in John's milieu (and surely also in Jesus' day). Why would a Jewish text by a Jewish writer have his Jewish protagonist polemically address other Jews as "the Jews"?

[36] I discovered both of these studies after this chapter went through multiple drafts. Both Esler and Parnell employ social-scientific approaches, though they make similar claims to my own. See Philip F. Esler, "From *Ioudaioi* to Children of God: The Development of a Non-Ethnic Group Identity in the Gospel of John," in *In Other Words: Essays on Social-Science Methods and the New Testament in Honor of Jerome H. Neyrey*, ed. Anselm C. Hagedorn, Zeba A. Crook, and Eric Stewart (Sheffield: Sheffield University Press, 2007), 106–37. I discovered Penwell's important monograph two days before I had to submit the final manuscript of this book and could only gain limited access through Google Books. I happily point readers to his material: Stewart Penwell, *Jesus the Samaritan: Ethnic Labelling in the Gospel of John*, BibInt 170 (Leiden: Brill, 2019). Note also the observation by John Pryor that "Jesus is the true Shepherd, gathering the flock of God not by racial exclusiveness, but out of all the nations (10:16)." See John W. Pryor, *John: Evangelist of the Covenant People: The Narrative & Themes of the Fourth Gospel* (Downers Grove, Ill.: InterVarsity Press, 1992), 158 (emphases original). Another interpretation of John's portrayal of "the Jews" with some similarities to my own is offered by Mathias Rissi, "Die 'Juden' im Johannesevangelium," *ANRW* II.26/3 (Berlin: De Gruyter, 1996), 2099–141. Rissi believes John is challenging Jewish Christians who are promoting a mystical spirituality premised on the Johannine ascent motif, and who are laying claim to their Jewish ethnic heritage and leadership influence in addition to their belief in Christ's word.

[37] See chapters 6, 7, and 8 in Gruen, *Ethnicity in the Ancient World*.

Because he is rhetorically attributing to his opponents the categorization they believe requisite for covenant membership: to be born among the Ἰουδαῖοι.[38]

John is not anti-Jewish or anti-Semitic—his provocative use of Ἰουδαῖος undermines not an ethnic group, but an envisaged social identity that is, in his view, wrongly restrictive. This Jewish text seeks to redefine group membership along confessional, not racial, grounds. The object of John's polemical use of "the Jews" is an ethnicizing of soteriology and ecclesiology (propped up by leadership figures). By the phrase "an ethnicizing of soteriology and ecclesiology," I mean an understanding of salvation and group membership premised on or guaranteed by ethnic identity, particularly by those monothetic connotations more easily perceived as fixed and immutable. At the heart of what is called anti-Judaism in John is actually an anti-ethnicizing of salvation, a deracializing of covenant identity. John is thus invested in an explicit exercise of *de-othering*, even as he rhetorically "others." Though salvation is from "the Jews" as Jesus puts it in John 4:22, it is a salvation that requires a resocialization not out of non-Jewishness into Jewishness nor out of Jewishness into some other ethnic or racial designation; Johannine soteriology and ecclesiology encompass a resocialization of an altogether different sort, *from the sphere of biological heritage into divine kinship*. This resocialization does not produce a new nation (ἔθνος, a word used only in the singular in John and largely as a political designation ostensibly for Roman Judea and its inhabitants and attending customs). Neither does this resocialization produce a new race (γένος) or tribe (φυλή), ethnic-related terms never appearing John.[39] This resocialization is into a divine *family* who collectively share, as Philip Esler puts it, "an identity that transcends ethnicity."[40] Barclay has commented that, when proselytes embraced Jewish religion, their identity "was so thoroughly

[38]   A similar argument is made regarding ethnic identity construction in Luke-Acts by Aaron Kuecker, *The Spirit and the "Other": Social Identity, Ethnicity and Intergroup Reconciliation in Luke-Acts*, LNTS 444 (London: T&T Clark, 2011).

[39]   The term λαός appears in 8:2, 11:50, and 18:14, but its connotation is generic in the first and final instances and likely parallel to the meaning of ἔθνος also in 11:50.

[40]   Esler, "From *Ioudaioi* to Children of God," 106.

redefined as to transfer them, practically speaking, into the Jewish nation,"[41] exemplifying the possibilities for mutable dynamics within Judaism. Though perhaps the exception, certain strands holding to a more monothetic view of inclusion certainly existed in early Judaism.[42] Within John's polemical sights is such an approach, possibly advanced within his own Jewish context, a stance that must have had some influence in the first century since it was challenged elsewhere by other early Christian writers (some of whom were Jewish).[43] John writes with the conviction that the arrival of Jesus as the Jewish

[41] John M. G. Barclay, *Jews in the Mediterranean Diaspora: From Alexander to Trajan (323 BCE–117 CE)* (Berkeley: University of California Press, 1996), 408.

[42] See Christine E. Hayes, *Gentile Impurities and Jewish Identities: Intermarriage and Conversion from the Bible to the Talmud* (Oxford: Oxford University Press, 2002), especially the chapter "Impurity, Intermarriage, and Conversion in Second Temple Sources" where she focuses on 4QMMT and Jubilees (pp. 68–91); see also the chapter "Jewishness as Genealogy in the Late Second Temple Period," in Matthew Thiessen, *Contesting Conversion: Genealogy, Circumcision, and Identity in Ancient Judaism and Christianity* (Oxford: Oxford University Press, 2011), 87–110. In his discussion of the debates surrounding Idumean inclusion among the Jews in the background, Thiessen reviews several early Jewish texts emphasizing genealogical boundary construction: the *Animal Apocalypse* (1 En. 85–90), 1 Esdras, and the depictions of (the Idumean) Herod in Pss. Sol. 17 and of Herod and Agrippa I in Josephus' *Antiquities* and in some rabbinical texts. For Thiessen's discussion on Jubilees, a text that clearly defines Jewishness via ancestral descent, see the chapter "Eight-Day Circumcision in *Jubilees*," 67–86. For a study on Philo's association of Jewish identity to one's mother, see Maren R. Niehoff, *Philo on Jewish Identity and Culture*, TSAJ 86 (Tübingen: Mohr Siebeck, 2020), 17–33.

[43] In addition to Matt 3:9 and Luke 3:8, discussed further below, Paul writes, "Just as Abraham 'believed God, and it was reckoned to him as righteousness,' so, you see, those who believe are the descendants of Abraham. And the scripture, foreseeing that God would justify the Gentiles by faith, declared the gospel beforehand to Abraham, saying, 'All the Gentiles shall be blessed in you.' For this reason, those who believe are blessed with Abraham who believed" (Gal 3:6-9 NRSV). Paul's references to his own ancestral heritage—e.g., "a member of the people (ἐκ γένους) of Israel, of the tribe (φυλῆς) of Benjamin, a Hebrew born of Hebrews" (Phil 3:5 NRSV); "I myself am an Israelite, a descendent of (ἐκ σπέρματος) Abraham, a member of the tribe (φυλῆς) of Benjamin" (Rom 11:1 NRSV)— attests to its legitimating power among early Jews, even if Paul himself ends up redefining covenant membership on christological grounds.

Messiah redefines the parameters of "the Jewish nation" and unsettles even the traditional polythetic means of covenant membership. The Fourth Evangelist vividly narrates how a divine Messiah who effects divine rebirth compels a renegotiation of monothetic notions of group identity—for anyone and everyone. One might accuse this Jewish evangelist of nullifying race itself as a human category of identification, calling for the deracialization of his own ethnic identity via conversion to a raceless Christianity, with the very idea of ethnicity or race under attack. Instead, I propose that John is simply *relativizing* race.[44] *What he is deracializing is not the ethnic nature of human identity, but the means of salvation made available to all humans through Jesus.*[45] In other words, race—as we would understand the term today—is not nullified or eradicated by this early Christian text; race is just removed as a predecided identity marker for group membership. For this Jewish writer, salvation is grounded in a participation not within an ethnic category but within the divine family itself. And since this new filial membership is effected by a divine re-origination "from above," Johannine resocialization is comparable to what later Christian theologians would call *deification*. Indeed, on the basis of Jesus' citation of Psalm 82 in John 10, belief in Jesus generates a new social group, the members of which are more appropriately understood as "gods" than "Jews," "Greeks," or "Gentiles."[46] Theosis

[44] Again for this dynamic in Luke-Acts, see Kuecker, *Spirit and the "Other."*

[45] Though he acknowledges the Johannine relativization of race, Andrew Benko believes that John succeeds not in eliminating race as a soteriological factor but in simply creating a different race, a "cosmic race." In his *"ethnos*-conscious approach," race is a dominant hermeneutical frame shaping his exegesis—Benko struggles to imagine a social identity except in racial or ethnic terms. Benko essentializes race and therefore sees John as taking race to a deeper (cosmic) level: "John consistently downplays the significance of various markers of earthly race, such as one's descent, and instead champions a new layer of racialized identity" (Benko, *Race in John's Gospel*, 205). In my view, this misses John's point of de-essentializing race and eliminating ethnicity as an identifying badge of covenant membership (see the summary comments in Benko, *Race in John's Gospel*, 205–6).

[46] On theosis in the use of Psalm 82 in John 10, see the discussion in Andrew J. Byers, *Ecclesiology and Theosis in the Gospel of John*, SNTSMS 166 (Cambridge: Cambridge University Press, 2017), 186–99.

trumps genetics. John, therefore, incessantly punctuates his narrative with the phrase οἱ Ἰουδαῖοι to destabilize rhetorically a social policy of restricting membership in the christologically reconfigured family of God to a category of race, promoting instead the vision of a regenerated divine community. Though he has his own exclusivist tendencies, John is undermining a program of ethnic othering sponsored by monothetic influences represented as "the Jews" in his narrative. John is negatively othering an alternative program of othering.[47]

In the contemporary debates within Johannine scholarship, the customary hermeneutical entry points for discussing John and "the Jews" are John 4:22, 8:44, and 9:22 (plus 12:42 and 16:2).[48] As intimated above, John 8:44 ("you are from your father, the devil") holds primary place for those who accuse John of being anti-Jewish; John 9:22 ("put out of the synagogue") is the interpretative key to the debate for those who envision an historical inter-Jewish conflict that blunts Johannine anti-Jewishness; and finally, John 4:22 ("salvation is from the Jews") holds pride of exegetical place for those keen to absolve John of anti-Jewish leanings.[49]

My own exegetical starting point will be the Gospel's opening.[50] Given the significance of the Prologue for establishing foundational thematic trajectories, I build my case by exploring themes related to divine and ethnic identity in John 1:1-18. Since meaning is conducted sequentially in a narrative, the next major section will trace the linear development and cumulative expansion of these ideas, demonstrating that John interweaves his vision of divine community with questions of ethnicity and alongside the polemical use of the phrase οἱ Ἰουδαῖοι.

[47]   As discussed in chapter 5, John maintains a basis for othering. He just refuses to ground it in ethnic terms.

[48]   The following translations are from the NRSV.

[49]   The comment, "We do not find convincing interpretations that use John 4:22 to deconstruct the anti-Jewishness of 8:44" is indicative of how exegetical entry points shape the debate. From Bieringer et al., "Wrestling with Johannine Anti-Judaism," 36.

[50]   In the exegetical part of his arguments on a non-ethnic identity for Johannine believers, Esler also begins with the Prologue ("From *Ioudaioi* to Children of God," 125–27).

Divine and Ethnic Identity in the Johannine Prologue

It is widely acknowledged that John's foundational narrative opening unveils the work's principal emphases and sets the basic plot trajectory into motion.[51] Though John 1:1-18 has been hailed as one of the most christologically significant texts in early Christianity,[52] it is often missed that inseparably wed to the Prologue's christological vision is an *ecclesial* vision, one in which ethnic determinism is subverted as a means of constructing the social identity of the people of God.[53] Of Barclay's six key indicators of Jewish ethnicity, three appear in the Prologue. Questions are raised, at least indirectly, over the efficacy of *common territory* and a *shared corpus of sacred texts* as group identifiers. More directly, the idea of *shared biological ancestry* is invalidated as a premise for defining God's people. John calls instead for an alternative ancestry that is divine and linked to the Incarnation of the Logos.

Redefining Geographical Domain: "He came to his own territory"

Though the Prologue opens with a protological setting in which God and the Logos are correlated as cosmic figures outside the terrestrial sphere, reference is soon made to the expansive physical domain of all creation. As the sweeping metaphysical terms θεός and λόγος accrue sharper definition along with categorizations for humanity (πᾶν

---

[51] Bruce J. Malina and Richard L. Rohrbaugh, *Social Science Commentary on the Gospel of John* (Minneapolis: Fortress, 1998), 5; Morna D. Hooker, "Beginnings and Endings," in *The Written Gospel*, ed. Markus Bockmuehl and D. A. Hagner (Cambridge: Cambridge University Press, 2005); Warren Carter, "The Prologue and John's Gospel: Function, Symbol and the Definitive Word," *JSNT* 39 (1990): 35–58; Elizabeth Harris, *Prologue and Gospel: The Theology of the Fourth Evangelist*, JSNTSup 107 (Sheffield: Sheffield University Press, 1994); Adele Reinhartz, *The Word in the World: The Cosmological Tale in the Fourth Gospel*, SBLMS 45 (Atlanta: Scholars Press, 1992), 16–28; John F. O'Grady, "The Prologue and Chapter 17 of the Gospel of John," in *What We Have Heard From the Beginning: The Past, Present, and Future of Johannine Studies*, ed. Tom Thatcher (Waco, Tex.: Baylor University Press, 2007), 215–28.

[52] Martin Hengel, "The Prologue of the Gospel of John as the Gateway to Christological Truth," in *The Gospel of John and Christian Theology*, ed. Richard Bauckham and Carl Mosser (Grand Rapids: Eerdmans, 2008), 289.

[53] A fuller treatment of this claim is found in Byers, *Ecclesiology and Theosis in the Gospel of John*, 27–48.

and ἄνθρωποι) throughout the Prologue's sequence,[54] so the spatial sphere contracts from the broader term κόσμος as the Logos comes εἰς τὰ ἴδια.[55] This neuter use of "his own" is immediately followed by a masculine use of "his own" (οἱ ἴδιοι). The referent of the former use is here largely understood as the territory of Israel,[56] with the masculine plural use referring to the relational sphere of the people associated with that spatial domain. The social and locational connotations of "his own" are lexically and semantically interlinked—the Logos came to his own place, and to his own people with whom that place is affiliated. Commentators have drawn attention to the parallels between the activity and function of the Logos in the Johannine prologue and the descent and indwelling of personified Wisdom in Sirach. Though originating from the divine realm, Wisdom searches for a physical dwelling place, settling amenably within the territorial domain of Israel (Sir 24:3-11; cf. Bar 3:29-37; 1 En. 42:1). The Johannine Logos, however, with conceptual parallels to the personification of Wisdom (and Torah), finds the same realm—physical and social—inhospitable to his aspirations for a terrestrial abode.

The rejections of the Word by "his own [people]" (masculine plural) as well as "his own [land]" (neuter plural) seem designed to contrast with this tradition of Wisdom's quest for a home. The striking irony of the landless and evicted status of the Word alerts readers and hearers to a program of reconfiguring standard means of determining and defining social identity: if the Logos is rejected by those within his own physical domain (as v. 11 makes clear), then *shared territory*—a common feature characterizing ethnicity—is problematized as a means of socially designating the people of God.

[54] On this pattern of "disambiguation," see Byers, *Ecclesiology and Theosis in the Gospel of John*, 50–58.

[55] The term κόσμος is not always spatial in its Johannine usage, but at this point in the Prologue it is associated with a material creation into which the Logos enters.

[56] John W. Pryor, "Jesus and Israel in the Fourth Gospel—John 1:11," *NovT* 32, no. 3 (1990): 201–218; D. A. Carson, *The Gospel According to John*, PNTC (Grand Rapids: Eerdmans, 1991), 124; Raymond E. Brown, *The Gospel According to John: Introduction, Translation, and Notes*, 2 vols., AB 29, 29A (Garden City, N.Y.: Doubleday, 1966, 1970), A:10; Marianne Meye Thompson, *John: A Commentary*, NTL (Louisville: Westminster John Knox, 2015), 30.

A subtle blow is thus delivered to the edifice of ethnicity as a mode of defining covenant membership. The blow that comes in v. 12 is less subtle: authentication of membership within the people of God is expressly stated as resulting from the believing reception of the Logos. This means of socialization sets up an alternative mode of othering (see chapter 5), but it undercuts attempts to define inclusion on ethnic terms.

The Johannine Genealogy

Perhaps in keeping with developing practices in Gospel writing, John supplies in his narrative opening a genealogy. This is not a genealogy of the Messiah, but of the Messiah's people. In Matthew and Luke, Jesus is depicted as a divine figure mysteriously irrupting into the earthly sphere through miraculous birth narratives. In John, Jesus' entrance into the world as a divine figure is not portrayed through an account of his birth. Readers are simply informed that "the Word became flesh." The Prologue's sparse chronicling of Jesus' appearance in the earthly realm, however, is coordinated with the irruption of a new people out of the heavenly realm.[57] Whereas the divine Logos becomes human, human beings become divine. This Johannine genealogy is not of God's Son, but of God's children who are brought into being through the reception of the Son. This creative spin on the established format of the Gospel birth narrative entails the dynamic of divine-human exchange that unequivocally eliminates as signifiers of religious group identity biological descent and genetic heritage—fundamental concerns for deterministic models of ethnicity.[58]

The emphatic Johannine severance of ethnicity from the social entity comprising God's people is found in the repetition in 1:13

---

[57] Tertullian famously believed Jesus' birth was being referred to in John 1 (*Carn. Chr.* 19). Edwin Hoskyns suggests that John intentionally used language associated with the virgin birth of Jesus to present the birth of Christians. See his *The Fourth Gospel*, ed. Francis Noel Davey, 2nd rev. ed. (London: Faber and Faber, 1947), 164–66.

[58] John makes similar reversal of roles in John 8:12. Whereas Matthew's Gospel presents the disciples as the "light of the world (τὸ φῶς τοῦ κόσμου)" in the Sermon on the Mount (5:14), John presents Jesus as "the light of the world (τὸ φῶς τοῦ κόσμου)" in 8:12.

of how the re-envisioned people of God are *not* formed. Birth is the image employed to articulate the means of their formation, but this is a birth "*not* out of bloods and *not* out of the will of the flesh and *not* of the will of a husband" (v. 13, emphases added). The threefold Greek negations of οὐκ . . . οὐδέ . . . οὐδέ are then followed by the conjunction ἀλλά ("not . . . and not . . . and not . . . but"). This conjunction introduces the unconventional genealogical source of the ecclesial identity: θεός. Believers in Jesus are born "out of God" (ἐκ θεοῦ) and thus re-originated from a heavenly sphere—this genesis is not genetic.[59]

Before the narrative proper even begins, this Johannine birth narrative in the Prologue immediately establishes that ethnic foundations for the ecclesial entity of God's children are inoperative in this social vision. The idea of birthright is retained but radically redefined as divinely construed. In spite of an influential (even if irregularly practiced) strand in Jewish tradition that encouraged endogamy for preserving ethnic identity,[60] the origin of believers cannot be traced through a bloodline. Though predating the ministry of Jesus by a few centuries, both the widespread postexilic practice of divorce and the legitimization of group membership through biological descent after the exiles' return to Jerusalem attest to a consciousness within some Jewish circles that genealogical identity markers contributed to their own "terminal identity."[61]

[59] Byers, *Ecclesiology and Theosis in the Gospel of John*, 46.

[60] Erich S. Gruen, "Judaism in the Diaspora," in *The Eerdmans Dictionary of Early Judaism*, ed. John J. Collins and Daniel C. Harlow (Grand Rapids: Eerdmans, 2010), 77–96 (here 86–87). See his lengthier treatment of this strand of tradition in Erich S. Gruen, *Rethinking the Other in Antiquity* (Princeton: Princeton University Press, 2011), 277–307, in which he also discusses alternative traditions of openness to outsiders. In his more recent *Ethnicity in the Ancient World*, Gruen stresses that mixed marriages are found throughout the Hebrew Bible and the chief concern of endogamy was not to preserve genetics but to avoid idolatry (see the chapter "The Chosen People and Mixed Marriages," 113–30). For early Jewish texts featuring endogamy, see Joseph and Aseneth and Tobit.

[61] In the biblical story of postexilic national reconstitution recounted in Ezra-Nehemiah, Jews fastidiously consulted genealogical records to certify their legitimate biological descent. Aaron Kuecker explains that "an individual's most basic identity is his or her *terminal identity*. This social identity orients other lower-level identities and can be conceived as the

The accentuated negations in John 1:13 and the insistence of "the Jews" in John 8 that their place in the household of God's family is assured due to their biological heritage highlight that, in spite of other more polythetic understandings of Jewish ethnicity, there must have persisted some tendency in Jesus' and/or John's context in which common ancestry and shared descent had become paramount in identity construction. In response, the Fourth Evangelist is not delegitimizing Jewish ethnicity. He is, however, reconceiving a group identity that certain leading figures ground solely in Jewish lineage. The people of God are identified not by their biological birth within an ethnically determined nation or tribe, but by their spiritual birth within a divinely determined family.

This new birth "out of God," soon to be described by the parallel phrase "from above" (3:3), is a "becoming" (from γίνομαι) correlated with the "becoming" that follows immediately after in the Prologue: "the Word *became* flesh" (1:14; emphasis added). Though the actual language of birth in John 1:1-18 is reserved for the new ecclesial entity, it is clearly implied that Jesus was also born because he has taken on flesh. As stated earlier, and as the Samaritan woman confirms in John 4, when the Logos took on flesh in the Incarnation, it was specifically *Jewish* flesh (σὺ Ἰουδαῖος ὢν, 4:9).[62] In a mysterious divine-human exchange, the heavenly-bound Logos becomes Jewish flesh and flesh-bound believers become re-originated "from above," to use Johannine language of 3:3 and 8:23.[63]

This divinely generated identity of Johannine believers invites the language of theosis or deification. Employing such terminology risks the accusation of anachronistic exegesis. In defense, this

---

answer to the question, '*Who are my people?*'" And "ethnic identities quite often function as terminal identities. . . ." See Aaron Kuecker, "Ethnicity and Social Identity," in *T&T Clark Handbook to Social Identity in the New Testament*, ed. J. Brian Tucker and Coleman A. Baker (London: T&T Clark, 2014), 59–77 (here 73).

[62]   "Flesh (σάρξ) itself is not an ethnic identifier. In stating that the Logos becomes flesh, rather than that the Logos becomes a Jew or a Greek or a Caucasian, the Prologue gestures toward the universality of Jesus' import." See Carlos Raúl Sosa Siliezar, *Savior of the World: A Theology of the Universal Gospel* (Waco, Tex.: Baylor University Press, 2019), 42.

[63]   For more on this dynamic of divine-human exchange in the Prologue, see Byers, *Ecclesiology and Theosis in the Gospel of John*, 60–71.

language derives from later generations of church leaders who were reading New Testament texts—with John prominent among them—and striving to give some theological account of the themes of transformation and participation.[64] The risk of accusations of anachronism, which I am willing to take, is measured against another risk, which I am not willing to take, and that is to fall short in the descriptive task of articulating John's striking vision of transformative participation. Though the Fourth Evangelist does not explicitly claim that believers are deified, his narrative insinuates in this direction through 1) the repeated reference to birth out of God and from above; 2) the inclusion of believers within the divine oneness language that stems from the Shema; 3) the diffusion of reciprocity statements in which believers share in roles and activities established within the Gospel as divine; 4) the "I AM" statement on the lips of the man born blind; and 5) the use of Psalm 82 in which "gods" are recognized as "those to whom the λόγος of God came," a highly suggestive phrase for a text that opens with divine birth effected by the positive reception of the Jesus, the λόγος.

With or without the language of theosis, the point here is that divine birth rather than biological descent is the Johannine means of constructing the identity of God's people.

The Prologue's Ecclesial Narrative Script

As this brief overview of the Gospel's vision of theosis and language of divine birth indicates, the Prologue sets into place for the narrative proper an "ecclesial narrative script," a pattern of group formation and social delineation evoked by the presence of the Logos in the earthly domain.[65] The christologically provoked social realignment found in John 1:11-13 is emplotted throughout the Gospel story as the Prologue's cosmic tensions are illustrated through a dualistic division between Johannine characters and collective character groups. In this reconfiguration of both othering and de-othering, "the Jews" will regularly appear on the unfavorable side of John's "dualism." As Adele Reinhartz puts it, the

---

[64]   See the rationale for using theosis language in interpreting John in Michael J. Gorman, *Abide and Go: Missional Theosis in the Gospel of John* (Eugene, Ore.: Cascade, 2018), 8–26.

[65]   For more on this idea of an "ecclesial narrative script," see Byers, *Ecclesiology and Theosis in the Gospel of John*, 82–102.

Beloved Disciple as implied author "employs a rhetoric of binary opposition," crafting a "dichotomous structure" that "ultimately banishes the Other."[66] Though she acknowledges that "it is unrealistic to expect the Beloved Disciple to anticipate and adhere to a postmodern ethos that values diversity and multiplicity," Reinhartz is nonetheless clear that her most fundamental reservation in embracing his worldview is the refusal to accommodate a model in which alternatives may arise to the sharp binary of belief and eternal life or unbelief and eternal condemnation.[67]

There is no doubt that John's soteriological "dualism" offends pluralistic sensibilities. *But what if the rhetorical program is to undermine another exclusivist claim, that one lies beyond the pale of God's children unless they are also the biological children of Abraham, and thus racially "Jews"?* The concern here is whether or not John's soteriological othering (and de-othering) is premised on race or ethnicity. In tracing the instantiations of the ecclesial narrative script by which "the Jews" are "othered," I hope to show how, throughout his narrative, the Fourth Evangelist is not attacking Jewish ethnicity but delegitimating Jewish genetics as a soteriological and ecclesiological precondition. And in this program, John casts a soteriological framework that opens certain boundaries even while forming new ones.

The Fourth Evangelist's Narrative Destabilization of an Ethnically Determined "Israel"

Moving beyond the Prologue, it is worth recalling that in response to the "irresolvable" question—why would a Jewish text portray Jews who negatively call other Jews "the Jews"?—I am building the case that John is inviting readers (many or even most of whom would be Jewish[68]) to adopt as their terminal identity one that is divinely generated rather than racially determined (though a dispensing of the latter basis of identity is nowhere demanded). Opposed to an ethnicizing of soteriology, John is relativizing race and deracializing

---

[66]   Reinhartz, *Befriending the Beloved Disciple*, 141.

[67]   Reinhartz, *Befriending the Beloved Disciple*, 141.

[68]   I am not convinced by Adele Reinhartz's suggestion that John envisions primarily a Gentile audience (*Cast Out of the Covenant*, 135–46 [here 161]). See my remarks in Andrew J. Byers, review of *Cast Out of the Covenant*, by Adele Reinhartz, *RBL* 6 (2019).

salvation. Does the rest of John's narrative bear this out? Like Peter and the Beloved Disciple in John 20, we now embark on a footrace of sorts, pausing briefly at a number of scenes to observe how John may be destabilizing the soteriological necessity of Jewish ethnic identity markers and affirming his ecclesial vision of a new social group divinely generated "from above" yet inhabiting the world, whether as Jews, Greeks, Romans, or Samaritans.

John 1:19–28, 47 | John the Baptist, οἱ Ἰουδαῖοι, and One Who Is ἀληθῶς Ἰσραηλίτις

Luke and Matthew use the ministry of John the Baptist to call into question the tendency to define salvation and covenant belonging along racial/ethnic lines:

> Do not presume to say to yourselves, "We have Abraham as our ancestor (πατέρα ἔχομεν τὸν Ἀβραάμ)"; for I tell you, God is able from these stones to raise up children to Abraham (τέκνα τῷ Ἀβραάμ). (Matt 3:9 NRSV)

> Bear fruits worthy of repentance. Do not begin to say to yourselves, "We have Abraham as our ancestor (πατέρα ἔχομεν τὸν Ἀβραάμ)"; for I tell you, God is able from these stones to raise up children to Abraham. (Luke 3:8 NRSV)

For the First and Third Evangelists, an axe lies ready to dismember the metaphorical trees that rely inordinately on their ancestral heritage. John the Evangelist is actually more subtle in his Gospel's opening material, but it is surely no mistake that we first encounter "the Jews" immediately after the Prologue has established a narrative script in which the children of God are defined by divine birth and not by ethnic status.

With rough parallels shared between Luke and Matthew, John's introduction of οἱ Ἰουδαῖοι into the narrative occurs in a dialogue scene with John the Baptist. As already discussed, their inaugural reference is surely foundational for the corporate character profile that will receive expanded elaboration throughout the narrative. Though they do not actually appear on stage at this point in the sequence (they are merely acknowledged as those who sent the

priests and Levites querying the Baptist), John establishes a hermeneutical point already mentioned—*whenever a broad-brush categorization occurs, look for qualifications.* And here, the Ἰουδαῖοι are
directly linked to leading figures among the Pharisees (1:24).

Soon after these "Jews" are introduced (as a leadership group
operating behind the scenes), we encounter someone whom
Jesus designates as "truly an Israelite in whom there is no deceit
(δόλος)" (1:47 NRSV). This salutation contrasts the prospective
disciple with the deceitfulness associated with Jacob, later named
Israel. Given that Jacob's dream of the ladder in Genesis 28:12
is referred to in John 1:51, C. K. Barrett suggests that the use of
δόλος in 1:47 evokes Jacob's theft of Esau's paternal blessing in
Genesis 27.[69] Isaac explains to Esau, "your brother came deceit-
fully (μετὰ δόλου), and he has taken away your blessing," to which
Esau replies, "is he not rightly named Jacob? . . . He took away my
birthright; and look, now he has taken away my blessing" (37:35-
36 NRSV). Though the Septuagint transliterates the Hebrew name
יעקב to Ιακωβ, the Greek lexeme behind the name's meaning is
δόλος. In Jesus' greeting of Nathanael, John recalls the problematic nature attending the origins of Jewish lineage and the birthright of Jacob/Israel.

Nathanael's designation as one without δόλος appears ironic at
first (since he is skeptical that anything good can come out of Naza-
reth), but the favorable epithet is actualized in his positive reception
of Jesus. Though deceit marks the legacy of the patriarch Israel, his
namesake bears redemptive possibilities ultimately available in the
Messiah, here identified with Jesus. The word Ἰσραηλίτης follows
not long after John the Baptist has explained his purpose for baptiz-
ing, so "that [Jesus] might be revealed to Israel" (1:31). Yet this prospect of the Christ's manifestation to Israel follows immediately after
the Baptist has hailed him in universalizing colors as "the Lamb
of God who takes away the sin of the κόσμος" (1:29).[70] Freighted
with theological connotations as the name for God's faithful people,

---

[69]   C. K. Barrett, *The Gospel According to St John: An Introduction with
Commentary and Notes on the Greek Text,* 2nd ed. (London: SPCK, 1978
[1955]), 185. Similarly, Thompson, *John,* 52.

[70]   See the discussion in Sosa Siliezar, *Savior of the World,* 13–18.

"Israel" is a positive term for John, the meaning of which is more porous than an ethnic modifier.[71]

In summary, the Ἰουδαῖοι are introduced in John 1:19–28 as authoritative figures seated in Jerusalem who are making concerned inquiries into the ministry of John the Baptist, a prophetic character whose role is to present Jesus to Israel as one who brings a salvation of universal scope, extending to the κόσμος (a theme that accords well with longstanding scriptural traditions). Though the Christology of Nathanael and the other disciples in John 1 is underdeveloped (as indicated by Jesus in 1:51), the evangelist is crafting a profile for his ideal Jewish reception of Jesus. Readers are introduced to two collective character groups: "Israel," emblematic of positive Jewish reception, and "the Jews," who will become increasingly associated with a negative reception of Jesus. The Logos has come to "his own," and in these early scenes "some receive him." Scope for the same response entails both Israel and the world.

John 3 | Nicodemus, a Leader of οἱ Ἰουδαῖοι

The Prologue's idea of divine re-origination reappears in Jesus' conversation with Nicodemus, a "ruler of the Jews (ἄρχων τῶν Ἰουδαίων)" who is also "out of the Pharisees" (ἐκ τῶν Φαρισαίων) (3:1). These coextensive group identifications place Nicodemus within the social sphere of those who have inquired about the ministry of John the Baptist. Significantly, his narrative role is as yet undetermined by those associations—since "Nicodemus 'came to [Jesus]' just as Jesus had come to John (1:29) and Nathanael had come to Jesus earlier (1:47),"[72] he is a Pharisee and a Jew open to the positive trajectory of the ecclesial narrative script. His coming "by night" certainly darkens his introduction and adumbrates Judas' hour of betrayal in 13:30. Judas, however, *departed from* Jesus,

[71] On "Israel" as a positive term in John, see Thompson, *John*, 52; D. Moody Smith, *The Theology of the Gospel of John*, NTT (Cambridge: Cambridge University Press, 1995), 172; Donaldson, *Jews and Anti-Judaism*, 89. In a recent monograph, Mark Blumhofer argues that John's Gospel narrates a vision for the future of "Israel" which is alternative to the vision embodied in John's Ἰουδαῖοι. See his *The Gospel of John and the Future of Israel*, SNTSMS 177 (Cambridge: Cambridge University Press, 2019).

[72] J. Ramsey Michaels, *The Gospel of John*, NICNT (Grand Rapids: Eerdmans, 2010), 177.

while Nicodemus *came to* Jesus, one who has been earlier referred to as the Light (1:4-9). As J. Ramsey Michaels puts it, "Nicodemus' motives and spiritual condition" must be left at this point in John as "an open question."[73]

The idea of birth "from above (ἄνωθεν)" re-articulates the divine genealogy of believers in John 1:12-13, an act of origination that accrues extra layers of meaning by the reuse of terms and ideas introduced after the Prologue. Birth "out of God (ἐκ θεοῦ)" in John 1 is expanded into birth "out of water and Spirit (ἐξ ὕδατος καὶ πνεύματος)" in John 3. The same idea of divine generation is clearly in place since the contrast of this birth from above is with *flesh*: "what has been born (τὸ γεγεννημένον) out of the flesh is flesh (ἐκ τῆς σαρκὸς σάρξ ἐστιν)" (3:6), an echo of how the children of God are *not* born according to John 1:13 ("not out of the will of flesh [οὐδὲ ἐκ θελήματος σαρκός]"). The procreative capability of flesh is limited solely to the generation of more flesh. In contrast, water and Spirit have been associated with eternal life offered through the ministry of Jesus. The people of God comprise those who have been regenerated as new beings sourced in the realm "from above."

As a Pharisee, a Ἰουδαῖος, "a teacher of Israel," and a ruler of "the Jews," this divine re-origination of the people of God is a truth of which Nicodemus should be cognizant (3:10). The clear implication is that if anyone should be able to grasp the idea of a divine social composition, it should be a "Jew" who teaches "Israel."[74] This dialogue prompts Jesus' statement that his salvific mission is grounded in God's love for the world. Because the scope of salvation extends to the κόσμος, what is required is a re-origination from the heavenly sphere that overrides any mortal, flesh-induced genealogies.[75]

---

[73]   Michaels, *Gospel of John*, 178.
[74]   Jerome H. Neyrey views "Israelite" as a term in direct contrast to Ἰουδαῖος, but in John 3 it seems as though "Israel" and "the Jews" are not necessarily binary categories. Potentially, at least, they could be parallels. Rejection is contingent—not inevitable—at this stage in the narrative. For Neyrey's observation, challenged here, see Jerome H. Neyrey, *The Gospel of John in Cultural and Rhetorical Perspective* (Grand Rapids: Eerdmans, 2009), 89–90.
[75]   Lars Kierspel has argued that "the Jews" are paralleled with "world" in John. The cosmos comprises the collective disposition of antagonism toward Jesus, and features primarily in the Prologue, the Farewell

Though he fades from view in John 3 and seems numbered among those who "do not receive our testimony" (3:11), Nicodemus will reappear in this Gospel as a "Jew" on a trajectory of receiving Jesus (7:50; 19:39), indicating that the group labeled οἱ Ἰουδαῖοι bears potential for a divine birthright as long as biological birthrights are recognized as soteriologically irrelevant.

John 4 | "Salvation is from οἱ Ἰουδαῖοι": ἡ Σαμαρῖτις and Jesus the "Jew"

The encounter with Nicodemus, a named member of the Jewish elite, stands in striking contrast with the next dialogue scene, in which Jesus encounters an unnamed Samaritan woman. Ethnic language is clustered throughout this account of Jesus' stopover in Samaria en route to Galilee. From the mouth of the Samaritan woman, the Fourth Evangelist makes clear the ethnic identity of Jesus: he is a Jew, a Ἰουδαῖος. The ethnic (and gender) distinctiveness of these two interlocutors is succinctly indicated in verse 9: "How is it that you, being a Jew (Ἰουδαῖος), ask to drink from me, a Samaritan woman (γυναικὸς Σαμαρίτιδος)?" (4:9).[76] The evangelist adds the editorial note that "Ἰουδαῖοι do not have dealings with Samaritans," further clarifying the developing narrative profile of "the Jews" as those who collectively view the Samaritans as *the other*. In this scene, we find a Ἰουδαῖος, Jesus, breaking out of the social expectations and practices (here, that of *othering*) associated with the ethnic identifier of the term Ἰουδαῖος. The Samaritan woman makes an appeal to her own ethnic heritage in asking,

---

Discourse, and in speech material. In the narrative, the Gospel writer presents "the Jews" as embodying the world in historical particularity. See Lars Kierspel, *The Jews and the World in the Fourth Gospel*, WUNT 2/220 (Tübingen: Mohr Siebeck, 2006).

[76] That Jesus agrees with her recognition of his ethnicity is made clear in 4:22. See Craig S. Keener, *The Gospel of John: A Commentary*, 2 vols. (Peabody, Mass.: Hendrickson, 2003), 1:601. Reinhartz is dismissive of this significance, however, pointing out that "while it [the word Ἰουδαῖος] is applied to Jesus (4:9), it is never used of a figure who is a believer; this despite the fact that almost all the followers of and believers in Jesus within the Gospel narrative, with the exception of the Samaritan woman, her compatriots, and, perhaps, the officer of John 4 are Jewish in the national and ethnic sense." See Reinhartz, "'Jews' and Jews in the Fourth Gospel," 220.

"Are you greater than *our father* Jacob?" (4:12, emphases added).

Then, in a discussion about which mountain summit holds pride of place between Gerizim or Zion as the site of authentic worship, Jesus reports in 4:22 that "salvation is from the Jews (ἡ σωτερία ἐκ τῶν Ἰουδαίων ἐστίν)."[77] This statement, however, is immediately qualified, succeeded by the adversative conjunction, "but" (ἀλλά). Though salvation emerges out of Jewish heritage and tradition, clearly affirmed here by Jesus,[78] a new situation is underway in which conventional ethnic identity markers such as geographical domain, sites of cultic observance, and ancestral lineage have no ultimate soteriological value. There is no indication here that Jesus wishes to dispense with his own ethnicity, or that he implores his interlocutor to forego her Samaritan identity. The point is not that ethnicity is wrong but that "God is Spirit" (4:24), and "spirit" is a category ultimately more soteriologically inclusive than ethnic particulars and the limitations of cultic geography,[79] whether Jewish or Samaritan.[80]

[77] See the discussion on this scene in Sosa Siliezar, *Savior of the World*, 30–38.

[78] Andrew Lincoln explains that this claim ("salvation is from the Jews") "constitutes an extremely positive statement, indicating that what Johannine Christians know affirms the validity of the promises of salvation God made to Israel and posits a continuity between those promises and the new epoch of worshipping the Father. As will become apparent in the ensuing dialogue, the statement can be made because in Jesus the Jew (cf. v. 9) the promises of salvation for Israel come to fulfilment." See Andrew T. Lincoln, *The Gospel According to Saint John*, BNTC (London: Continuum, 2005), 177.

[79] "It is the spirit that gives life; the flesh is useless" (6:63). On the point of territorial identity, Raymond Brown puts it nicely: "The idea that God would be worshiped neither in Jerusalem nor on the Samaritan mountain but in Spirit and truth (4:21-23) means there are no second-class Christians geographically." See Raymond E. Brown, *The Churches the Apostles Left Behind* (New York: Paulist Press, 1984), 109.

[80] Adele Reinhartz argues that this so-called positive statement about the Ἰουδαῖοι in 4:22 "is consistent with the anti-Jewish rhetoric that pervades John's Gospel" (*Cast Out of the Covenant*, 73) since the only reason Jesus makes such a claim is ultimately to point to himself, not to the Jews collectively or Judaism. Salvation is from the Jews only because it is from the Jew Jesus (a claim slightly at odds with her insistence on "the

From the Prologue and John 3, readers know by this point in the narrative that belief in Jesus effects a divine re-origination understood as birth from above "out of water and Spirit" (3:5) into a categorically new relationship with God who, as made clear in John 4, is to be worshiped in Spirit and in truth. In John 4, Jesus the Jew offers the Samaritan woman living water. When she leaves her now unneeded water bucket behind, she reports to her village that she has found the "savior (ὁ σωτὴρ) of the world (κόσμος)." The Ἰουδαῖος from *Galilee* leaving *Judea* via *Samaria* brings a salvation in which spatial borders blur and ethnic boundary lines fade.[81] The soteriology on offer may arise from a context characterized by ethnic and geographical particularities and certainly entails its own confessional particularities, but its invitational scope is universalized through Jesus the "Jew."[82]

John 5–7 | "All will be taught of God" (Including "Greeks"): Universal Language at Jewish Festivals

John's negative portrayal of "the Jews" in the scenes leading up to the dialogue in John 8 seems rhetorically designed to extend the salvation that is "from the Jews" beyond Jewish cultic practices and territory. This rhetorical program is conducted in part by Jesus' attendance at three Jewish festivals in John 5–7. Significantly, where the polemical instances of οἱ Ἰουδαῖοι occur, they are directly linked with 1) Sabbath-breaking (the breach of a religious practice marking Jewish distinctiveness) in John 5; 2) the universalizing of divine teaching beyond Jewish contexts in John 6; and 3) the supposed extension of Jesus' teaching among the Greeks (Ἕλληνές) in John 7, an ethnic category that will receive further development in John 12.

Gospel's ambivalence about Jesus's own status as a *Ioudaios*") (*Cast Out of the Covenant*, 81).

[81] A similar reading of this passage is offered by Kobus Kok, "As the Father Has Sent Me, I Send You: Towards a Missional-Incarnational Ethos in John 4," in *Moral Language in the New Testament: The Interrelatedness of Language and Ethics in Early Christian Writings*, ed. Ruben Zimmerman and Jan G. van der Watt, WUNT 2/296 (Tübingen: Mohr Siebeck, 2010), 168–93.

[82] Esler uses the phrase "trans-ethnic identity" as well as "non-ethnic" to express the inclusion of other groups like the Samaritans ("From *Ioudaioi* to Children of God," 133).

The first two scenes open with a reference to a festival of "the Jews," and then the phrase "the Jews" goes on narrative silence *until Jesus does or says something that threatens the more restrictive parameters of group identity.*

After Jesus heals the man at the pool of Bethesda, John makes four references to "the Jews" after supplying the narrative detail, "but that day was a Sabbath" (5:9). Thus far in the Gospel, the Ἰουδαῖοι have merely posed challenging questions, first to John the Baptist (through their representatives)—

> "Who are you?" . . . "What then? Are you Elijah?" . . . "Are you the prophet?" . . . "Who are you?" . . . "What do you say about yourself?" . . . "Why then are you baptizing if you are neither the Messiah, nor Elijah, nor the prophet?" (from 1:19-25)

and then to Jesus—

> "What sign can you show us for doing this?" (2:18)

> "This temple has been under construction for forty-six years, and will you raise it up in three days?" (2:20)

> "How can anyone be born after having grown old? Can one enter a second time into the mother's womb and be born?" . . . "How can these things be?" (from 3:4-9)[83]

In John 5, however, the Ἰουδαῖοι become more than questioners and begin "persecuting Jesus" precisely because he was "doing these things on the Sabbath" (5:16). In his cumulative development of what is often perceived as anti-Jewish polemic, it is important to attend to this initial scene of direct conflict between Jesus and "the Jews." At the heart of the controversy is not only the reconfiguration of Jewish theology (in which Jesus makes himself equal to God in 5:18), but also the subtle challenge leveled against the construction of Israel's identity on ethnic terms. The "observance of Sabbath was one of the most prominent boundary

---

[83] These citations are from the NRSV. Though Nicodemus asks the questions in 3:4-9, he is presented as a ruler of "the Jews" and initially addresses Jesus in the first-person plural (οἴδαμεν, 3:2) as a representative voice.

markers setting Jewish communities apart from Gentiles"[84] and thus a critical component in the set of ethnic identity practices Barclay calls "constitution." In his program of de-ethnicizing soteriology and group membership within his vision of the people of God, the evangelist depicts Jesus not undermining Sabbath-keeping but affirming it as a celebration of divine creative power and thus expanding its acquired restrictions: "If a man receives circumcision on the sabbath in order that the law of Moses may not be broken, are you angry with me because I healed a man's whole body on the sabbath?" (7:23 NRSV). Both circumcision and Sabbath-keeping reinforce group boundaries. John presses instead for a Sabbath practice of restorative healing and the consequent resocialization of someone whose chronic illness had limited his participation in the broader Jewish community.

After setting the stage with a reference to the Passover, another "festival τῶν Ἰουδαίων," the narrative silence on the Ἰουδαῖοι obtains until 6:41, where the spark of controversy is once again linked to the openness of John's ecclesial vision beyond a predominantly ethnic scope. In his retelling of divine provision in the Exodus story, Jesus emphasizes that God, not Moses, sent the manna, and the recipients of the christological iteration of this nourishment are not limited to those whose ancestors ate the bread in the wilderness: "For the bread of God is that which descends out of heaven and gives life to the κόσμος" (6:33). As the Bread of Life, the soteriological benefits of Jesus are offered to any who might come to him (ὁ ἐρχόμενος) and to the one who might believe in him (ὁ πιστεύων) (6:35). This universal availability of God's salvific nourishment of the world (on the particular condition of Christ-belief) is reinforced by the repeated use of "all" (πᾶς)[85]:

---

[84]   Daniel K. Falk, "Sabbath," in *The Eerdmans Dictionary of Early Judaism*, ed. John J. Collins and Daniel C. Harlow (Grand Rapids: Eerdmans, 2010), 1174–76 (here 1174).

[85]   See the important discussion on the universalizing language of John 6 in Sosa Siliezar, *Savior of the World*, 52–59. His observations about Jesus' use of Isa 54, with its wider universal themes of God's salvation, in contrast with "the Jews'" use of the more particularizing Ps 78, is insightful, even if it must be remembered that underway is a Jewish (as well as a Christian) form of universalism that bears particularizing conditions.

Everything (πᾶν) that the Father gives me will come to me, and anyone who comes to me I will never drive away. . . . And this is the will of him who sent me, that I should lose nothing of all (πᾶν) that he has given me, but raise it up on the last day. This is indeed the will of my Father, that all (πᾶς) who see the Son and believe in him may have eternal life; and I will raise them up on the last day. (6:37-39 NRSV)

Responding to the murmurings of "the Jews" (which echo the grumblings of Israelites in the wilderness[86]), Jesus cites Isaiah 54:13—"they will 'all be taught of God (πάντες διδακτοὶ θεοῦ)'" (6:45), highlighting the scriptural foundation of universalism.[87] Building on this use of "all (πᾶς)," Jesus then twice uses the indefinite pronoun "anyone (τις)" to describe the potential beneficiary of eternal life (6:50–51). The theme of universal access to Jesus' salvation has its climactic rhetorical moment in the line "the bread that I give on behalf of the life of *the world* (κόσμου) is my flesh" (6:51).[88]

In this interaction, "the Jews" continue their narrative script of questioning:

"Is not this Jesus, the son of Joseph, whose father and mother we know?" (6:42)

"How can he now say, 'I have come down from heaven'?" (6:42)

"How can this man give us his flesh to eat?" (6:52)[89]

---

[86] The of γογγύζω in 6:41 and 6:61 (cf. 6:43) draws on the use of the verb in Exod 17:3, Num 11:1; 14:27, 29; 16:41; and 17:5.

[87] It seems that the "all" of πάντες διδακτοὶ θεοῦ receives further clarification through the use of "all" that immediately follows: "Everyone (πᾶς) who has heard and learned from the Father comes to me" (6:45 NRSV).

[88] It is important to acknowledge here the continuation of a Johannine understanding of divine election (expressed earlier in John 3:27). Twice in the John 6 discourse, Jesus points out that, in spite of the universal availability of the salvation he brings, those who actually come to him are drawn to him (6:44, 65). As Sosa Siliezar points out, though, drawing on a range of significant interpreters, God draws from further afield than the Jewish people (*Savior of the World*, 57, n. 41).

[89] These citations are from the NRSV.

The middle question concerns the audacity of Jesus' self-evaluation. The first question has the rhetorical aim of circumscribing the extent of Jesus' import. Roughly parallel with the Synoptics (Mark 6:3 // Matt 13:55 // Luke 4:22), this question highlights a particular mode of Jewish resistance to the universality of divine salvation. By appealing to Jesus' biological ancestry, they dismiss a christological vocation that encompasses the "world." And the final question expresses not only incredulity over the literal act of consuming Jesus, but also reservations over dietary practices. Eating Jesus' flesh and drinking his blood is not only bizarre; it is also offensive. Along with Sabbath-keeping and circumcision, a kosher diet demarcated Jews from other ethnic groups. Again, at the heart of the Jesus-Ἰουδαῖοι conflict is a soteriology of cosmic proportions and a social identity beyond ethnic delineations. What limits participation in the new society Jesus envisions is not the identity of one's father or mother, but one's willingness to embrace the challenging message of Jesus as the bread of God, a message that puts off not only "the Jews," but also many of the (surely Jewish) disciples (6:60-65).

Moving into John 7, five questions are directly attributed to "the Jews"[90] during Booths, another "festival τῶν Ἰουδαίων" (7:2):

"Where is he?" (7:11)

"How does this man have such learning, when he has never been taught?" (7:15)

"Where does this man intend to go that we will not find him?" (7:35)

"Does he intend to go to the Diaspora among the Greeks and teach the Greeks?" (7:35)

"What does he mean by saying 'You will search for me and will not find me' and 'where I am, you cannot come?'" (7:36)[91]

[90]   Again, the term Ἰουδαῖοι must be understood within its narrative frame. In the sequential account of John 7, "the Jews" seem synonymous with the Pharisees (7:32, 45, 47-48) and the "chief priests (οἱ ἀρχιερεῖς)," who seem to be collectively presented as "the rulers (οἱ ἄρχοντες)" (7:26, 48).

[91]   These quotations are taken from the NRSV. Note the other questions in John 7, asked largely by the crowd and its various divisions, in 7:25-26, 31, 41-42. The Pharisees are implicitly co-identified with the

The final two questions are joined together and demonstrate that "the Jews" are wise to the scope of Jesus' ministry. Having heard Jesus speak of "all," "anyone," and "the world" in John 6, their natural assumption after Jesus makes an elusive reference to an imminent departure is that he envisions another stage of his mission, one that will cross geographical and ethnic boundaries well beyond Samaria and Samaritans. The term Ἑλληνές most likely refers to ethnic Gentiles, not merely diaspora Jews (for which Luke's term Ἑλληνισταί would perhaps be more fitting—see Acts 6:1, 9:29, 11:20).[92] Either way, a soteriological trajectory that is "from the Jews" (4:22) and radiating outwards is recognized by Jesus' opponents. In his narrative destabilization of ethnic particularity as a means of membership within Israel, the evangelist links the questioning of the Ἰουδαῖοι with the de-ethnicizing program of his protagonist, hailed by Nathanael as Israel's "king" (1:49).

John 8 | "You are of [your] father, the devil": οἱ Ἰουδαῖοι and Jesus the "Samaritan"

Turning to John 8, we enter the scene that lies at the heart of what is understood as Johannine anti-Semitism and anti-Judaism. Jesus' controversial accusation that "the Jews" originate from the devil occurs during an argument over biological paternity, and thus ethnic particularity. Surprisingly, the words "you are of your father the devil" are specifically addressed to a group of "Ἰουδαῖοι who had believed in him" (8:31 NRSV). Their belief, however, is exposed as

---

Ἰουδαῖοι and ask questions in 7:45, 47-48; Nicodemus, "being one of them (εἷς ὢν ἐξ αὐτῶν)" (7:50) asks the final question of the scene in v. 51.

[92] The question is a perennial concern in Johannine interpretation: Does John mean with this term to denote diaspora Jews or Gentile God-fearers throughout the Mediterranean world who have attached themselves to Jewish beliefs and practices? The genitive construction can be read either way, but the strongest case is for the latter. Keener points out that the term always applies to Gentiles in its use not only in the NT but also in the LXX (Keener, *Gospel of John*, 1:721). See also Brown, *Gospel According to John*, 1:314; Johannes Beutler, *A Commentary on the Gospel of John*, trans. Michael Tait (Grand Rapids: Eerdmans, 2017 [2013]), 332; Sherri Brown, "The Greeks: Jesus' Hour and the Weight of the World," in *Character Studies in the Fourth Gospel: Narrative Approaches to Seventy Figures in John*, ed. Steven A. Hunt, D. Francois Tolmie, and Ruben Zimmermann, WUNT 314 (Tübingen: Mohr Siebeck, 2013), 397–402 (here 400).

untenable because they ultimately reject the soteriological necessity (a *Johannine* particularity) of entering a social group that is divinely generated rather than biologically determined. They profess instead that their soteriological status is sufficiently premised on ethnic heritage: "we are the seed of Abraham (σπέρμα Ἀβραάμ ἐσμεν)" (8:33). As in his conversation with the Samaritan woman, Jesus moves the dialogue beyond questions of ethnicity and physical paternity and shifts to a cosmic or metaphysical horizon. In John 8, Jesus claims that these "Jews" are in bondage to sin, imprisoned within a household as slaves to its power and in need of a transfer of status that can only be granted by the heir, the household owner's son.[93] "The slave does not remain in the house forever" (8:35) is strong language implying that the Ἰουδαῖοι must acknowledge their standing (along with other sinners) as household servants, a position that can only be altered by a re-origination from "above."[94]

Jesus acknowledges that these Ἰουδαῖοι are the biological heirs of Abraham (οἶδα ὅτι σπέρμα Ἀβραάμ ἐστε, v. 37) and after the jibe about the devil's paternity, he even reaffirms their claim to Abraham as father (Ἀβραὰμ ὁ πατὴρ ὑμῶν).[95] But as the Prologue has made unequivocally clear, biological birth—and thus ethnic descent—is no true guarantor of covenant belonging.[96] Even so, the Ἰουδαῖοι here continue to assert their legitimacy on the basis of their progenitor, hastening to add that "we are not born out of sexual immorality" (v. 41). Yet it is not enough simply to have *not* been born

---

93   See Paul's similar depiction of Abraham's household in Rom 9:6-13 and Gal 4.

94   Jesus' interaction with "the Jews" here draws on the previous interaction in John 6 in which the "Living Father" (6:57) is contrasted with "fathers" of the Jews (6:31, 49, 58).

95   "Being children of Abraham is certainly not antithetical to being children of God; so it is not the fatherhood of Abraham (and therefore ethnic Israel) that Jesus condemns per se, but the fatherhood of Satan." See Byers, *Ecclesiology and Theosis in the Gospel of John*, 92.

96   Raimo Hakola does not see a difference between the language of "seed of Abraham" and "children of Abraham." I think there is indeed a difference. The phrase "children of Abraham" functions as a positive parallel to "children of God," who, according to the Prologue, are not born out of bloodline or the will of a husband, means of conception more closely linked with the biological language of "seed." See Hakola, *Identity Matters*, 190–91.

ἐκ πορνείας ("out of sexual immorality"), nor is salvation ensured by the pedigree of Abrahamic lineage because, as John has claimed from the beginning, no human birthright—no mortal means of reproduction—can bear the weight of Johannine soteriology.

The soteriological logic of the Ἰουδαῖοι, on the other hand—the logic John intends to expose and undermine throughout his narrative—is this: *since we are not products of fornication but biologically descended from Abraham, we are therefore children of the One God of the Shema* (ἕνα πατέρα ἔχομεν τὸν θεόν, 8:41).[97] On the contrary, for John, one cannot be qualified or disqualified as a member of God's people on the basis of a legitimate or illegitimate human genealogy. Again, a divine birth is necessary, and is enacted from above through the reception of Jesus, the Logos, as the embodiment of Israel's one God, who will soon declare "I and the Father are one" and who repeatedly voices the divine self-declaration ἐγώ εἰμι in chapter 8 ("if you do not believe that I AM, you will die in your sins," 8:24).

That the entire dialogue concerns the exaltation of ethnic identity and biological descent over divine re-origination is confirmed in vv. 47 and 48. In 8:47 the Johannine Jesus summarizes what the discussion has illustrated: "The one who is from God (ἐκ τοῦ θεοῦ) hears the words of God; for this reason you do not hear, because you are not from God (ἐκ τοῦ θεοῦ)." That these particular Ἰουδαῖοι are viewing Jewish genealogy as a basis of covenant belonging is affirmed by their reply to Jesus in v. 48. To the offensive accusation that their father is the devil, these Ἰουδαῖοι offer as a commensurate riposte: "Do we not rightly say that you are a Samaritan and you have a demon?" (the latter accusation, "you have a demon," has already been lodged in 7:20). The charge that Jesus is a Samaritan is likely intended to exclude him from the very means that these Ἰουδαῖοι believe justify their claims to the fatherhood of God: ethnic identity. And the ethnic identity of "Samaritan" becomes an epithet paired with the demonic, intentionally echoing Jesus' perceived association with Jewish ethnicity to the diabolic. How Jesus responds in 8:49 is telling: "Jesus answered, 'I do not have a demon.'"

---

[97] On the use of the Shema in 8:41, see the next chapter, plus Byers, *Ecclesiology and Theosis in the Gospel of John*, 131–34; Beutler, *Commentary on the Gospel of John*, 241–43; Lincoln, *Gospel According to St. John*, 272.

He could have rightly added, "Nor am I a Samaritan," yet there is no protest about the first part of the accusation, which involves an ethnic identity. Being a Ἰουδαῖος or a Σαμαρίτης is relativized to a divine pedigree sourced from above.

To be clear, Jesus seems positive about the label "children of Abraham (τέκνα τοῦ Ἀβραάμ)" (8:39). A claim to that status, however, is not legitimated by being Abraham's "seed" but by an appropriate ethic.[98] And any desire to put Jesus to death certainly falls well beyond the evangelist's notion of an Abrahamic ethic. Even so, it is crucially significant that Jesus does not here tie immorality to a race. The intent to kill is not inherently *Jewish*—it is inherently *diabolical*. For John, group identity is elective and participatory. One can choose one's alignments, whether with cosmic evil or with divine goodness. The Ἰουδαῖοι here are accused of immorality not because they are Ἰουδαῖοι but because they have allied themselves with the immoral agenda of a malevolent paternity.

Again, in his rhetorical use of "the Jews," John is likely himself a Jew targeting a specific set of ideas that are held by a limited group of Jews amidst a narrative populated with other Jews of both undefined commitments and the potential for making a choice one way or another. In the controversial dialogue of John 8, the Johannine Jesus is challenging the forging of links between a fixed ethnic identity and the covenant people of God. John himself stands as a Jewish representative of alternative ways of thinking about Jewish identity that are not limited to ancestral descent. The evangelist is thus rejecting what contemporary specialists might call a "primordialist" or "essentialist" way of thinking about ethnicity and promoting instead a more "constructivist" model (albeit christologically figured, and thus marked by a different set of parameters discussed more in chapter 5).[99]

---

[98]   In this regard, John is still operating within Jewish parameters. Like John, Philo deems virtue as important as bloodline in determining Jewish identity. See *Virt.* 195, 206–207, and 211–216, briefly discussed in Horrell, *Ethnicity and Inclusion*, 98, 144–45.

[99]   For these terms, see the discussions in Horrell, *Ethnicity and Inclusion*, 69, and Gruen, *Ethnicity in the Ancient World*, 1–7, both drawing in part on Hutchinson and Smith, introduction to *Ethnicity*, 8–9.

John 11–12, 19–20 | INRI: οἱ Ἕλληνές, οἱ Ῥωμαῖοι and "The King τῶν Ἰουδαίων"

So far in John's Gospel, the negative instances of "the Jews" have been associated with a resistance to the universalizing scope of covenant belonging along with a refusal to relinquish biological birthright and ethnic-specific religious customs as soteriological conditions. In John 11, other important values for Jewish ethnic identity rise to the narrative surface. After "many of the Jews" have believed in Jesus following Lazarus' resurrection, the chief priests and Pharisees convene what appears to be an emergency council meeting under the perceived threat that, should Jesus continue to gain followers, "the Romans will come and take away from us both the place (τὸν τόπον) and the nation (τὸ ἔθνος)" (11:48). Territory (and/or the Temple and its symbolic locale) and Roman political recognition—both painfully lost at the time of John's writing—are here shown with striking irony as other ethnically charged values (along with common ancestry) constituting the taxonomy of peoplehood John is criticizing. As Jo-Ann Brant puts it, "[t]heir conviction that the temple in Jerusalem and their leadership are necessary for the preservation of God's people is precisely the supposition that this Gospel refutes."[100]

The model of the Jewish leadership for securing group identity is contrasted with the model of Johannine ecclesiology as the council seeks to shore up ethnic and territorial identity by eliminating the distraction of Jesus, whose death will actually serve to cast a wider social net by gathering "the dispersed children of God into one" (11:52). As the evangelist puts it, Jesus was about to die "on behalf of the nation (ὑπὲρ τοῦ ἔθνους), and *not on behalf of the nation only* (καὶ οὐκ ὑπὲρ τοῦ ἔθνους μόνον), but in order that he might gather the dispersed children of God into one" (from 11:51-52, emphases added). Commenting on this verse, Richard Hays writes, "John's reference to gathering the dispersed children of God who are not part of the nation completely overspills the boundaries of the immediate narrative setting in Jerusalem, and it suggests a

[100] Jo-Ann Brant, *John*, Paideia (Grand Rapids: Baker Academic, 2011), 177.

universal dimension to the saving significance of Jesus' death."[101] Reading this scene in John 11 with the reference to "other sheep" lingering from John 10 and the anticipation of approaching Greeks in John 12, "it would suggest that John's ecclesiology is not limited to a vision for a restored ethnic Israel, but that it has universal dimensions."[102]

The machinations that lead to Jesus' crucifixion are instantly set into place after this council meeting ("from that day on they planned to kill him," 11:53). The Johannine emphasis on the universal import of Jesus' death, first indicated by the Baptist's testimony that the Lamb would be slain for the sins of the κόσμος, is repeated with vivid clarity in John 12 as Jesus exclaims, "And I, when I am lifted up from the earth, will draw all people to myself" (12:32 NRSV). This assertion is made in response to the request of Greeks (οἱ Ἕλληνές) to see Jesus, a request made immediately after the exasperated statement by "the Pharisees" in 12:19, "Look, the κόσμος has gone after him!" (NRSV). The reappearance of the "Greeks" (cf. John 7:35) in this scene and the reiteration of the cosmic ambit of Jesus' salvation evidence that John's soteriological trajectory is broad and ever stretching across assumed boundaries, all the while redrawing a singular boundary line on the grounds of Christ-belief.

In the Johannine passion narrative, where almost a third of John's uses of Ἰουδαῖοι appear, this universalizing of salvation beyond ethnic classifications is symbolically inscribed in Latin, Greek, and Aramaic on the placard above the cross: "Jesus the Nazorean, King of the Jews" (19:19). Moments earlier, Pilate had presented this King of "the Jews" to the Jewish leaders. In a disturbing scene of grim irony, fearful of losing their place and their "nation (ἔθνος)," John depicts them pledging allegiance instead to the king of the Romans: "we have no king but Caesar" (19:15). On the other side of the Praetorium's walls, Jesus had claimed a kingdom not of this world, a kingdom that is not geographically or ethnically defined but otherworldly and rising above the horizons

---

[101] Richard B. Hays, *Echoes of Scripture in the Gospels* (Waco, Tex.: Baylor University Press, 2016), 341.

[102] Hays, *Echoes of Scripture in the Gospels*, 342.

of national and racial identity. That inscription above the cross on Golgotha proclaimed in ethnic particulars a soteriology of trans-ethnic scope. Jesus, "the Nazorean, King of the Ἰουδαῖοι," a title scrawled into the local, official, and universal languages of the day, is presented as the Jewish Lamb of God slain to release the κόσμος from the metaphysical power of sin.

What John "Others": The Ἰουδαῖοι or Something Else?

In John's Gospel, Jesus is creating a community. The foregoing is an account of the evangelist's destabilization of Jewish ethnicity as a prerequisite for inclusion. Membership is still particularized, though solely by divine re-origination through belief in Jesus. All other criteria for belonging are eradicated. Ancestral bonds are soteriologically inadequate, territorial space and national status are ecclesiologically irrelevant, and Jewish cultic rites find their significance only in their relation to the Ἰουδαῖος Jesus. According to John, ethnicity and all its connotations have no determinative bearing on salvation and the group identity of Christ-believers. The effect is, at least potentially, an expansive de-othering of certain exclusionary ideas, and a recasting of "the other" along a confessional wall that has Jesus as its "door" or "gate." Though first-century Jews would have variously weighted each component of Barclay's retrospective inventory of ethnic identity markers in a diverse range of configurations, the Fourth Evangelist writes to challenge a rigid, more exclusive mode of constructing group identity: a common ancestry and a common territory are no longer necessary; language barriers are dissolved as Aramaic, Greek, and Latin crown the cross of the "King of the Jews"; and the sacred scriptures, religious constitution, and temple are reconfigured around him. The boundaries of geographical distance and immutable biological descent erected walls of othering. The Fourth Evangelist (along with the Jewish writer Paul the Apostle) would see such walls crumble and erect a different sort of partition, though one that comes with the invitation to "come and see" via a christological gate.

Why would a Jewish text polemically target "the Jews"? With John's Gospel, this Jewish author ironically labels "Ἰουδαῖοι" those Ἰουδαῖοι who demand that one must become a Ἰουδαῖος to become a member of Israel. Salvation is most certainly "from the Jews" (4:22), but that does not mean that one must become a Jew in order to be saved. Given the number of questions John portrays them asking, "the Jews" are readily identifiable as a character group bearing rhetorical functions. Though surely reflective in some sense of historical situations and figures underlying the text, their primary rhetorical purpose is to embody a strand of resistance to the Christian message that restricted covenant membership to ethnic constraints. John persistently hammers cracks into the conceptual foundation that ethnicity decides the membership status of God's people. This salvation and ecclesial membership are offered to "all," to "anyone"; indeed, it is available to the "world." In Johannine thought, no one is "cast out of the covenant"—as Adele Reinhartz puts it, employing Johannine language—for being ethnically Jewish per se, but for rejecting the vision of expanded covenantal membership in Israel as it is christologically reconfigured.[103]

But there is certainly "the other" in this vision of community. In John 8, the *locus classicus* of the topic at hand, the alterity between "the Jews" and Jesus is sharpest when Ἰουδαῖοι who initially believe in Jesus are insisting that their genealogy is the primary basis of covenant membership (8:31-33), plotting violence against Jesus (8:39-44), and allegedly operating in the realm of falsehood directly opposed to divine truth. In the first instance, these "Jews" refuse to accommodate the Johannine soteriology that requires divine regeneration. In the second and third instances, they are aligning themselves with the ultimate negative "other" for John: the one in whom cosmic darkness is personified. The signature activities of the devil are killing and lying. What is diabolical is not Jewishness, but murder and falsehood. The Ἰουδαῖοι are not described as being children of the devil because they are "children of Abraham." Their self-identification as "children of Abraham" is challenged, but explicitly because they are betraying an Abrahamic ethic in wanting to commit murder.[104]

---

[103]   The title of Reinhartz's most recent study on John's anti-Judaism is drawn from Jesus' parable of the vine in John 15, particularly v. 6 (a parable addressed, in my reading, to disciples who are Jewish). See her important discussion in *Cast Out of the Covenant*, 51–62.

[104]   As Marianne Meye Thompson writes of John's polemic against "the Jews" in John 8, "Jesus warns that appealing to Abraham as their father avails nothing if they do not act as Abraham did" (*John*, 197).

Jesus will insinuate that he is "greater than" their father Abraham (8:53), but Abraham is nonetheless portrayed as a positive figure in John 8. Though the language is certainly conducive for dangerous misapplication, calling "the Jews" the offspring of Satan is not intended as a defamation of ethnicity or a racial slur; *Jesus is condemning not ethnicity in 8:44 but the falsehood and violent agenda* of those who insist on ethnic heritage as an identity marker for "Israel." The immediate basis supplied for calling his interlocutors children of the devil is murderous intent: "you are of [your] father, the devil, and you want to do the desires of your father.[105] That one was a murderer (ἀνθρωποκτόνος) from the beginning." As 1 John 3:8 confirms, what constitutes satanic paternity in Johannine thought is not ethnicity, but sinfulness expressed in violence: "the one committing sin is from the devil (ἐκ τοῦ διαβόλου), because the devil has been sinning from the beginning." The negative prototype is Cain, who was "of the evil one" (ἐκ τοῦ πονηροῦ) and "murdered his brother" (1 John 3:12), and "every murderer does not have eternal life."[106] The polemical force of John 8:44 is ultimately directed against a violent ethic, *not an ethnicity*. Had Jesus been confronted by a belligerent group of Gentiles set on his death, surely he would just have readily identified them as "children of the devil," offspring of the one who was a "murderer from the beginning." Any Christian who desires to murder a Ἰουδαῖος on the basis of John 8:44 would actually find themselves *condemned* by its logic.

Though understandably confusing in a day that is rightly vigilant against racial othering, what John is othering is thus more ethical than ethnic. What he is "anti-" is not Jewishness per se, but the ethnicizing of salvation that restricts group membership. The

---

[105] Similarly, Christopher Blumhofer writes that "*inherent to the charges in John that a person or group acts under the power of the devil is an awareness that the primary role of the devil or a demon is to prevent Israel from embracing its identity as the people of God and to hold God's people captive to the falsehood and violence that have always marked the devil's ways*" (*Gospel of John and the Future of Israel*, 158; emphases original).

[106] The context in 1 John is a contrast between the one who sins and originates from the devil and the one who does righteousness and thus demonstrates that she is "born of God (ὁ γεγεννημένος ἐκ τοῦ θεοῦ)." The word ἀνθρωποκτόνος is only in the Johannine literature in the NT and found in 8:44 and in this discussion in 1 John 3 (v. 15).

appropriate application of John's portrait of "the Jews" is not the demonization of a particular ethnicity but the elimination of ethnic particularities as conditions for covenant membership. Surely, the Johannine Jesus would be just as vehemently opposed to any modern-era program that assumes Christianity is primarily the possession of Caucasians. Any attempt to anchor Christian identity in national citizenship or denomination or gender or class or race would be deemed in a Johannine hermeneutic as false and inappropriately restrictive.[107] Imagine, for example, European missionaries who preach to sub-Saharan African people groups that they must adopt Western practices and cultural ideologies in order to become "Christian." In such a scenario, a modern-day "John" might write as a fellow Westerner to a mixed audience of African, Asian, and European Christians a testimonial narrative about the Logos who entered, for the sake of love, the cultural realm of "the other." And to highlight the error of equating Westernization with salvation, he might just ironically label his fellow Europeans, inordinately confident in their particularized identity, as "the Westerners."

Though John denounces soteriological particularism based on race or ethnicity, a different sort of "other" arises from his soteriological particularism based on christological confession. This mode of othering will be discussed later in chapter 5. For now, it is important to affirm that the Johannine Jesus who directed such harsh language against a collective intent to kill would surely also view as diabolical falsehood the later European rhetoric that led to pogroms. And the Third Reich's murderous campaigns against

---

[107] Referring to John 8:44, Craig Koester writes, "The passage cannot be used to demonize an ethnic or religious group. More importantly, deception, hatred, and violence are what Jesus opposes . . . In this passage Jesus engages in a sharp debate, but when it comes to throwing stones, Jesus does not participate (8:59)." See Craig R. Koester, *The Word of Life: A Theology of John's Gospel* (Grand Rapids: Eerdmans, 2008), 76. Paul Anderson has also rejected any Johannine motivations for violence (Anderson, "Anti-Semitism," 273–75). David Rensberger, who certainly agrees that John opposes violence, nevertheless believes that the dehumanization of his enemies lays a "groundwork for violence" should the tables of power be overturned. See the discussion in David K. Rensberger, *Johannine Faith and Liberating Community* (Philadelphia: Westminster, 1988), 116–17, 125–26.

Jews and recent attacks on synagogues in the United States and else-where he would surely decry as deriving from the twisted figure of personified evil. The "children of the devil" are not those born with a particular shade of skin or biological heritage but those who align themselves with violence and cosmic darkness (and thus find them-selves in violent opposition to John's idea of Jesus). In my view, the Fourth Gospel is not anti-Jewish or anti-Semitic but anti-falsehood, anti-violence, anti-evil (as understood in Johannine thought), and opposed to soteriological particularism based on ethnicity.[108]

Conclusion: John's Ecclesiology of Divine Identity

John 8:44 has become a hermeneutical entry point into the Fourth Gospel, so that any attempt at explaining or defending the charge of anti-Judaism becomes in the minds of many interpreters a col-lusion with some of the darkest forces in distant and recent history. My approach in this chapter has been to allow the Prologue to serve as an entry point, and to offer carefully reasoned exegesis, even if it goes some way toward making a defense on the evangelist's behalf and with the acknowledgement that my own locatedness within a Christian and Western tradition has its own interpretive liabilities and blind spots. I certainly recognize the dangerous hermeneuti-cal potential inherent within John's polemical use of the phrase οἱ Ἰουδαῖοι. But I also believe that the evangelist, who never autho-rizes violence and never commands hatred except to the believer, who must be willing to hate his own life in order to preserve it, would surely want the opportunity to correct how his narra-tive has been employed in its complicated history of reception. In response to the question, "Why would Jews in a Jewish text negatively call other Jews, 'Jews'?" I have proposed this answer: because the Gospel writer intends to de-ethnicize soteriology and

[108] It may be worth noting that "the Jews" are not without universal-izing tendencies in their Johannine portrayal. Though they certainly view the label "Samaritan" and probably even "Galilean" as negative epithets (8:48; 7:52), the "Greeks" are not disparaged as a group, perhaps indicating that, though different from Judean "Jews," there is no reason to suspect that these Ἕλληνές (whether diaspora Jews or Gentiles) are othered by Ἰουδαῖοι in John's presentation.

point to a terminal identity that is sourced from above, permitting inclusion to others regardless of their ethnic identity. An ecclesiology of a divine social identity does not deracialize its members. Jews are the seed of Abraham regardless of their cosmic origin. An ecclesiology of divine group identity, rather, makes participation universally open on new grounds of membership: belief in the Word who became Jewish flesh to save Romans, Greeks, Samaritans, Jews, and the κόσμος.

Since not all will share in this belief, appeals to a Christian inclusiveness or universalism are not entirely warranted. Again, the degree to which this confessional line constructs "the other" will be discussed in chapter 5. For now, we look to another group of "others" as perceived by the sectarian hermeneutic. We have considered here John and other Jews. We now turn to the topic of John and other Christians.

3

John and Other Christians I

Evangelists, Schismatics, Secessionists, and Strangers

As the previous chapter has argued, John did not other "the Jews" because they were Jews. He and his fellow community members, perceived as a divine kinship group, were most probably, like Jesus, Ἰουδαῖοι themselves.[1] The distance erected within the Gospel narrative between believers and those labeled "the Jews" was not along racial lines but along the lines of theology, Christology, ecclesiology, and ethical intent as the evangelist proffered a divine social identity configured around a divine Christ. The "John" behind the Gospel and Epistles canonically bearing his name, however, is not just viewed by many as anti-Jewish, but also as contrarian toward other Christ-confessing Jews and to other forms of what we now

[1] The Epistles provide further evidence that the wider Johannine network was predominantly Jewish. One example is the reference to the ἐθνικοί in 3 John 7, understood as a reference to non-Christian pagans. A second is the description in 1 John 2:22 of the "antichrist" as one who denies that Jesus is the Christ. The docetic denial that Jesus came in the flesh is a feature that might be shared between Jews and Gentiles. Denying or embracing Jesus as the Messiah, however, are positions most rationally attributed to Jews. See John Painter, *1, 2, and 3 John*, SP 18 (Collegeville, Minn.: Liturgical Press, 2002), 200; and Paul Trebilco, *The Early Christians in Ephesus from Paul to Ignatius*, WUNT 166 (Tübingen: Mohr Siebeck, 2004), 384–85.

call "Christianity."[2] In biblical scholarship we often modify early
Christian traditions with terms like "Petrine," "Pauline," "catholic"
or "mainstream," with the latter two often understood as a confla-
tion of the former two. Though early Christianity was sectarian (by
certain sociological definitions) as a minority movement experi-
encing some degree of tension with its surrounding milieu, "Johannine" Christianity is viewed as a sect within the sect, as a minority
strand within a marginal phenomenon. The Gospel and Epistles
of John are indeed the products of a marginal community (which
surely warrants sustained attention given contemporary concerns
to heed minority voices). Yet in a scholarly climate in which differences are regularly stressed—whether for the promise of undertak-
ing comparative studies or perhaps for the sake of problematizing
canonical sensibilities—Johannine diversity is axiomatically inten-
sified as adversarial. This early Christian movement's antagonism
is viewed not only as externally focused. The dissonance was also
internalized. "John" could not get along with others on the proverbial playground, and even othered those within his own playgroup.[3]

The purpose of this chapter and the next is to provide grounds
for re-narrating the nature of Johannine Christianity's external
and internal dynamics toward other Christians. These Johannine
believers were not inclusive of any and all views and practices,
but neither were they closed and disapproving of every outsider
or outlying idea within the broader Christian purview. Just like

---

[2]   The shift in chapter titles from "John and Other Jews" to "John
and Other Christians" is not intended to demarcate early Jews from early
Christians. Most first generations of Christians were of course Jews. The
purpose is to explore another realm of possible Johannine "othering." As
this opening paragraph explains, John is often viewed not only as hostile
(or at least inhospitable) towards Jews who did not believe in Jesus, but
also towards Christians who did.

[3]   A recent collection of studies on the Johannine Epistles takes on a
title epitomizing these angles of conflict: "Communities in Dispute." See
R. Alan Culpepper and Paul N. Anderson, eds., *Communities in Dispute:
Current Scholarship on the Johannine Epistles*, SBLECL 13 (Atlanta: SBL
Press, 2014), 3. The title (of this helpful and important volume) is meant to
capture not only the internal tensions within Johannine Christianity, but
also the disagreements about the Epistles among contemporary Johannine
scholars (see "Introduction," 2).

Petrine and Pauline Christianity—along with Markan, Lukan, and Matthean—there are degrees of openness and flexibility alongside the cautionary and at times resistant stance required by any social movement premised on deeply held convictions. In the following chapter, attention is given to the ecclesiology of "Johannine Christianity," often understood as anti-hierarchical, anti-institutional, and charismatic to a fault. Here, we consider John amidst other evangelists, other Johannine Christians, and other "others" who are envisaged on the horizons.

John and Other Evangelists

The canon of Christian Scripture is a textual embodiment of unified plurality.[4] A sort of literary de-othering occurs as diverse written works are aggregated into a collective whole. The formation of the Fourfold Gospel is an act of de-othering, perhaps most pronounced in its inclusion of John. Yet the Fourth Gospel's canonical placement accentuates the degree to which it is "other" to Matthew, Mark, and Luke. Conscious of the distinctiveness of John's work vis-à-vis what later scholarship would call the "Synoptics," Clement of Alexandria's oft-cited observation that John wrote a "spiritual Gospel" (πνευματικὸν εὐαγγέλιον) is a *comparative* statement.[5] He is making some provision as to why John is so different. Does the uniqueness of the Fourth Evangelist's narrative of Jesus imply, however, that he is fundamentally "anti-" as in antagonistically sectarian? Clement's impulse is to supply an apologetic for the otherness, not to problematize it. Eusebius, who records Clement's remark on John's "spiritual" nature, makes a similar move when he writes this of the Fourth Evangelist:

> The three gospels which had been written down before were distributed to all including himself; it is said that he welcomed (ἀποδέξεσθαι) them and testified to their truth but said that there was only lacking to the narrative the account of what was done by Christ at first and at the beginning of the preaching. The story is surely true.[6]

4   This is true, of course, for the Jewish scriptures as well.
5   Cited in Eusebius, *HE* 4.14.7.
6   Eusebius, *HE* 3.24.7 (Lake, LCL).

Eusebius and Clement perceive John's canonical relation to Matthew, Mark, and Luke as one of supplementation. Yet in contemporary scholarship (prompted by Bauer, and not without some
justification), such an approach is naïve, and Johannine diversity
funds the perception of Johannine polarity. John is the "other"
Gospel written in contradistinction from the mainstream textual
witnesses to Jesus.

With difference so quickly interpreted as sectarian antipathy in
the study of Gospel of origins, it is unsurprising that something of a
consensus has emerged that Gospel writing was a competitive practice, part and parcel of the early Christian maelstrom of divisive
diversity.[7] In his study *Writing the Gospels*, Eric Eve notes that "Matthew probably aimed at not just competing with Mark but replacing
it."[8] The evidence seems clearer in Luke's Preface.[9] Acknowledging
that "many (πολλοί)" have set their hand to the task of composing a
Jesus narrative, Luke writes that "it seemed good to me also (ἔδοξεν
κἀμοὶ)" (1:3) to provide an alternative account that is penned "accurately" and "orderly" (from ἀκριβῶς and καθεξῆς, respectively).[10]

[7]   Though he understands Gospel writing as constituent of a broader
act of reception that involves the (corrective, and possibly competitive)
rewriting of prior material, Francis Watson understands the Fourfold Gospel as a composite text that celebrates diversity in the early Christian reception of Jesus. See *Gospel Writing: A Canonical Perspective* (Grand Rapids:
Eerdmans, 2013) and *The Fourfold Gospel: A Theological Reading of the New
Testament Portraits of Jesus* (Grand Rapids: Baker Academic, 2016).

[8]   Eric Eve, *Writing the Gospels: Composition and Memory* (London:
SPCK, 2016), 29. See the wider discussion in 29–32. Eve is in some respects
following the arguments of David C. Sim, "Matthew's Use of Mark: Did
Matthew Intend to Supplement or to Replace His Primary Source?" *NTS*
57 (2011): 176–92. (And for Sim, the answer is "yes.")

[9]   See also the comments of Papias who reports that Mark, as Peter's
interpreter, penned everything accurately (ἀκριβῶς) just not in order (οὐ
μέντοι τάξει), an order that Matthew later corrects for the Markan sayings/
oracles (τὰ λόγια συνετάξατο). See Eusebius, *HE* 3.39.15–16. Francis Watson urges interpreters not to miss the connection between Markan disor-
der and Matthean order in *Gospel Writing*, 124–28.

[10]   The word καθεξῆς that I have translated "orderly" can imply
chronological sequence (as Watson takes it [*Gospel Writing*, 124–31]). It
can also refer to interpretative arrangement. On this reading, see David
P. Moessner, "The Appeal and Power of Poetics (Luke 1:1-4): Luke's Superior Credentials (παρακολουθηκότι), Narrative Sequence (καθεξῆς), and

With tongue in cheek, Luke is writing not merely to supplement but to replace.[11] His Gospel will be superior to previous attempts (why else would he take on the project of producing another?).[12]

Because he diverges so sharply from the collective Synoptic material, the Fourth Evangelist is at times viewed not merely as a corrective or competitive Gospel writer, but as one who has set out to usurp and upend the standing traditions.[13] Surely it is John's distinctiveness from Matthew, Mark, and Luke that has generated the consensus in New Testament studies that the testimonies of the Beloved Disciple are at odds with mainstream Christianity. Robert Kysar writes,

> The very title now given to the first three Gospels among students of the New Testament stresses the peculiarity of the fourth. They are called the Synoptic Gospels. This means that they have a common point of view, that they see their subject in a similar fashion. The Fourth Gospel is not synoptic, then, but sees its subject in a way that stands quite apart from its three colleagues in the Christian canon. If you will, the Fourth Gospel is a maverick among the Gospels. It runs free of the perspective presented in Matthew, Mark, and Luke. It is the non-conformist Gospel of the bunch. No wonder that so many of the heretical movements in

---

Firmness of Understanding (ἡ ἀσφάλεια) for the Reader," in *Jesus and the Heritage of Israel*, ed. David P. Moessner (Harrisburg: Trinity Press International, 1999), 84–123; and "Dionysius's Narrative 'Arrangement' (οἰκονομία) as the Hermeneutical Key to Luke's Re-Vision of the 'Many,'" in *Paul, Luke and the Graeco-Roman World: Essays in Honour of Alexander J. M. Wedderburn*, ed. Alf Christophersen et al., JSNTSup 217 (Sheffield: Sheffield University Press, 2002), 149–64.

[11] Joel Green, however, writes, "Luke mentions other attempts at orderly accounts not to disparage them, but to place his project in their company." See Joel B. Green, *The Gospel of Luke*, NICNT (Grand Rapids: Eerdmans, 1997), 37.

[12] For a measured approach to Gospel writing as rewriting for the sake of "revision, supplementation, or substitution," see Watson, *Gospel Writing*, 121–31, 286–90 (the quotation is from 286).

[13] Hans Windisch, *Johannes und die Synoptiker: Wollte der vierte Evangelist die älteren Evangelien ergänzen oder ersetzen?* WUNT 12 (Leipzig: Hinrichs, 1926). Windisch's answer to the question of his subtitle is that John wrote to do the latter (to replace, rather than supplement, the Synoptics).

the history of the Christian church have used the Gospel of John as their authority in the New Testament.[14]

As Gospel scholarship shifts back toward the view that John knew the Synoptics,[15] should this Fourth Evangelist be viewed as a perpetrator of textual violence in his use of their material? Is Johannine Gospel writing a sectarian exercise designed to "other" established evangelists and their traditions and social networks?

No—at least, not necessarily.

John's two attempts at narrative closure reveal much about his perspective on other Gospels, or at least on other accounts

---

[14]   Robert Kysar, *John: The Maverick Gospel*, 3rd ed. (Louisville: Westminster John Knox, 2007 [1976, 1993]), 2.

[15]   In anglophone scholarship the turn away from John's dependence on the Synoptics was secured by P. Gardner Smith, *Saint John and the Synoptic Gospels* (Cambridge: Cambridge University Press, 2011 [1938]). For a book-length treatment on the scholarly twists and turns in the debate, see D. Moody Smith, *John among the Synoptics: The Relationship in Twentieth-Century Research*, 2nd ed. (Columbia: University of South Carolina Press, 2001 [1992]). The shift in identifying John's use of the Synoptics has been supported by C. K. Barrett, *The Gospel According to St John: An Introduction with Commentary and Notes on the Greek Text*, 2nd ed. (London: SPCK, 1978 [1955]) and the "Leuven hypothesis." See Frans Neirynck, "John and the Synoptics," in *L'Évangile de Jean: Sources, redaction, théologie*, ed. Marinus de Jonge, BETL 44 (Leuven: Leuven University Press, 1977), 73–106; Adelbert Denaux, ed., *John and the Synoptics*, BETL 101 (Leuven: Leuven University Press, 1992); Michael Labahn and Manfred Lang, "Johannes und die Synoptikser: Positionen und Impulse seit 1990," in *Kontexte des Johannesevangeliums: Das vierte Evangelium in religions- und traditionsgeschichtlicher Perspektive*, ed. Jörg Frey and Udo Schnelle, WUNT 175 (Tübingen: Mohr Siebeck, 2004), 443–515. A number of recent and forthcoming studies are also arguing for some form of John's dependence on the Synoptics. See Richard Bauckham, "John for Readers of Mark," in *The Gospels for All Christians: Rethinking the Gospel Audiences*, ed. Richard Bauckham (Grand Rapids: Eerdmans, 1998), 147–71; Harold W. Attridge, "John and Other Gospels," in *The Oxford Handbook of Johannine Studies*, ed. Judith M. Lieu and Martinus C. de Boer (Oxford: Oxford University Press, 2018), 45–62; Wendy E. S. North, *What John Knew and What John Wrote: A Study in John and the Synoptics*, Interpreting Johannine Literature (Lanham, Md.: Fortress, 2020); Eve-Marie Becker, Helen K. Bond, Catrin H. Williams, eds., *John's Transformation of Mark* (London: T&T Clark, 2020); and Elizabeth J. B. Corsar, "John's Use of Mark: A Study in Light of Ancient Compositional Practices" (PhD diss., University of Edinburgh, 2018).

promoting the significance of Jesus.[16] If Matthew and Luke envisioned their task of Gospel composition as corrective, competitive, and polemical, the Fourth Evangelist may be viewed as more irenic. John certainly wrote to supplement existing Jesus-material, but he does not envision displacing them. In both concluding sections he openly acknowledges the possibility of other extant accounts as well as the likelihood that future accounts will emerge onto the literary scene:

> Now Jesus did many other signs (πολλὰ . . . ἄλλα σημεῖα) in the presence of his disciples (ἐνώπιον τῶν μαθητῶν[17]), which are not written in this book (ἐν τῷ βιλίῳ τούτῳ). (20:30 NRSV)

> But there are also many other things (ἄλλα πολλὰ) that Jesus did; if every one of them were written down, I suppose that the world itself could not contain the books (βιβλία) that would be written. (21:25 NRSV)

In a recent study, however, Chris Keith has identified these colophons as evidence that John is more competitive a Gospel writer than Luke:

> John 20:30–31 and 21:24–25 represent the most competitive instances of textualization in contemporary Jesus tradition. Luke's Gospel asserts superiority to its competitors, but John's Gospel asserts superiority to its competitors on the basis of continuing the scriptural textuality of Moses. John asserts the value of "this book" (20:30) about Jesus implicitly over any predecessors or current rivals and explicitly over any books about Jesus that may yet come (21:25).[18]

---

[16]   John 21 may, of course, have been a later addition. Though this "epilogue" may clear up a few matters on the relationship between Peter and the Beloved Disciple, it still ends inconclusively.

[17]   NA 28 leaves the pronoun "his (αὐτοῦ)" that immediately follows this phrase within brackets to indicate its presence as contested yet not without strong attestation.

[18]   Chris Keith, *The Gospel as Manuscript: An Early History of the Jesus Tradition as Material Artifact* (New York: Oxford University Press, 2020), 154. I came across Keith's study after having completed the draft of my chapter here. His arguments should be carefully weighed, but I am not convinced that the evidence leads to the conclusion that John is a polemical evangelist.

For Keith, John's reference to that which is written specifically "in *this* book (ἐν τῷ βιβλίῳ τούτῳ)" (20:30, emphases added) targets other books and dismisses their comparative worth.[19] Keith acknowledges that it is quite a lot of weight to attribute to a pronoun ("this"/οὗτος). For his argument to work, he marshals two other points: 1) John writes as if he is composing and continuing Scripture and thus supplies an authoritative work that brooks no rivals and forestalls any future attempts at replacement; and 2) John is clearly correcting Mark in certain narrative scenes (as in when Jesus carries his own cross and prays differently about the cup of suffering), which Keith takes as evidence that the entire Fourth Gospel is designed to supplant its textual forebears.[20]

I suggest an alternative way of reading John's colophons.

This Gospel writer acknowledges openly that beyond his own pages is a surplus of other material that may yield an unending proliferation of other works. For John, the Jesus tradition is marked by inexhaustible plurality—there are (many!) *other* things, *other* signs, and (both potentially and actually) *other* books. The evangelist (and also the redactor, if John 21 is a later addition) does not end his narrative as if it were a capstone work that finalizes the foregoing attempts at Gospel writing and closes off all future projects.[21] The Jesus story is fecund, capable of an uncontainable and unmanageable reception process that has been underway for some time.[22] John's open acknowledg-

---

[19] Similarly, see Tom Thatcher, *Why John WROTE a Gospel: Jesus—Memory—History* (Louisville: Westminster John Knox, 2006), 149–50.

[20] See the wider discussion in Keith, *Gospel as Manuscript*, 131–54.

[21] "The closing remarks here allow for other traditions, perhaps even other ways to tell the story of Jesus, so long as they are consonant with the truthful witness borne" by the Fourth Evangelist. See Marianne Meye Thompson, *John: A Commentary*, NTL (Louisville: Westminster John Knox, 2015), 447. J. Ramsey Michaels observes that John here "leaves the door open for other narratives." See J. Ramsey Michaels, *The Gospel of John*, NICNT (Grand Rapids: Eerdmans, 2010), 1058. He also notes that 21:25 serves as a fitting ending to the Fourfold Gospel in the Christian canon (1057–58).

[22] For a list of other ancient writers who used similar hyperbolic language to speak of the excess of material, see Craig S. Keener, *The Gospel*

ment of other things and other signs left unrecorded in his own composition indicates that he anticipates members of his audience to detect his intentional omissions, most likely because he envisions some familiarity with other Gospel-like compositions. These concluding remarks are therefore, at least in part, apologetic in that the writer is hedging off any criticism for failing to incorporate other well-known scenes.

Yet John is not being deferential, either. He is confident in the veracity and worth of his own product ("we know that his testimony is true," 21:24; see also 19:35); and he seems convinced that his composition is sufficient for his specific purpose ("these are written so that you may [come to] believe," 20:31). But the concluding materials in 20:30 and 21:25 are not necessarily the statements of an author presenting an alternative account wholly incompatible with existing options. To be sure, "this book" is indispensable. It must be situated alongside existing and possible future works and it serves an additional and important pastoral and missional purpose.

What about Keith's two main points? Though I am not convinced John thinks he is writing Scripture per se, I would certainly affirm that he is writing *scripturally*. Yet it is clear that John would not envision his own Gospel as a *replacement* for the scriptures of Israel—as Wendy North has recently pointed out, he regularly works with authoritative scriptural texts and expands or reinterprets their meanings without intending to replace them.[23] In short, *John can write authoritatively alongside and in the stream of other authoritative works.* Just as this evangelist offers unique interpretations of Scripture, he offers unique interpretations of Jesus. Scripture, and other renderings of the Jesus tradition, are not thereby denounced. Penning another Gospel is not evidence that John deems Synoptic writers as falling short of their shared literary vocation of exploring christological inexhaustibility.

As for Keith's second argument, John's alteration of Synoptic accounts does not necessarily evidence a Johannine determination

---

of John: A Commentary, 2 vols. (Peabody, Mass.: Hendrickson, 2003), 2:1240–41.

23   See North, *What John Knew and What John Wrote.*

to replace other Gospels. Garrick Allen has shown that the evangelists actively engaged in the rewriting of prior works, a compositional practice well attested in early Jewish literary convention. Rewriting was an exercise in acknowledging the surplus of revelatory potential in extant material. To use a synoptic example, Allen claims that

> What underwrites Matthew's reworking of Mark is the idea that Mark did not have a monopoly on revelatory traditions. The totality of Jesus tradition was not localized within Mark, and the importance of the character generated more textual material about him. Mark's presentation of Jesus was contingent. Matthew too does not claim comprehensiveness in his work. NT authors recognized that the totality of revelation is something that one text cannot contain, nor is revelation defined purely in textual terms.[24]

Rewriting antecedent texts was not the rejection of those texts perforce, but an expression that those texts were not "comprehensive,"[25] something John acknowledges about his own work in his concluding statements. The Fourth Gospel's value is not in its power to usurp other Gospels, but in its capacity to offer a unique and truthful vista—alongside "others"—into the significance of Jesus.

It is also possible that, given John's later date, other Gospels had circulated widely enough that usurping or displacing them was out of the question in the evangelist's provenance. If he was indeed familiar with the Synoptics or even other similar narratives, then the enterprise of Johannine Gospel writing was only plied within a pluralistic field. He clearly did not feel compelled to cite directly his antecedent texts or appropriate their material into his own (the approach established by Matthew and Luke); nor did he imagine himself obliged to operate within the contours of their narrative details. These compositional freedoms, however, do not necessitate an interpretation of John as a maverick out to derail prior traditions

[24] Garrick V. Allen, "Rewriting and the Gospels" *JSNT* 41, no. 1 (2018) 58–69 (here 66).
[25] Allen, "Rewriting and the Gospels," 67.

or to "other" his predecessors. The Fourth Gospel is written out of a Johannine theology of excess ("Jesus did many other signs" and "many other things") and the world is not spacious enough for the outflow of countless publications.[26] John may be the "other" Gospel in his comparative relation to the Synoptics in modern scholarship, but the evangelist himself does not ineluctably "other" Matthew, Mark, and Luke.

John and Other Johannine Christians:
Schismatics, Secessionists, and Strangers

The prayer that believers may be "one" in John 17 and the sparse reference to "those who went out from us" in 1 John 2 are two key coordinates along which an historicizing approach maps reconstructions of Johannine Christianity.[27] Through mirror-reading, scholars reason that a prayer for "unity" implies internal strife, and the departure of the "secessionists" in 1 John corroborates suspicions that the "Johannine community" was fractious and schismatic.[28] In such an interpretive construct, these Johannine Christians had the tendency to "other" one another. Is the sectarianism so toxic that they cannot get along with their own fictive kin, much less with the wider world of emerging Christian networks?

To counter the trend of caricaturing Johannine Christianity as splitting apart at the communal seams, I consider three points in turn. The first is that the oneness for which Jesus prays in John 17 is less concerned with internal social unity than it is with a group identity grounded in the Shema. Next, I will suggest that the church

[26] John may well have envisioned Gospel writing to continue beyond his own work. For how his Gospel was used by later writers, see the studies by Lorne R. Zelyck, *John among the Other Gospels: The Reception of the Fourth Gospel in the Extra-Canonical Gospels*, WUNT 2/347 (Tübingen: Mohr Siebeck, 2013); Francis Watson, "A Gospel of the Eleven: The *Epistula Apostolorum* and the Johannine Tradition," in *Connecting Gospels: Beyond the Canonical/Non-Canonical Divide*, ed. Francis Watson and Sarah Parkhouse (Oxford: Oxford University Press, 2018), 189–215.

[27] Others include John 9 and the mission to the Samaritans in John 4.

[28] Judith M. Lieu offers an incisive account of this hermeneutical circle in "The Audience of the Johannine Letters," in Culpepper and Anderson, *Communities in Dispute*, 123–40 (esp. 123–24).

split of 1 John 2:19 has become unnecessarily overblown in biblical scholarship. The discussion ends with a look at the "strangers" whom the Elder encourages Gaius not to "other" but to *host*.

John 17 as a Prayer for Participation, Not Social Harmony

The term "one" in the Fourth Gospel is normally read as a gloss for "unity." But the oneness motif undergoes a careful narrative development that complicates this interpretation.[29] Jesus prays "that they may be one, as we are one" (17:11, 22) after readers have been conditioned to understand oneness within a complex thematic range. Two sets of scriptural texts lie in the background—the Shema of Deuteronomy 6:4 where God is proclaimed as "one," and Ezekiel 34 and 37 where God refers to "one" people under "one" Davidic shepherd.[30] Each time the term "one" appears in John's Gospel, the evangelist is alternating between these two Old Testament texts and their variant meanings of oneness. When the Shema is first echoed, the primary connotation is, as expected, theology.[31] When Ezekiel 34/37 is in view, Johannine oneness connotes Christology ("one shepherd") and ecclesiology ("one flock"). But expanded meanings accrue over the course of the narrative as Jesus includes himself within the divine oneness of the Shema in 10:30 ("I and the Father are one"). The term "one" at this point in the narrative (roughly halfway) now comprises theology and Christology. In John 17, all three oneness connotations—theological, christological, and ecclesiological—are fused together in climactic fashion:

---

[29] Since I have written extensively on these ideas already, I offer here a brief summary of the Johannine oneness motif. For more, see Andrew J. Byers, *Ecclesiology and Theosis in John's Gospel*, SNTSMS 166 (Cambridge: Cambridge University Press, 2017), 103–52.

[30] John's creative appropriation of divine and communal oneness in these scriptural texts demonstrates a determination to work out his "Christian" faith within his Jewish convictions and traditions.

[31] For recent studies on the Shema in John, see Lori Baron, "The Shema in John's Gospel and Jewish Restoration Eschatology," in *John and Judaism: A Contested Relationship in Context*, ed. R. Alan Culpepper and Paul N. Anderson, RBS 87 (Atlanta: SBL Press, 2017), 165–73; "The Shema in Mark and John and the Parting of the Ways," in *The Ways That Often Parted: Essays in Honor of Joel Marcus*, ed. Lori Baron, Jill Hicks-Keeton, and Matthew Thiessen, SBLECL 24 (Atlanta: SBL Press, 2018), 187–210.

Oneness Passage	Deut 6:4 Theology	Deut 6:4 Christology	Ezek 34/37 Christology	Ezek 34/37 Ecclesiology
John 8:41 "one Father: God"	√			
John 10:16 "one flock, one Shepherd"			√	√
John 10:30 "I and the Father are one"	√	√		
John 11:49-52 "One man" to die to gather God's people into "one"			√	√
John 17:11, 21-23 "that they may be one, as we are one"	√	√	√	√

What Jesus prays for in John 17 is not social harmony for a schismatic sect.

There are two dimensions to the social dynamics of Johannine oneness, and they are only indirectly deployable for shoring up disunity. The first social dimension of "one" is an associative and participatory group identity with the "one" God of Israel, and the second is the outward-oriented act of gathering in others beyond the immediate fold.

On the narrative level, the imminent threat addressed by Jesus' prayer for oneness is not *internal* but *external*—"you will be scattered" (16:32). This language of dispersal recalls the prophetic oracles of Ezekiel 34 and 37 in which God's people will be regathered (see John 11:49-52) under the benign rule of a messiah-figure. For John, this messiah-figure is the divine Logos who belongs within the theological oneness of the Shema. For believers to be reckoned as "one" with the "one Shepherd" and "one Father" is to be identified as the true people of the one God of Israel, an identification that is surely meaningful for what is likely a network of Jewish Christians whose Christ-devotion is being questioned by fellow Jews. One-ness certainly implies group solidarity—the re-formation of Israel envisioned by Ezekiel includes the reunification of Israel and Judah, and divine unity is surely reflected in social unity. But the primary accents in Jesus' prayer are on (Jewish) Christian social identity in the face of external threat and on participation within the divine interrelation of the one Father and one Shepherd.

Johannine oneness is not ultimately an appeal for peaceful coex-istence.[32] It is "sectarian" to the extent that it establishes a group iden-tity for those who have received the Logos, sketching a distinctive confessional boundary. The outlook, however, is invitational, not merely protective or insular. In both its social dimensions—binding their group identity to Israel's God and gathering in those scattered far afield—*Johannine oneness is inclusive of the other*. Divine one-ness opens to include Jesus, and the disciples are invited to partic-ipate within it.[33] Through their testimony, others will be included

[32]   For Bultmann, the unity prayed for in John 17 is unrealized because it is "a thing of the future" as the "other sheep" are gradually added to the fold over time. See Rudolf Bultmann, *Theology of the New Testament*, trans. Kendrick Grobel (Waco, Tex.: Baylor University Press, 2007 [1955, 1951]), 2:92.

[33]   In a 1998 essay, Fernando Segovia offered an "intercultural read-ing" of John 17 and criticized the dichotomy between the disciples and the world that is rhetorically constructed by Jesus' prayer. Segovia is personally alert to the dangers of imperial and colonial forces and understands John's Gospel as a work produced within the political teeth of imperial Rome. Moreover, he wisely identifies power inversion as a potential danger when critiques from the margins undermine and eventually topple the forces at the center. For Segovia, John's marginal and powerless voice does not pro-mote a reorganization of sociopolitical structures; instead, the evangelist simply reinforces the dynamics of center vs. margins and seeks a reversal of roles, upholding an unjust system. Such "strategies of inversion," though understandable, "may quite easily slip into similar situations of outright disdain and oppression of the 'other' and become enormously destruc-tive, for both body and mind." See Fernando F. Segovia, "Inclusion and Exclusion in John 17: An Intercultural Reading," in *"What is John?"* vol. 2: *Literary and Social Readings of the Fourth Gospel*, ed. Fernando F. Segovia, SBLSS 7 (Atlanta: Scholars Press, 1998), 183–209 (here 208). I agree with Segovia's analysis of power dynamics, but I would question their appli-cability to the Johannine sociopolitical vision. For one, the powers John

since Jesus prays for oneness "not only on behalf of these, but also on behalf of those who will believe in me because of their word, that they may all be one" (17:20-21a NRSV). Oneness is ultimately outward in its orientation, not inward, since its purpose is "so that the world may know that you have sent me and have loved them even as you have loved me" (17:23 NRSV).[34] The situation, therefore, that makes the most sense of John's narrative development of oneness is not an insular community fractured by internal schism but a network of (predominantly Jewish) believers who openly seek an expanded membership yet require assurance that their Christ-belief includes them within the "one" people of Israel's "one" God.

The Over-Dramatization of the Secessionists

"They went out from us," declares the author of 1 John. Little else is said. Yet this brief clause offers an irresistible temptation for us in the act of interpretation: not only does 1 John 2:19 afford a rare glimpse into *history*, but also evidence of early Christian *conflict*. What we know from the actual text is that a particular group of unknown number made an exit. Latching on to this unique instance of an historical event in the Johannine social life, however, scholars have produced elaborate profiles not only of these "opponents," "apostates,"

---

challenges are ultimately cosmic—Jesus' interactions with Pilate betoken an ambivalence toward Roman authority, which is merely the latest face of darker forces. As David Rensberger writes in the same volume as Segovia's essay, "The Johannine Christians did not seek to regain control of the levers of their society but instead offered a critique and an alternative vision—a witness—in their messianic community of unhierarchical love." See David Rensberger, "Sectarianism and Theological Interpretation in John," in Segovia, *"What is John?"* 2:139–56 (here 156). My second challenge to Segovia's reading is that the prayer for oneness in John 17, as argued above, blurs the boundaries of Johannine dichotomies since the term "one" is ultimately inclusive, relational, and invitational.

[34]   Raymond Brown suggested that "when Jesus prays, 'That they may all be one' (17:20–21), he is praying for the oneness of the Apostolic and the Johannine Christians. Here the Johannine attitude is just the opposite of the outlook of a sect." See Raymond E. Brown, *The Community of the Beloved Disciple: The Life, Loves, and Hates of an Individual Church in New Testament Times* (New York: Paulist Press, 1979), 90.

"schismatics," or "secessionists," but also of their positions.[35] We may cautiously deduce that they adhered to a range of ideas that were ultimately exposed as incompatible with Johannine Christology (1 John 2:18, 22-23; 3:23; 4:1-6, 15; 5:1, 5; cf 2 John 7-11), and that they seemed to have refused to live according to certain Johannine ethical practices (1 John 1:10; 2:3-9; 3:22-24; 4:20; 5:3). Pneumatology and eschatology may also have been points of contention.[36] But the author of 1 John writes for many reasons and covers a vast range of themes. Does the specter of a targeted group of deserters and their traumatic exit lurk behind every line? Many take this route and thereby understand 1 John as a "polemical" text.[37]

Mirror-reading is an important methodology for sketching a range of possibilities that lies behind an extant text. But when these sketches become concretized as hermeneutical entry points, their contingency is ignored and much questionable ink is spilled. With "history" so dearly prized, access to any clue like the one in 1 John 2:19 may lead to excess.[38] I referred earlier to Walter Bauer's exaggerated polemical language, portraying this leaving party as full of "hellish, fratricidal hatred."[39] Bauer may be on the extreme end of over-

[35]   Horst Han has called 1 John 2:18-27 an *Einstiegstext*, that is, the textual entry point for studies on the Johannine Letters (and even for Johannine Christianity). See Horst Han, *Tradition und Neuinterpretation im ersten Johannesbrief* (Zürich: Theologische Verlag Zürich, 2009), 25–37.

[36]   See Raymond Brown's detailed analysis in *Community of the Beloved Disciple*, 109–44.

[37]   The polemical reading has been established through major commentaries like those of Brown in Raymond E. Brown, *The Epistles of John: A New Translation with Introduction and Commentary*, AB 30 (New Haven, Conn.: Yale University Press, 1982); John Painter, *1, 2, and 3 John*; Rudolf Bultmann, *The Johannine Epistles: A Commentary on the Johannine Epistles*, trans. R. Philip O'Hara, with Lane C. McGaughy and Robert W. Funk, Hermeneia (Philadelphia: Fortress, 1973 [1967]); and Rudolf Schnackenburg, *The Johannine Epistles: A Commentary*, trans. Reginald Fuller and Ilse Fuller (New York: Crossroad, 1992 [1965]).

[38]   An alternative approach is offered by Judith Lieu. See, e.g., her account of how rhetorical includes and excludes in Judith M. Lieu, "Us or You? Persuasion and Identity in 1 John," *JBL* 127, no. 4 (2008): 805–19.

[39]   Walter Bauer, *Orthodoxy and Heresy in Earliest Christianity*, ed. Robert A. Kraft and Gerhard Krodel, trans. the Philadelphia Seminar on Christian Origins (Philadelphia: Fortress, 1971 [1934]), 92 (trans. David Steinmetz).

dramatizing this instance of Johannine conflict, but his interpretation belongs to a wide circle. John Painter's comments are representative:

> If this literature [i.e., 1 John] rose out of and addressed a particular crisis in the life of the Johannine community that crisis is not only part of the 'supposed background,' it is also the central subject matter addressed. Once this is recognized the reader is aware that the presence of the opponents pervades the whole book. That presence would have been more obvious to the original readers for whom the schism of the opponents was a recent, painful, traumatic experience. Because the meaning of the book is bound up with that situation some attempt must be made to reconstruct it if 1 John is to be understood.[40]

The comment begins with an "if" but proceeds with certainty that a "painful" and "traumatic" schism has indeed occurred, and an accurate interpretation of 1 John depends on recognizing and reconstructing it. Painter acknowledges the requisite "caution" and the potential "danger" of historical reconstructions,[41] but once the hermeneutical circle is in play, there is no escaping the constructed reality of a dramatic split whose perpetrators are now pervasively present throughout the text. His own reconstruction is compelling as a possible scenario. But does the text warrant his creative elaboration on the identity of these "opponents"?

Such "polemical" readings of 1 John have themselves encountered opponents in more recent decades of biblical scholarship.[42]

---

[40]   John Painter, "The Opponents in 1 John," *NTS* 32 (1986): 48–71 (here 49–50). See also his commentary *1, 2, and 3 John*, 84–94.

[41]   Painter, "Opponents in 1 John," 50.

[42]   Pheme Perkins, *The Johannine Epistles*, New Testament Message 21 (Wilmington, Del.; Glazier, 1979); Ruth B. Edwards, *Johannine Epistles*, New Testament Guides (Sheffield: Sheffield Academic Press, 1996), 64–67; Judith M. Lieu, "Authority to Become Children of God: A Study of 1 John," *NovT* 23, no. 3 (1981): 210–28; Terry Griffith, "A Non-Polemical Reading of 1 John: Sin, Christology and the Limits of Johannine Christianity," *TynBul* 49, no. 2 (1998): 253–76; Griffith, *Keep Yourselves from Idols: A New Look at 1 John*, JSNTSup 233 (Sheffield: Sheffield Academic Press, 2002); Hansjörg Schmid, "How to Read the First Epistle of John Non-Polemically," *Biblica* 85, no. 1 (2004): 24–41; Schmid, *Gegner im 1. Johannesbrief? Zu Konstruktion und Selbsreferenz im johanneischen Sinnsystem*, BWANT 159 (Stuttgart: Kohlhammer, 2002); Daniel R. Streett, *"They Went out from Us"*:

With a disappointed nod toward the Bauer thesis, Judith Lieu observes in a 1981 essay that "It has become accepted practice to interpret 1 John within a framework of the conflict between orthodoxy and heresy."[43] Though the reconstructions offered by Painter, Brown, and many others are truly ingenious, their models are ultimately unprovable. Non-polemical readings have thus appeared that demand less imaginative—but no less plausible—exegetical work. In his monograph on the opponents in 1 John, Daniel Streett challenges the mirror-reading approach in a tour de force, discussing multiple reasons for dispensing with the polemical interpretations. If the Johannine author's polemics are so central to his purpose in writing, why is there no mention of these adversaries until a third of the way into the letter? Streett points out that the actual secession receives minimal attention and that the pastoral warnings are often generalized and perhaps even more preventative than corrective.[44] For Streett, the polemical interpretations of the Epistles arise from "subjective and unregulated maximalist mirror-reading," leading exegetes to "detect polemic where none is intended."[45]

There is no doubt that a disruption occurred within the Johannine network. Given the strong emphasis on kinship language and κοινωνία, this social breech—whether consisting of a large group or merely of a handful of discontents—surely caused some degree of pain. But the tendency to overdramatize conflict suggests some modification may be required in the terms used to describe 1 John: "departure" rather than "secession"; "pastoral" and "paraenetic" rather than "polemical"; "challenging" or "difficult" rather than

---

The Identity of the Opponents in First John, BZNW 177 (Berlin: De Gruyter, 2011). Some voices are less recent—in his 1912 commentary, Alan Brooke claimed that the purpose of 1 John "is not exclusively, or even primarily, polemical." See Alan Brooke, *A Critical and Exegetical Commentary on the Johannine Epistles*, ICC (Edinburgh: T&T Clark, 1912), xxvii.

[43]   Lieu, "Authority," 210. Though Lieu does not read 1 John polemically, she does believe that the primary occasion of the text is the "schism" (225). As for which "heresy," the usual suspects have been Cerinthianism, Docetism, and Gnosticism. See Bultmann, *Johannine Epistles*.

[44]   See his arguments in Streett, *"They Went out from Us,"* 2. Similar arguments are found in Lieu, "Authority," and in Trebilco, *Early Christians in Ephesus*, 277–83.

[45]   Streett, *"They Went out from Us,"* 118–31. See his broader critique of this mirror-reading approach in 112–31.

"traumatic." The author is certainly writing to shore up the integrity of Johannine orthodoxy amidst the recipients, and also to affirm them in the face of some defection. Connecting every ethical (even every theological) exhortation in 1 John, however, to these former community members is an unnecessary step pushed by a sectarian hermeneutic. The departure may have prompted the author to write, but that does not mean that his audience was not also in need of hearing afresh reminders to love one another, to resist and confess sin, and to hold firm to their tradition. What early (or contemporary!) Christian community does *not* need such pastoral encouragement, whether in times of crisis or not?

The overall point is that the Epistles do not necessarily evince a community so sectarian in outlook that it internally disintegrates as members "other" certain factions. It is true that boundaries are reaffirmed (defined by christological confession and ethical action). As with other early Christian groups, there is certainly a recognizable profile for both insiders and outsiders. The Elder goes so far as to forbid entertaining and even greeting "those who go beyond and do not remain in the teaching of Christ" (2 John 9). And surely one of the most (ostensibly) sectarian lines in all the Johannine literature is the command, "if anyone comes to you and does not bring this teaching, do not receive him into the house-church (οἰκίαν) and do not even greet him" (2 John 10). Yet it would appear as though this prohibition of hospitality is not a standard Johannine practice, but a special case. Furthermore, in spite of the admonition against dangerous influencers in 2 John, this social network is not so rigidly sectarian that it cannot host and accept others beyond its own borders. Not only do certain people "go out" (1 John 2:19) from this group, they also "go out" (3 John 7) from others and enter in.[46]

The Johannine Welcoming of Strangers (and the Inhospitality of Diotrephes)

Any claim that John is sectarian and resistant to outsiders must wrestle with the praise of Gaius in 3 John for welcoming the "strangers" (ξένοι):

> Beloved, you do faithfully whatever you do for the friends (ἀδελφοὺς), even though they are strangers (ξένους) to you;

---

46   The term ἐξέρχομαι is used in both texts.

they have testified to your love before the church. You will do well to send them on in a manner worthy of God; for they began their journey for the sake of Christ, accepting no support from non-believers (τῶν ἐθνικῶν). Therefore we ought to support such people, so that we may become co-workers (συνεργοί) with the truth. (3 John 5-8 NRSV)

The proper Johannine treatment of itinerant Christians is not just tolerance, not even mere acceptance, but active partnership. The Elder is here insisting that his ecclesial confederation become "co-workers" with "strangers," συνεργοὶ with ξένοι. What we find here is not merely an openness to the "other" but an *embrace* of the "other." And it is not just this one particular group of strangers that warrant such treatment; they are concrete representatives of a broader group—"such people," as the NRSV translates τοὺς τοιούτος, a generic assemblage to which countless others might belong.[47] Demetrius seems to be included within this broader group of "such people" (3 John 12) as a stranger to Gaius, yet possibly the bearer of the letter whom the Elder commends.[48]

---

[47] A standard reading of ἀδελφοί here is that it is "a term for inner-Johannine affection" (Brown, *Epistles of John*, 270). Paul Trebilco writes that "the term is not used for all Christians, but rather is an insider self-designation for 'those who belong' to 'our group.'" Though he acknowledges that the ἀδελφοί in 3 John are "clearly unknown to the readers," they are ἀδελφοί "because they were part of the same wider movement," by which he surely means the orbit of house churches directly affixed to the Johannine tradition. This limited sematic scope of ἀδελφοί seems based on assumptions of the sectarian hermeneutic that Johannine Christianity is insular. Though this more circumscribed meaning of ἀδελφοί may be correct, it is also possible (and perhaps more likely) that these itinerants are simply Christians who maintain a Christology other early Christians throughout the Empire would have held as orthodox (that Jesus was divine and came in the flesh). See Paul Trebilco, *Self-Designations and Group Identity in the New Testament* (Cambridge: Cambridge University Press, 2012), 62–64.

[48] Abraham J. Malherbe, "The Inhospitality of Diotrephes," in *Light from the Gentiles: Hellenistic Philosophy and Early Christianity: Collected Essays, 1959–2012*, ed. Carl R. Holladay et al., NovTSup 150 (Leiden: Brill 2014), 69–82 (here 78). Earlier versions of Malherbe's essay appeared in 1977.

There are certainly "others" within the Johannine letters. The ἐθνικοί mentioned in 3 John 7 are understood as "other,"[49] though not necessarily in a hostile way. More importantly, it is the departed "antichrist" group that holds the position of "arch-other" in this social system, to whom the doors of hospitality are closed and for whom the prospect of cooperation proscribed. From 2 John:

> Many deceivers have gone out into the world, those who do not confess that Jesus Christ has come in the flesh; any such person is the deceiver and the antichrist! Be on your guard, so that you do not lose what we have worked for, but may receive a full reward. Everyone who does not abide in the teaching of Christ, but goes beyond it, does not have God; whoever abides in the teaching has both the Father and the Son. Do not receive (λαμβάνετε) into the house or welcome anyone who comes to you and does not bring this teaching; for to welcome is to participate in the evil deeds of such a person. (2 John 7-11 NRSV)

Gaius is praised for his welcoming of strangers, but the "elect lady" is stringently warned to withhold any form of welcome (even a greeting, as the Greek makes clear[50]) from the "deceivers" and "antichrists." And those who "go beyond (προάγων)," who are "not abiding in the teaching of Christ (μὴ μένων ἐν τῇ διδαχῇ τοῦ Χριτοῦ)," are external threats that must never be accommodated (2 John 9). How are these two different strategies of hospitality to be understood?[51]

Significantly, the dual themes of sending and receiving are prominent in John's Gospel. The Father sends the Logos/Son into the world and some receive (ἔλαβον) him, becoming children of God. In turn, the Son sends the children into to the world, and blessed are those who embrace them and receive their testimony.[52] As discussed in more detail presently, such reciprocity is a standard

[49] Paul Trebilco, *Outsider Designations and Boundary Construction in the New Testament: Early Christian Communities and the Formation of Group Identity* (Cambridge: Cambridge University Press, 2017), 172–73.

[50] "χαίρειν αὐτῷ μὴ λέγετε· ὁ λέγων γὰρ αὐτῷ χαίρειν κοινωνεῖ τοῖς ἔργοις αὐτοῦ τοῖς πονηροῖς" (2 John 10b–11).

[51] See also the related instructions in Did. 11 and Ign. *Smyrn.* 4.1; 7.1. New Testament exhortations to show hospitality to strangers are also found in Rom 12:13 and Heb 13:2.

[52] In addition to John 1:12, see 3:11, 27, 32-33; 5:43-44; 12:48; 13:20.

feature of Johannine Christianity. The reciprocal nature of *sending* is succinctly articulated by Jesus near the end of John's Gospel: "As the Father has sent me, so I am sending you" (20:21). Likewise, the reciprocal nature of *receiving* finds clear expression in Jesus' line, "Truly, truly, I say to you, the one who receives whomever I may send receives me, and the one receiving me receives the one who sent me" (13:20). Though hospitality was part of the warp and woof of the Greco-Roman world and practiced distinctively by Christians throughout the Empire, Gaius' reception and support of these "strangers" falls within this Johannine frame of reciprocal sending and receiving. He has received these strangers who "went out" (ἐξῆλθον) from somewhere outside the Johannine sphere and is exhorted to send them on in a manner worthy of God, the ultimate agent of sending in Johannine theology. Though a disruptive coterie "went out" (ἐξῆλθαν) from their common fellowship into the world (1 John 2:19), the social boundaries delimiting Johannine Christianity can open both ways, not only for some to secede, but for others to join in while passing along in their journey.

These movements of going in and out of communal contexts recalls the imagery of the Gospel's Shepherd Discourse in which members of Christ's flock are brought in and out through him as a "gate" (the connection between John 10 and the instances of exit and entry in the Epistles is reinforced by the use of ἐκβάλλω in 3 John 10[53]). The gate opens in both directions, and it is clear that there are those who belong and those who do not among the fold. Entry and egress are monitored and guarded christologically. Though the Elder does not directly draw on John 10 in his letter to Gaius, it is clear that Christology is the gateway, the determinative factor in receiving or rejecting. If the Christology is wrong, insiders become outsiders and outsiders remain outside. If the Christology is sound, outsiders are enthusiastically welcomed and supported. Those who "went out" because they deny that Jesus has come in the

---

[53]   Cf. John 10:4, and also its use in the preceding scene of the blind man's synagogue expulsion in 9:34-35. Lieu acknowledges a "possible parallel" between this use of ἐκβάλλω and its use in John 9. See Judith M. Lieu, *I, II, & III John: A Commentary*, NTL (Louisville: Westminster John Knox, 2008), 278.

flesh are indeed outsiders, even if they emerge from within; those who "went out" are welcomed as insiders if they have done so "on behalf of the Name" (3 John 7), even if they arrive from elsewhere.

The Elder's charge to refuse hospitality in 2 John 10-11 is harsh, yet hardly representative of Johannine social consciousness broadly speaking, as the sectarian hermeneutic in contemporary scholarship seems to assume. Though this strand of early Christianity erected boundaries, there was nonetheless a social porosity that could joyfully receive outsiders. In fact, the refusal of hospitality (to appropriate visitors) is one of the chief transgressions of Diotrephes.[54] He not only refuses the Elder and any delegations sent on his behalf (3 John 9); Diotrephes' inhospitality extends to a broader group, the ἀδελφοί (3 John 10, translated "friends" in the NRSV), paralleling the group (or one of the groups[55]) Gaius has been praised for receiving in 3 John 5.

[54]   Influential scholars have suggested a range of possible historical scenarios underlying 3 John. The nature of the conflict between the Elder and Diotrephes may be ecclesiastical, theological, sociological, or some combination of the three. Those perceiving an ecclesiastical conflict, in which Diotrephes is acting as if with episcopal authority, include Theodor Zahn et al., *Introduction to the New Testament*, 3 vols. (Edinburgh: T&T Clark, 1953 [1909]), 3:375ff; Adolf von Harnack, "Über den dritten Johannesbrief," TU 15, no. 3 (1897): 3–27. Walter Bauer and Ernst Käsemann are among those who have detected a theological dispute: Bauer, *Orthodoxy and Heresy*, 93–94 (trans. Gerhard Krodel); Ernst Käsemann, "Ketzer und Zeuge: Zum johanneischen Verfasserproblem," ZTK 48 (1951): 292–311 (Käsemann understands Diotrephes as a representative of more mainstream Christian tradition to which the Elder is an outlier). Abraham Malherbe's sociological reconstruction, in which Diotrephes' refusal of hospitality amounts to a rejection of the Elder as sender, has won strong support ("Inhospitality"). John Painter and Raymond Brown take on much of Malherbe's argument but expand it in different ways. Painter argues that a theological conflict is still in view and evidenced in the linguistic connection between 2 John 11 and 3 John 10 of πονηρός—Diotrephes was thus a sympathizer with the antichrist party (Painter, *1, 2, and 3 John*, 363–65). Brown believes the Elder and Diotrephes have been aligned against those who left the community (1 John 2:18-19 and 2 John 10-12), though the latter went an unfortunate step further and withheld hospitality from all itinerant Christians (Brown, *Epistles of John*, 738–39).

[55]   The phrase in 3 John 5, τοὺς ἀδελφούς καὶ τοῦτο ξένους, may be understood as a single collective entity ("the brothers, even though they are strangers") or two different groups ("brothers" and "strangers"). For

In summary, John's missional dynamics of sending and receiving illumine these instances of hospitality granted, withheld, and called for. The elect lady is urged to refuse hospitality, Gaius is praised for showing it, and Diotrephes is criticized for refusing it. The practices differ for each situation, but the Elder's rationale is consistent in at least the first two. The grounds of receiving "the other" are christological: itinerants who serve "on behalf of the Name" are warmly welcomed and energetically supported; those who deny or misrepresent that Name are denied access.[56] We see enacted in the letters of John the christological and ecclesial imagery of John 10, in which a Shepherd guards and guides his flock across multiple folds or courtyards and even stands in the position of communal entryway ("gate"). He grants access to those he knows by name, and those who would access his flock without license are the dangerous "others": "the one who does not enter (ὁ μὴ εἰσερχόμενος) through the gate (θύρας) into the courtyard of the sheep but climbs up

---

our purposes, the Elder's openness to outsiders is affirmed regardless of the translation option. See the discussion in Karen H. Jobes, *1, 2, & 3 John*, ZECNT (Grand Rapids: Zondervan, 2014), 300.

[56]   I am taking the reference to the "Name" (ὄνομα) in 3 John 7 as a reference to the name of the Father that is shared with Jesus according to John 17, "your name that you have given me" (appearing twice, in 17:11 and 17:12). Debate continues on what this name may be. Options include "I am" (Raymond E. Brown, *The Gospel According to John: Introduction, Translation, and Notes*, AB 29, 29A [Garden City, N.Y.: Doubleday, 1966], 2:755–56); "YHWH/יהוה" (Barrett, *Gospel According to St John*, 505; and, more recently, see Charles A. Gieschen, "The Divine Name that the Son Shares with the Father in the Gospel of John," in *Reading the Gospel of John's Christology as Jewish Messianism: Royal, Prophetic, and Divine Messiahs*, ed. Benjamin E. Reynolds and Gabriele Boccaccini, AJEC 106 [Leiden: Brill, 2018], 387–410); the LXX's equivalent of the Tetragrammaton, "Lord"/κύριος (Thompson, *John*, 352–53; Joshua Coutts, *The Divine Name in the Gospel of John: Significance and Impetus*, WUNT 447 [Tübingen: Mohr Siebeck, 2017], 130–31). Coutts makes the strong case that John's name theology derives primarily from Deutero-Isaiah (not simply from Exodus 3:14), where the concept is both eschatological and associative (with another—perhaps divine—figure). See *Divine Name*, 2–3, 144, and throughout. I argue that this shared "Name" is "one," drawing on the Shema and encompassing both "Lord/κύριος," the tetragrammaton, and the "I am" sayings. See Byers, "One Flock, One Shepherd, One God" (forthcoming).

another (ἀναβαίνων ἀλλαχόθεν) way is a thief and a bandit" (John 10:1). But the Shepherd knows of "other sheep (ἄλλα πρόβατα)" (10:16) beyond the boundaries of individual folds, and these "others" who would access the sheep through the Shepherd—through the Name—are admitted with joy. The scenes of going and coming in the Epistles are instantiations of the Shepherd Discourse and encompassed within the Johannine motif of sending/receiving.

Though epistolary literature entices the historical imagination with suggestive clues but frustratingly little else, I hope it is clear from this brief treatment of John's letters that the Johannine social network need not be regarded as aggressively sectarian or fundamentally insular. Safeguarded, yes—but in a carefully qualified way that retained an openness to the other, as is the case for any healthy household, ancient or modern. In the sectarian hermeneutic challenged throughout this study, emphasis seems to lie on the conflict with Diotrephes in 3 John and on the resistance to outsiders found in 2 John 10-11, which together reinforce the idea that this community is internally fractious and externally closed off. The purpose in this section has been to highlight that there are other factors at play, namely Gaius' celebrated welcoming of strangers in 3 John 5-8 and also the nature of Diotrephes' offense, which is the resistance not only to the Elder's authority, but also to other "friends" (ἀδελφοί) that belong within the wider circle of Johannine welcome. With a well-established hermeneutical tradition in contemporary New Testament scholarship that is so quickly drawn toward early Christian conflict, focus centers on the so-called schismatics, secessionists, and the anathematized itinerants of 2 John rather than on the welcomed strangers of 3 John. Attention lands not so much on Gaius but on Diotrephes. Societies of all times define vice and virtue through their depictions of villains and heroes. In many readings of John and his eponymous letters, the villains get the spotlight. We need to bring Gaius out from Diotrephes' shadow.

Conclusion: John and Other Sheep

The "John" behind the Fourth Gospel and the Johannine Epistles, though often understood as a contrary leadership figure of an introverted sect, has been shown throughout this study as more open to "the other" than his standard caricature has allowed. Though many assume his external stance is standoff-ish and guarded even toward other Christians, as an evangelist, this "John" seems not only cognizant of other Gospels, but also invested in a Christology of excess that may even compel the ongoing work of Gospel writing. The Elder of the Epistles is only resistant to *certain types* of outside influence and committed to a communal openness to the itinerant stranger as seen in his praise of Gaius and in his indictment of Diotrephes. And John's internal relations, though troubled as elsewhere in early Chris-tianity, may not have been as volatile as many have claimed. Though some form of group exit occurred in the Johannine network, the actual impact of these "secessionists" may be over-blown in scholarly paradigms. Along related lines, the prayer for oneness may be an appeal not so much for unity but for a participatory association with the one God of Israel as Jewish coreligionists asserted the incompatibility of Christ-belief with a faithful observance of their own scriptural traditions.

Hints abound throughout the Gospel and the Epistles that Johannine Christianity was fundamentally open to "the other." As seen in the chapter "John and Other Jews," the Johannine Jesus pushed against constrictive social boundaries that limited soteri-ology and ecclesiology to narrow particulars of ethnicity. Though the sheep must be protected and carefully bounded within a fold, there are "other sheep" (John 10:16) for which the Johannine Jesus is ever scanning the social horizons.[57] The internal dynamics and external relations of this emerging stream of early Christianity were certainly fraught with challenges and marked by various degrees of boundary-construction. *But the problems normally denoted as "sectarian" may have actually emerged from a gen-eral openness to outsiders and a determination to seek after "other*

[57]   Does John envisage these "other sheep" in John 10:16 as Gentiles or as diaspora Jews? I think the question is unanswerable from what the text makes available. What I intend to capture above is the Johannine orienta-tion that is outward and open. The social inclusion of Samaritans, the hint that Greeks are included as well, the statement about "other sheep," and the multilingual titulus over the cross all demonstrate the Johannine impulse to widen the circle of inclusion.

sheep." The Gospel's Samaritans and Greeks and the strangers and brothers of 3 John are among those welcomed into the Johannine fellowship. This network may have fences, but it also has a "gate" (John 10:1-2), and this gate opens as well as closes.

4

John and Other Christians II

Ecclesiology and Pneumatology

In the view of many scholars of Christian origins, John did not get along with other Christians, and Johannine Christianity did not get along with other versions of Christianity.[1] Having evaluated in the previous chapter the longstanding assumption that this Christian stream perennially resisted those outside its own tradition and struggled intensely with factions from within its own ranks, attention now turns from John and other specific *Christians* and Christian *groups* to John and other Christian *ideas and ecclesial traditions* (with reference to specific leading figures who embodied them).

The distinctiveness (the otherness) of the Johannine literature is said to lie not only in its language and historical situation, but also in the internal dynamics of its ecclesial life. Though the Christology is high, the ecclesiology is reckoned as "low." John purportedly

---

[1]   In these introductory remarks and in the following section, I rely heavily, and sometimes reproduce (with permission) my article, Andrew J. Byers, "Johannine Bishops? The Fourth Evangelist, John the Elder, and the Episcopal Ecclesiology of Ignatius of Antioch," *NovT* 60 (2018): 121–39. I am grateful to Dr. Jonathon Lookadoo for his helpful suggestions and comments in reading this material before its earlier publication.

promoted individualism,[2] minimized the sacraments,[3] and subverted the more formal leadership structures that were being established in the late first century and beyond.[4] This anti-institutional
and anti-clerical model of leadership, authority, and polity stands
at odds with the more formalized hierarchies that many scholars
detect emerging in the Pastoral Epistles and giving rise to models like the one found in the *Epistles* of Ignatius of Antioch. Furthermore, Johannine scholarship tends to assume that an anti-
hierarchical and anti-institutional community like John's required
no leadership offices given the presence of the Paraclete and the
supposed spiritual self-sufficiency and authority of each individual.
As James Dunn writes, "*Throughout these writings there is no real
concept of ministry, let alone of office.* Everything is seen in terms of
the individual's immediate relationship to God through the Spirit
and the word."[5] Not only is John's pneumatology seen as part of its
sectarian consciousness (reinforced by its later links with Montan-
ism[6]), it is also viewed as inciting internal strife.

[2]   See the discussion below in the section on Johannine pneumatology.
[3]   See Eduard Schweizer, "The Concept of the Church in the Gospel and Epistles of St John," in *New Testament Essays: Studies in Memory
of Thomas Walter Manson, 1893–1958*, ed. A. J. B. Higgins (Manchester:
Manchester University Press, 1959), 230–245; more recently, see Meredith J. C. Warren, *My Flesh Is Meat Indeed: A Nonsacramental Reading of
John 6:51–58* (Minneapolis: Fortress, 2015). Other interpreters, of course,
assigned the apparent eucharistic language in John to later ecclesiastical
revision. See Günther Bornkamm, "Die eucharistische Rede im Johannes-
Evangelium," *ZNW* 47 (1956): 161–69; and Rudolf Bultmann, *The Gospel
of John: A Commentary*, trans. George R. Beasley-Murray, R. W. N. Hoare,
and J. K. Riches (Philadelphia: Westminster, 1971), 218–19, 234–37.
[4]   See Schweizer, "Church"; Hans-Josef Klauck, "Gemeinde ohne
Amt? Erfahrungen mit der Kirche in den johanneischen Schriften," *BZ* 29,
no. 2 (1985): 193–220; and Robert Kysar, *John: The Maverick Gospel*, 3rd
ed. (Louisville: Westminster John Knox, 2007 [1993, 1976]), 132–42.
[5]   James D. G. Dunn, *Unity and Diversity in the New Testament: An
Inquiry into the Character of Earliest Christianity*, 3rd ed. (London: SCM
Press, 2010), 129 (emphases original).
[6]   See the comments in Walter Bauer, *Orthodoxy and Heresy in Earliest Christianity*, ed. Robert A. Kraft and Gerhard Krodel, trans. Philadelphia Seminar on Christian Origins (Philadelphia: Fortress, 1971 [1934]),
141 and 145 (trans. Robert F. Evans), 187 (trans. Howard Bream and Robert L. Wilken), and 225 (trans. Paul J. Achtemeier).

Raymond Brown suggested that the combination of a low-church ecclesiology and a robust pneumatology led to the failure and dissolution of this early Christian tradition: "The most serious weakness in Johannine ecclesiology and the one most apparent in the Epistles centers on the role of the Paraclete."[7] The problem is that Jesus "who sends the Paraclete never tells his followers what is to happen when believers who possess the Paraclete disagree with each other."[8] Brown is not being fanciful, but as ever postulating on the basis of a close reading of the texts. Similarly, D. Moody Smith highlights the potential for strife and confusion when he asks rhetorically,

> If the author of I John demands that his fellow Christians should not believe every spirit but test the spirits, since there are now many false prophets (4:1), may he not reflect a situation in which spirit-inspired prophets uttering words of the risen Lord have become a distinct problem in the church?[9]

In an ecclesiology lacking institutional roles of authority, multiple members or cliques among Johannine Christians could easily legitimate their ideas or decisions by direct appeals to the Paraclete. If a corporate charismatic authority holds the day, the community is then bereft of any formalized means of arbitrating between competing claims to inspiration. For Brown, this (mis)alignment of a strong pneumatology alongside a low-church ecclesiology was ultimately pathological, leading to an ecclesial demise: "In my judgment, there is no way to control such a division in a Paraclete-guided community of people. The Johannine community discovered that, *for it split up and went out of existence.*"[10] Ironically, it is Diotrephes who auspiciously seems to have read the writing on the wall and embraced a survivable mode of ecclesial leadership—for

---

[7] Raymond E. Brown, *The Churches the Apostles Left Behind* (New York: Paulist, 1984), 121.

[8] Brown, *Churches the Apostles Left Behind*, 121.

[9] D. Moody Smith, *Johannine Christianity: Essays on Its Setting, Sources, and Theology* (Columbia: University of South Carolina Press, 1984), 16.

[10] Brown, *Churches the Apostles Left Behind*, 123 (emphases added).

Brown, Diotrephes stands in the tradition as an early adopter of the episcopal ecclesiology found in Ignatius.[11]

Though surely different from other streams in the complex matrix of early Christianity, Johannine pneumatology and ecclesiology need not be envisaged as fundamentally dysfunctional nor as fundamentally opposed to other modes of church life (and "the other" Christians who embraced them). The consensus view that John's vision of the church and understanding of the Spirit stand at odds with the mainstream tradition(s) is premised on exegesis. But other interpretations are exegetically plausible, and perhaps even preferable.

An alternative reading will emerge from a discussion in two parts. After demonstrating the compatibility of Johannine thought with the underlying ideas of Ignatius' episcopal ecclesiology, I will then evaluate the assumption that John's notion of individualism, egalitarianism, and charismatic authority automatically invalidate hierarchical leadership. Our contemporary assessments about the Spirit-inspired church-life intimated in the Johannine Letters may be influenced more by contemporary instantiations of the twentieth- and twenty-first-century charismatic movement than by ecclesial ideas in first- and second-century Christianity. As I hope to show, the sort of pneumatology suggested in this literary corpus is not necessarily resistant to nascent and emerging ecclesiastical structures promoting ordered worship under clerical authority. The unhelpful dichotomization in which charismatic and prophetic leadership is pitted against episcopal and hierarchical leadership is a major force in the contemporary relegation of Johannine ecclesiology to the sidelines of the emerging Great Church.

But first to John and Ignatius of Antioch . . .

John and the Episcopal Ecclesiology of Ignatius of Antioch

Martin Hengel draws connections between John and Ignatius, but he is absolutely clear that the Syrian bishop's ecclesiastical hierarchy derives from elsewhere:

> What connects Ignatius with the Gospel and the letters of John is not a direct 'literary dependence' in the strict sense but a

[11]   Brown, *Churches the Apostles Left Behind*, 123.

kindred theological milieu—in christology, Eucharistic doctrine, and abrupt repudiation of the "docetic" heresy. *At the same time his excessive stress on the hierarchy is a point of difference.* Here Ignatius looks anxiously at the future of the church, requiring strict obedience of the bishops and the presbyters, while the Johannine writings still live completely under the charismatic authority of the Lord and his spirit, 'who will guide into all truth.' *Possibly Ignatius does not mention 'Elder John' because he had been an antihierarchical, charismatic teacher, without any interest whatsoever in ecclesiastical offices like bishops, presbyters and deacons.*[12]

It is in Ignatius' *Epistles* that the paradigm of monepiscopacy seems first to take root in early Christianity,[13] a leadership structure purportedly alien to John's tradition yet possibly adumbrated in Matthew 16:18-19 when Jesus christens Peter as the church's foundational rock. The exact contours of Ignatius' unique vision of the threefold church order comprising one bishop and a tiered group of elders and deacons is modified elsewhere and over time in early Christianity.[14] Still, Ignatius' configuration of ecclesial leadership was a determinative precursor to later clerical models and seems to

[12] Martin Hengel, *The Johannine Question*, trans. John Bowden (London: SCM Press, 1989), 15 (emphases added). Likewise, Raymond Brown writes, "There may be close similarities between Ignatius and John in matters of high christology and the eucharist, but they are very unlike each other in ecclesiology, especially in matters of church structure." See Raymond E. Brown, *The Community of the Beloved Disciple: The Life, Loves, and Hates of an Individual Church in New Testament Times* (New York: Paulist Press, 1979), 158.

[13] Thomas A. Robinson, *Ignatius and the Parting of the Ways: Early Jewish Relations* (Peabody, Mass.: Hendrikson, 2009) 95–102.

[14] See Hans von Campenhausen, *Ecclesiastical Authority and Spiritual Power in the Church of the First Three Centuries*, trans. J. A. Baker (Peabody, Mass.: Hendrickson, 1997), 106. Allen Brent, though, writes that, in spite of later adjustments, "the normative structure of liturgy and Order of a given Christian community was to remain essentially as Ignatius of Antioch had described it." See Allen Brent, *The Imperial Cult and the Development of Church Order: Concepts and Images of Authority in Paganism and Early Christianity before the Age of Cyprian*, VCS 45 (Leiden: Brill, 1999), 1–2; see also Brent's *Ignatius of Antioch and the Second Sophistic: A Study of Early Christian Transformation of Pagan Culture*, STAC 36 (Tübingen: Mohr Siebeck, 2006), 22, 25.

have enjoyed wide acceptance among the Asian churches addressed in his letters.[15] How can any form of resonance persist between Johannine Christianity and the Ignatian notion of episcopacy?

In an influential essay on Johannine ecclesiology, Eduard Schweizer observed that the community of the Fourth Evangelist "has no priests or officials." In fact, "there is no church order at all," and neither are there any "'offices' except among Jesus' enemies—the Jews, Judas (12:6), Diotrephes (3 John 9)."[16] In a similar vein, Brown has pointed out that the titular use of the term "apostle" is "completely absent from the Johannine writings."[17] For Smith, John's "downplaying of the Twelve would be commensurate with an ecclesiology in which the concept of apostolic authority was not espoused or emphasized as the touchstone of churchly ministry."[18] Harold Attridge suggests that the reason Diotrephes was recognized as an enemy to this group of believers is because he "probably represents the new style of leadership, like Ignatius of Antioch, that emerged in the early second century."[19] A Johannine aversion to hierarchical leadership models is also regularly identified in the Fourth Evangelist's undermining of Petrine authority through his

---

[15]   The rise of monepiscopacy is often deemed operative before Ignatius, a view for which the *Epistles* serve as the first evidence, or altogether invented by him. See, e.g., B. H. Streeter, *The Primitive Church* (New York: Macmillan, 1929), 168–83, and, more recently, Frances M. Young, "Ministerial Forms and Functions in the Church Communities of the Greek Fathers," in *Community Formation in the Early Church and the Church Today*, ed. Richard N. Longenecker (Peabody, Mass.: Hendrickson, 2002), 157–176 (here 161); and Allen Brent, *Ignatius of Antioch: A Martyr Bishop and the Origins of Episcopacy* (New York: T&T Clark, 2007). The underdetermined wording above ("seems") is intentional to account for Alistair C. Stewart's cogent arguments that a *monepiskopos* was not a bishop holding office within a local church but a bishop who oversaw the life of multiple congregations in a given locale. For Stewart, Ignatius was no such thing. See his detailed discussion in Alistair C. Stewart, *The Original Bishops: Office and Order in the First Christian Communities* (Grand Rapids: Baker Academic, 2014), 237–98.

[16]   Schweizer, "Concept of the Church," 237.

[17]   Brown, *Churches the Apostles Left Behind*, 91.

[18]   Smith, *Johannine Christianity*, 212.

[19]   Harold W. Attridge, "Johannine Christianity," in *Essays on John and Hebrews* (Grand Rapids: Baker Academic, 2010), 3–19 (here 12). Similarly, Brown, *Community of the Beloved Disciple*, 160.

literary juxtaposition of Peter with the Beloved Disciple (discussed presently). Though nuances abound from diverse approaches to early Christianity, the interpretation of the Gospel and Letters of John has been largely anchored within the reference frame of a sectarian hermeneutic perceiving the Johannine community as an anti-authoritarian "conventicle" standing in awkward tension against the wider trends toward "*Frühkatholizismus*."[20]

Contrary to these standard approaches, the hierarchical leadership structure of Ignatius of Antioch is actually compatible with Johannine theology.[21] The aim here is not to argue for Ignatian dependence on John,[22] nor even to argue that the Fourth Evangelist envisioned an ecclesial theology of formal clerical hierarchies; and it is certainly not my purpose to re-narrate early Christianity as uniform or homogenous or even perfectly irenic. But diversity need not mean anti-ecclesiastical enmity in the case of

[20]   Again, on this reading see Ernst Käsemann, *The Testament of Jesus According to John 17*, trans. Gerhard Krodel (Philadelphia: Fortress, 1978 [1966]), 27–32. For a careful analysis on the Johannine Epistles and what many scholars have called "early Catholicism," see C. Clifton Black, "The Johannine Epistles and the Question of Early Catholicism," *NovT* 28, no. 2 (1986): 131–58.

[21]   For comparative studies between John and Ignatius, see Christian Maurer, *Ignatius von Antiochien und das Johannesevangelium* (Zürich: Zwingli-Verlag, 1949); Helmut Koester, "History and Cult in the Gospel of John and in Ignatius of Antioch," *JTC* 1 (1965): 111–23; Titus Nagel, *Die Rezeption des Johannesevangeliums im 2. Jahrhundert: Studien zur vorirenäischen Aneignung und Auslegung des vierten Evangeliums in christlicher und christlich-gnostischer Literatur*, ABG 2 (Leipzig: Evangelische Verlagsanstalt, 2000), 207–51; and Wolfram Uebele, *"Viele Verführer sind in die Welt ausgegangen": Die Gegner in den Briefen des Ignatius von Antiochien und in den Johannesbriefen*, BWANT 151 (Stuttgart: Kohlhammer, 2001). See also the brief overview of the discussions in scholarship on the relationship between John and Ignatius by Christine Trevett in *A Study of Ignatius of Antioch in Syria and Asia*, SBEC 29 (Lampeter: Edwin Mellen, 1992), 20–22.

[22]   The negative assessment that Ignatius demonstrates negligible knowledge of John by Paul Foster, however, seems overstated and too reliant on exact citations. See Paul Foster, "The Epistles of Ignatius of Antioch and the Writings that Later Formed the New Testament," in *The Reception of the New Testament in the Apostolic Fathers*, ed. Andrew F. Gregory and Christopher M. Tuckett (Oxford: Oxford University Press, 2005), 159–85 (esp. 183–84).

John's Gospel and Letters. The purpose here is to continue desta-bilizing, at least partially, the axiomatic narrative of Johannine antipathy by showing how an early second-century ecclesiology, in spite of its formalities and sacerdotal tendencies, is as amena-ble to John's writings as the anticlerical readings that feature in many of the scholarly reconstructions of the movement behind them. The contemporary attribution of John's Gospel and Epistles to an errant social group self-consciously divergent from more mainstream Christian movements is problematized if the earli-est form of episcopal ecclesiology in the second century can be understood, at least in certain respects, as "Johannine." This early Christian movement may have indeed embodied "low church" ecclesiology, and John did not directly promote an episcopal model of leadership. Ignatius, however, may have premised his "high church" ecclesiology on Johannine ideas—and it is possible that "John" would have even found it compelling.

The Syrian bishop wrote as he journeyed to Rome from his (for-mer?) see of Antioch,[23] long guessed as the provenance of Matthew's Gospel.[24] Yet Ignatius does not ground his ideas of ecclesiastical authority on Matthew's account of Peter's role as a "rock" or even on apostolic succession, an approach that became more universal in subsequent generations.[25] Ignatius seems interested in themes more Johannine than Matthean when it comes to his theology of church

[23]   As for the phrase ἐπίσκοπον Συρίας in Ign. *Rom.* 2.2, the meaning can be "bishop from Syria" as easily as "bishop of/over Syria." See Stewart's detailed discussion in *Original Bishops*, 237–98.

[24]   See the discussions in Raymond E. Brown and John P. Meier, *Antioch & Rome: New Testament Cradles of Catholic Christianity* (Mah-wah, N.J.: Paulist Press, 2004 [1983]), 11–86; Michelle Slee, *The Church in Antioch in the First Century CE: Communion and Conflict*, JSNTSup 244 (London: Sheffield University Press, 2003), 118–25, 146–55; Robinson, *Ignatius and the Parting of the Ways*, 89–94. On the complex relationship between Matthew's Gospel and Ignatius in the social life of Antiochene Jews and Christians, see additionally Magnus Zetterholm, *The Formation of Christianity in Antioch: A Social-Scientific Approach to the Separation between Judaism and Christianity* (New York: Routledge, 2003), 211–16.

[25]   Francis A. Sullivan, *From Apostles to Bishops: The Development of the Episcopacy in the Early Church* (New York: Newman Press, 2001), 16. But see 1 Clem. 44 for an emphasis on apostolic appointments to ministry written nearer the time of Ignatius' letters.

leadership. Klaus Berger has observed that what can be found in Ignatius is "biete johanneische Theologie plus kirchliche Hierarchie."[26] In what follows I will seek to demonstrate that "johanneische Theologie" and Ignatius' additional "kirchliche Hierarchie" are potentially more consonant than is normally perceived and as Berger's estimation suggests.

Ignatius' Theology of Church Order

For Ignatius, the church is set apart from "the rest of humankind" (Ign. *Eph.* 10.1) and comprises individuals who are collectively "members (μέλη) of [God's] son" (Ign. *Eph.* 4.2), "participants together in a shared worship (σύνοδοι)," "God-bearers (θεοφόροι)," "temple-bearers (ναοφόροι), Christ-bearers (χριστοφόροι)" and "bearers of holy things (ἁγιοφόροι)" (Ign. *Eph.* 9.2).[27] Unified through the eucharistic feast, the church is to cultivate an internal harmony that promotes a supernatural peace "by which all warfare among those in heaven and those on earth is abolished" (Ign. *Eph.* 13.2). As one historian has put it, Ignatius envisions the church as a "supra-terrestrial, cosmic entity"[28] and "a mysterious divine reality belonging to the eternal order."[29]

No part of this ecclesial vision can be enacted or sustained apart from those holding leadership offices, who ground this ethereal community within the earthly sphere:

---

[26] Klaus Berger, *Theologiegeschichte des Urchristentums: Theologie des Neuen Testaments* (Tübingen: Francke, 1994), 692.

[27] Throughout this essay I am trusting in the reliability of the Middle Recension and using as my text Michael W. Holmes, ed., *The Apostolic Fathers: Greek Texts and English Translations*, 3rd ed. (Grand Rapids: Baker Academic, 2007). For an introductory discussion on the Middle Recension (in addition to Holmes' comments on pp. 166–81), see William R. Schoedel, *Ignatius of Antioch: A Commentary on the Letters of Ignatius of Antioch*, Hermeneia (Philadelphia: Fortress, 1985), 3–7.

[28] Campenhausen, *Ecclesiastical Authority*, 100. Similarly, Jochen Wagner suggests that "der Kirchenbegriff des Ignatius ist weniger ein rechtlich-verfassungsmäßiger als der eines lebendigen Mysteriums." See Jochen Wagner, *Die Anfänge des Amtes in der Kirche: Presbyter und Episkopen in der frühchristlichen Literatur*, TANZ 53 (Tübingen: Francke, 2011), 258.

[29] Campenhausen, *Ecclesiastical Authority*, 98.

> Let no one do anything that has to do with the church without the bishop. Only that Eucharist which is under the authority of the bishop (or whomever he himself designates) is to be considered valid. Wherever the bishop is, there let the congregation be. . . . It is not permissible either to baptize or to hold a love feast without the bishop. (Ign. *Smyr.* 8.1-2)

Serving alongside the bishop are presbyters and deacons. This threefold order of church leadership is fundamentally constitutive of Ignatian ecclesiology: "Without these [three leadership offices] no group can be called a church" (Ign. *Tra.* 3.1). Accordingly, Christians "must not do anything without the bishop and the presbyters" (Ign. *Mag.* 7.1).

These ecclesial leaders embody and represent the entire congregation they serve.[30] As a prisoner en route from Asia to Rome, Ignatius is convinced that he has seen the entire church in Magnesia in "the persons of Damas, your godly bishop, and your worthy presbyters Bassus and Apollonius" (Ign. *Mag.* 2.1; see also 6.1). To the Ephesians he writes, "I have received in God's name your whole congregation in the person of Onesimus, a man of inexpressible love who is also your earthly bishop" (Ign. *Eph.* 1.3a; see also 2.1b). Along with representing their respective congregations, the three offices also embody and represent God, Jesus, and the deceased apostles, whom Ignatius understands as a sort of "himmlischen Ratskollegium"[31]:

> Let everyone respect the deacons as Jesus Christ, just as they should respect the bishop, who is a model (τύπον) of the Father, and the presbyters as God's council (συνέδριον) and as the band (σύνδεσμον) of the apostles. (Ign. *Tra.* 3.1)

---

[30]   For this reason, Allen Brent emphasizes *typology* over against *hierarchy*, thus weakening the juridical authority usually associated with a monarchical episcopacy, of which Ignatius is often considered the earliest example. See Allen Brent, *Cultural Episcopacy and Ecumenism: Representative Ministry in Church History from the Age of Ignatius of Antioch to the Reformation with Special Reference to Contemporary Ecumenism*, SCM 6 (Leiden: Brill, 1992), 80–85.

[31]   This phrase is from Wagner, *Die Anfänge*, 260.

> You must all follow the bishop as Jesus Christ followed the
> Father, and follow the council of presbyters as you would the
> apostles; respect the deacons as the commandment of God.
> (Ign. *Smyr.* 8.1)

How can an ecclesiology with such a strong emphasis on episcopal authority bear affinities with the Gospel of John and its
(widely assumed) anticlericalism? Raymond Brown asked a similar question (to which he expected a negative response) regarding
Ignatius' leadership theology: "Could Johannine Christians have
accepted such an ecclesiology wherein the bishop is given the
prerogatives of the Paraclete?"[32] In a 1963 article, Robert Grant
anticipates Brown's rhetorical question and provides what could
be understood as a positive reply: "In Ignatius' view the model
for the relation between Christians and their bishop is provided
by the relation between Jesus and the Father. *This relationship
is described in terms almost certainly derived from the Gospel of
John.*"[33] In step with Grant's proposal, I sketch below a narrative
pattern of reciprocity depicted by the Fourth Evangelist through
a series of "inclusive parallels." Ignatian episcopacy may well
have been recognized as a form of Johannine reciprocity by early
Christians familiar with John's Gospel.

Inclusive Parallelism and Participatory Reciprocity in Ignatius' *Epistles* and John's Gospel

Fundamental to the threefold order in Ignatius is the reciprocal
interchange between divinity and humanity generally expressed in
the literary pattern of *just as . . . so also*, that is, *just as* with God
or Jesus, *so also* with the ecclesial leaders and sometimes with the
congregation:

---

[32] Brown, *Community of the Beloved Disciple*, 159. He answers his
own question by stating that the Ignatian hierarchical model "could not
have been seen as harmonious with Johannine tradition" (159). In Brown's
reconstruction of Johannine groups in the second century, the more orthodox faction eventually agreed to accept the emerging leadership models for
the sake of merging into the mainstream of the Great Church (155–62).

[33] Robert M. Grant, "Scripture and Tradition in St. Ignatius of
Antioch," *CBQ* 25, no. 3 (1963): 322–35 (here 329; emphases added).

For Jesus Christ . . . is the mind of the Father, *just as* the bishops appointed throughout the world are in the mind of Christ. (Ign. *Eph.* 3.1)

You . . . are united with him, *as* the church is with Jesus Christ and *as* Jesus Christ is with the Father. (Ign. *Eph.* 5.1)

As the Lord did nothing without the Father . . . *so you* must not do anything without the bishop and the presbyters (Ign. *Mag.* 7.1)

Be subject to the bishop and to one another, *as* Jesus Christ in the flesh was to the Father, and *as* the apostles were to Christ and to the Father. (Ign. *Mag.* 13.2)

You must all follow the bishop as Jesus Christ followed the Father, and follow the council of presbyters *as* you would the apostles. (Ign. *Smyr.* 8.1)

These reciprocal expressions have the effect of extending some divine function or honorary status into the earthly sphere in which the congregation conducts its life and gathers for worship.[34]

---

[34] Cognizant of the influential trend of reading the Fourth Gospel as anti-ecclesiastical, Allen Brent has suggested that the sacramental representation of bishops, presbyters, and deacons is amenable to the Johannine tradition. A threefold leadership model by which heavenly reality is incarnated during liturgical worship is in keeping with this understanding of John's sacramental theology. Along similar lines, Brent also finds the idea of representation in the Johannine portrayal of certain characters or character groups. See Brent, *Cultural Episcopacy*, 75, 78–79. (On the representative function of individuals in the Fourth Gospel, see Stephen C. Barton, "Christian Community in the Light of the Gospel of John," in *Christology, Controversy and Community: New Testament Essays in Honour of David R. Catchpole*, ed. David G. Horrell and Christopher M. Tuckett, NovTSup 99 [Leiden: Brill, 2000], 294–95.) It should be noted, though, that in more recent work Brent has sought to show that the actual threefold order of ministerial office is ultimately sourced in the pagan religious practices and the civic institutions of second-century Asia Minor. In fact, the "typology of Order" is explicitly "non-Johannine" and drawn, rather, from "the ideology of the Imperial Cult." See his *Imperial Cult*, 210–50; *Ignatius of Antioch and the Second Sophistic*; "Ignatius and Polycarp: The Transformation of New Testament Traditions in the Context of the Mystery Cults," in *Trajectories through the New Testament and the Apostolic Fathers*, ed. Andrew

Alongside these reciprocity statements are related "inclusive parallels" by which *episkopoi* are included within the role or status of God:

> Let us, therefore, be careful not to oppose the *bishop*, in order that we may be obedient to *God*. (Ign. *Eph.* 5.3b)

> It is good to acknowledge God and the bishop. *The one who honors the bishop has been honored by God*; the one who does anything without the bishop's knowledge serves the devil. (Ign. *Smyr.* 9.1)

In these excerpts, episcopal authority is paralleled with the authority of God. The divine roles and activities of bishops in the Ignatian correspondence are grounded in these parallels and repeatedly stressed through reciprocity statements.

Thematically and stylistically, these unique features are found elsewhere in early Christianity, *most prominently in John's Gospel.*[35] The "just as . . . so also" pattern appears all throughout John as a literary means of binding the activities and roles of Jesus to those of God. Later in the Gospel narrative, this reciprocity gradually opens to include the disciples. The following sequence is indicative:

> The Father is in me and *I am in the Father.* (10:38)

> *I am in my Father,* and you in me, and I in you.[36] (14:20)

Like Ignatius, the evangelist employs inclusive parallels in which certain actions, descriptions, or statements portraying God and Jesus are repeated later in the narrative but applied to certain human characters or character groups, depicting believers as participants

---

F. Gregory and Christopher M. Tucker (Oxford: Oxford University Press, 2007), 325–49; and *Ignatius of Antioch: A Martyr Bishop*, 79–94.

[35] See the detailed treatment of reciprocity in Mark L. Appold, *The Oneness Motif of the Fourth Gospel: Motif Analysis and Exegetical Probe into the Fourth Gospel*, WUNT 2/1 (Tübingen: Mohr, 1976), 18–47; and, more recently, see the discussion in Andrew J. Byers, *Ecclesiology and Theosis in the Gospel of John*, SNTSMS 166 (Cambridge: Cambridge University Press, 2017), 202–6.

[36] The italicized phrases above read in Greek as κἀγὼ ἐν τῷ πατρί and ἐγὼ ἐν τῷ πατρί μου, respectively.

in divine speech and activity. The following verses about prayer serve as an example:

> Martha to Jesus: "But even now I know that whatever you ask from God, God will give you." (11:22; see also 11:41-42)

> Jesus to the disciples: "Whatever you ask the Father in my name, he may give it to you." (15:16; see also 14:13-14; 15:7, 17; 16:23-24)

Both sets of examples above from John's Gospel depict the wider group of Jesus' disciples. Participating in the Son's mutual indwelling with the Father (as in John 10:38 || 14:20) and sharing in Jesus' own access to the Father through prayer (as in John 11:41-42 || 15:16) are collective experiences that may serve to reinforce interpretations of Johannine ecclesiology as more egalitarian, anti-institutional, and anti-hierarchical.

The reciprocity expressed through inclusive parallels, however, is at times applied to prominent individuals.[37] These specific characters include Peter and the Beloved Disciple, whose narrative coordination has been read by a large number of scholars as a Johannine assault against the hierarchical authority of the emerging "Great Church." In what follows, I will demonstrate that these two disciples could also be understood as episcopal figures not unlike the bishops addressed in the Ignatius correspondence.

Peter, the Beloved Disciple, and a Johannine Episcopacy?

A standard reading of the joint characterization of Peter and the Beloved Disciple in John is one of inter-relational friction betraying an anti-ecclesiastical dispute behind the scenes over Peter's dominant leadership role in the early church.[38] Yet the tension between

[37]   Cf. John 1:39 with 1:46; 4:29; 11:34. Note also that Jesus' "I am" statement appears on the lips of the man born blind in John 9:9.

[38]   See e.g., Graydon F. Snyder, "John 13:16 and the Anti-Petrinism of the Johannine Tradition," *BR* 16 (1971): 5–15; Oscar Cullmann, *The Johannine Circle: Its Place in Judaism, among the Disciples of Jesus and in Early Christianity*, trans. John Bowden (London: SCM Press, 1976 [1975]), 63–85; Colleen M. Conway, *Men and Women in the Fourth Gospel: Gender and*

the two is overplayed in the sectarian hermeneutic that habitually tends to view early Christianity through the reconstruction of conflict theories.[39] I submit that it is possible to understand the coordinated portrayal of these two disciples as a prefiguration of episcopal collegiality, not far from the mark of Ignatius' own self-understanding of his relationships with Polycarp, Damas, Polybius, or Onesimus, his counterpart bishops in Asia Minor.[40]

The Inclusive Parallels of Peter and the Beloved Disciple

Peter and the Beloved Disciple are both depicted within individualized inclusive parallels, one of Ignatius' preferred means of expressing his episcopal theology. Just as Jesus is symbolically understood

---

Johannine Characterization, SBLDS 167 (Atlanta: SBL Press, 1999), 163–99; Pheme Perkins, *Peter: Apostle for the Whole Church*, Studies on Personalities of the New Testament (Minneapolis: Fortress, 2000); William W. Watty, "The Significance of Anonymity in the Fourth Gospel," *ExpTim* 90, no. 7 (1979): 209–12; James H. Charlesworth, *The Beloved Disciple*, 392. For a survey of the literature (and a more positive stance toward the Peter–Beloved-Disciple interrelation), see Bradford B. Blaine Jr., *Peter in the Gospel of John: The Making of an Authentic Disciple*, SBLABib 27 (Atlanta: SBL Press, 2007), 8–18. Other challenges to the paradigm of a harsh tension between these two figures are found in Markus Bockmuehl, *Simon Peter in Scripture and Memory: The New Testament Apostle in the Early Church* (Grand Rapids: Baker Academic, 2012), 57–67; Nicolas Farelly, *The Disciples in the Fourth Gospel: A Narrative Analysis of Their Faith and Understanding*, WUNT 290 (Tübingen: Mohr Siebeck, 2010); Cornelis Bennema, *Encountering Jesus: Character Studies in the Gospel of John* (Milton Keynes: Paternoster, 2009), 53–63; and Kevin Quast, *Peter and the Beloved Disciple: Figures for a Community in Crisis*, JSNTSup 32 (Sheffield: Sheffield Academic, 1989); Byers, *Ecclesiology and Theosis in the Gospel of John*, 213–22.

[39] As discussed previously, Markus Bockmuehl points out that this interpretative trend became established in mainstream scholarship by F. C. Baur. See the discussion in Bockmuehl's *Simon Peter*, xv.

[40] It has often been argued that Ignatius writes as an early (perhaps the first) *monarchical* bishop. But this view has been challenged by recent interpreters. See Paul Trebilco, *The Early Christians in Ephesus from Paul to Ignatius*, WUNT 166 (Tübingen: Mohr Siebeck, 2004), 642–43; Brent, *Ignatius of Antioch and the Second Sophistic*, 29–30; and most vigorously and recently by Stewart, *Original Bishops*, 257–68. For arguments that Ignatius himself created the monepiscopacy, see Patrick Burke, "The Monarchial Episcopate at the End of the First Century," *JES* 7 (1970): 499–518.

as positioned in the bosom of the Father in John 1:18, so also the
Beloved Disciple is shown to be in the bosom of Jesus in 13:23.

> No one has ever seen God. God the only Son who is in the
> bosom of the Father (ὁ ὢν εἰς τὸν κόλπον τοῦ πατρός) has
> made him known. (1:18)

> One of his disciples—whom Jesus loved—was reclining in the
> bosom of Jesus (ἐν τῷ κόλπῳ τοῦ Ἰησοῦ). (13:23)[41]

Similarly, the way Jesus' impending death as the Good Shepherd is
described in 12:33 and 18:32 parallels the way Peter will die as an
ecclesial shepherd in 21:19:

> And he said this signifying by what kind of death (σημαίνων
> ποίῳ θανάτῳ) he [Jesus] was about to die. (12:33)

> so that the word of Jesus might be fulfilled that he spoke signi-
> fying by what kind of death (σημαίνων ποίῳ θανάτῳ) he [Jesus]
> was about to die. (18:32)

> And this he said signifying by what kind of death (σημαίνων
> ποίῳ θανάτῳ) he [Peter] will glorify God. (21:19)

As already shown, participation in the divine life of the Father and
Son is universally open to any who believe. Certain figures, however,
are singled out with more specific instantiations of reciprocity to bol-
ster this Johannine theme (e.g., the mysterious ἐγώ εἰμι statement of
the man born blind in 9:9[42]). The inclusive parallels featuring Peter
and the Beloved Disciple are given structural significance due to
their placement in the Gospel—the latter appears at the opening of
the Farewell Discourse and parallels a statement about Jesus made

---

[41]   In both 1:18 ("who is close to the Father's heart") and 13:23 ("was
reclining next to him"), the clear parallel in the Greek is obscured by the
NRSV (and other translations).

[42]   See the arguments in Mikeal C. Parsons, "A Neglected ΕΓΩ ΕΙΜΙ
Saying in the Fourth Gospel? Another Look at John 9:9," in *Perspectives
on John: Method and Interpretation in the Fourth Gospel*, ed. Robert B.
Sloan and Mikeal C. Parsons, NABPR Special Studies Series 11 (Lampeter:
Edwin Mellen Press, 1993), 145–80; and in Byers, *Ecclesiology and Theosis
in the Gospel of John*, 206–13.

in the narrative's magisterial opening; at the end of the Gospel (in John's extant form), Peter is enlisted into the divine pastoral vocation already established for Jesus in the narrative's center (John 10).

Peter and the Beloved Disciple are select individuals intimated as ecclesial leaders sharing in unique leadership roles amidst a wider congregation that also participates in divine life. That depiction is not a far cry from Ignatius' own model of church life. The reciprocity and parallelism by which the evangelist assimilates Christ-believers within the cosmic sphere of the Christian God and includes certain individuals within divine roles and functions is potentially serviceable to the emergence of an episcopal ecclesiology like that of Ignatius.[43]

Even if the Fourth Evangelist would have disagreed with the rigid hierarchical leadership model of the Asian churches in Ignatius' correspondence, he would have understood and perhaps even championed the logic that led to its formation. As uncharacteristically Johannine as it may seem with the sectarian hermeneutic shaping our understanding, the sentiment behind Ignatius' claims that "wherever the bishop is, there let the congregation be" and "it is not permissible either to baptize or to hold a love feast without the bishop" (Ign. *Smyr.* 8.1-2) may explain, in part, the supposed anxiety associated with the death of the Beloved Disciple. Perhaps Johannine Christians needed the sort of pastoral assurance that seems to be in view in John 21:23 because of that disciple's proto-episcopal role and the sense that, without his leadership, the church itself was compromised, a situation that may be roughly analogous to Ignatius' own eventual absence from the Antiochene church. And as an *episkopos* who may have viewed his own death as sacrificial on behalf of others (Ign. *Pol.* 2.3, 6.1), Ignatius would be quite at home within the imagery assigned by the Fourth Evangelist to Peter, who dies on behalf of Christ's flock.

---

[43] Andrew Lincoln reasons that the addition of John 21 was designed, in part, to provide Johannine validation of the emerging movements toward monepiscopal ecclesiology (as envisioned by Stewart, *Original Bishops*). See Andrew T. Lincoln, "John 21," in *From Paul to Josephus: Literary Receptions of Jesus in the First Century CE*, ed. Helen K. Bond, vol. 1 of *The Reception of Jesus in the First Three Centuries*, ed. Chris Keith et al. (London: T&T Clark, forthcoming), 209–22 (here 218, 221, 222).

Revisiting the Tension between Diotrephes and John the Elder

Having provided grounds for understanding Peter and the Beloved Disciple as possible prototypes of what would later emerge as episcopal leadership in Ignatius' epistolary corpus, I return now to the tension between John the Elder and Diotrephes discussed in the previous chapter. As already noted, Diotrephes has been profiled as a proponent of the sort of episcopal leadership that stood in strident friction with the longstanding view that the Johannine tradition was more egalitarian and averse to formal leadership structures.[44] The logic does not work—at least, not as convincingly as assumed.

Both figures are established leaders of some kind. The author of the Johannine Epistles writes to house churches in the Johannine network as a "presbyter" bearing some degree of recognized authority,[45] and since Diotrephes holds the power to refuse hospitality, it is likely that he is a householder within the same ecclesial network. Alistair Stewart has recently argued that Diotrephes "is no 'monarchical bishop,' as his position as householder is sufficient for him to hold authority."[46] The problem of this antagonist, who loves to be first among others (ὁ φιλοπρωτεύων αὐτῶν), is that he "does not receive us (οὐκ ἐπιδέχεται ἡμᾶς)" (v. 9).[47] As

[44]   In addition to those sources already cited (Schweizer, "Concept of the Church," 237; Black, "Johannine Epistles and the Question of Early Catholicism," 142–43; Attridge, "Johannine Christianity," 12; Klauck, "Gemeinde ohne Amt?" 217–18; Brown, *Community of the Beloved Disciple*, 160), see Adolf von Harnack, "Über den dritten Johannesbrief," TU 15, no. 3 (1897): 3–273.

[45]   For a cogent argument that the Elder is "one in whom considerable ecclesiastical authority has been invested," see Karl Paul Donfried, "Ecclesiastical Authority in 2–3 John," in *L'Evangile de Jean: Sources, Rédaction, Théologie*, ed. Marinus de Jonge, BETL 44, no. 2 (Leuven: Leuven University Press, 1977), 325–33 (here 333).

[46]   Stewart, *Original Bishops*, 28.

[47]   Margaret Mitchell has shown that the translation (as in the NRSV) "does not acknowledge our authority" is premised on faulty definitions of ἐπιδέχομαι in the lexicographical history. See Margaret M. Mitchell, "'Diotrephes Does Not Receive Us': The Lexicographical and Social Context of 3 John 9-10," JBL 117, no. 2 (1998): 299–320. Mitchell shows that the context of the verb ἐπιδέχομαι generally pertains to receiving diplomatic relations between two parties. A contest of authority between Diotrephes and the Elder may be implied in 3 John 9, but the issue may

suggested in the previous chapter, Diotrephes' refusal to receive the Elder (and "the brothers," as reported in v. 10) is less likely to be a rejection of Johannine charismatic anti-clericalism than a rebellion against a more established ecclesial authority held by the Elder and recognized by Gaius and Demetrius of 3 John and "the elect" lady of 2 John. It can be easily imagined that Diotrephes was not seeking to initiate a leadership hierarchy akin to Ignatius' among anti-hierarchical Johannine Christians, but that he was failing to honor recognized leaders appointed within an existing hierarchy or even within an episcopal polity that was in the process of being established.[48] In other words, the problem with Diotrephes in the Johannine network may not be that he was aspiring to an alien model of hierarchical authority, but that *he was failing to recognize the hierarchical authority that was already in place.* Rather than a prototype of an Ignatian *episkopos*, Diotrephes may actually be a prototype of those whom Ignatius would criticize for resisting episcopal authority (Ign. *Mag.* 4.1, 7.1; Ign. *Tra.* 2.2, 7.2; Ign. *Phld.* 7.2; Ign. *Smyr.* 8.1, 9.1). Paul Trebilco has suggested that those in Ephesus whom Ignatius urges not "to oppose the bishop (ἀντιτάσσεσθαι τῷ ἐπισκόπῳ)" (Ign. *Eph.* 5.2)

---

be simply one of refusing fellowship (on grounds ultimately unavailable to us) ("Diotrephes," 317–20). Even so, Judith Lieu grants that, with a reasonable degree of likelihood, "the problem was organizational." See Judith M. Lieu, *I, II, & III John: A Commentary*, NTL (Louisville: Westminster John Knox, 2008), 278.

48   Polycrates, Bishop of Ephesus in the final stretch of the second century, refers to John, the Beloved Disciple of the Fourth Gospel, who "who was a priest wearing the breastplate (ὃς ἐγενήθη ἱερεὺς τὸ πέταλον πεφορεκώς)" (Letter to Victor in Eusebius of Caesarea, *HE* 5.24 [Lake, LCL]). Richard Bauckham has argued that the reference to the breastplate signifies that this John was understood as serving in the capacity of the Jewish High Priest (Richard Bauckham, "Papias and Polycrates on the Origin of the Fourth Gospel," *JTS* 44 [1993]: 24–69; *Jesus and the Eyewitnesses: The Gospels as Eyewitness Testimony*, 2nd ed. [Grand Rapids: Eerdmans, 2017 (2006)], 438–52). Proponents of Johannine anticlericalism must at least acknowledge that what appears to be the first reference to a "priest" in the early church is accorded to none other than John. See Joseph Blenkinsopp, "Presbyter to Priest: Ministry in the Early Church," *Worship* 41, no. 7 (1967): 428–38 (here 431).

are Johannine Christians.[49] Though episcopal opposition is often understood as a Johannine peculiarity, it could also be argued that Johannine Christians, nurtured in their past under the shepherding authority of one like John the Elder and with the disruptive insubordination of Diotrephes still in memory, would welcome Ignatius' later exhortation not "to oppose the bishop."

Johannine Leadership Theology and the Sectarian Hermeneutic: A Summary of the Argument

The Fourth Evangelist narrated his account of Jesus with the conviction that divine reality is something in which human beings can participate in reciprocal fashion. Though this participation is made universally available to all believers, certain leadership figures were assigned specific relational honors or functional roles. The Beloved Disciple, the guarantor of the Johannine tradition, is depicted in the bosom of Jesus in the opening of the intimate Farewell Discourse, just as Jesus is depicted in the bosom of the Father in the magisterial opening of the Gospel. Moreover, the model of Jesus laying down his life for the sheep as the Good Shepherd became a derivative pastoral (episcopal?) vocation assigned to Peter. Both Peter and the Beloved Disciple are coordinated as authority figures whose ministries stand in collegial juxtaposition comparable to the relationships between early apostolic leaders as found in the book of Acts, and not unlike that which is found among the bishops who lead Asian churches some decades later. These relationships between leadership colleagues could certainly be strained at times, but the tension between Paul and Peter at the table in Antioch was surely sharper than what can be explicitly derived from any scene in John featuring Peter and the Beloved Disciple. The tension between John the Elder and Diotrephes, therefore, may not be emblematic of an egalitarian polity versus an episcopal polity; it may well be that Diotrephes is simply

[49] For Paul Trebilco, Ignatius' letter to the Ephesians encompasses all the Christians in that municipality, which would have included the network of Johannine believers (*Early Christians in Ephesus*, 645–83). He observes possible evidence in the Ignatian corpus that the bishop anticipated resistance to his leadership model by these Johannine Christians and also by Christians more comfortable with the charismatic and prophetic leadership valorized by John the Seer in Revelation (e.g., Ign. *Eph.* 5.1; 20.2; and Ign. *Phld.* 7). See Trebilco, *Early Christians in Ephesus*, 669–83.

out of order, insubordinate to an emerging hierarchical authority that was steadily being established in Johannine networks.

The goal of this discussion has been to demonstrate compatibility between Johannine theology and a later hierarchical ecclesiology in order to complicate supposed schismatic trajectories within the early church that have become axiomatic narratives in the study of Christian origins. The traditions underlying the Gospel and Epistles of John allow hermeneutical space for the later development of an episcopal ecclesiology the likes of which can be found in the writings of Ignatius of Antioch. For a generation of New Testament scholars whose historical imaginations have been shaped by Raymond Brown's impressive reconstruction of Johannine Christianity, this claim will surely appear absurd, abrading also against the previously cited judgment by Martin Hengel that Ignatius and John ideologically part ways precisely on the issue of ecclesial hierarchy. It should be noted, however, that John Webster once offered an indictment against the trend in biblical scholarship to find individualism and anticlericalism in early Christianity, observing that "the search for origins is always driven by interests, so that doctrinal judgments masquerade as historical observations."[50] The widespread assumption that the Johannine tradition stood on the ecclesial fringes in the late first and early second centuries may be premised on certain (relatively recent) theological impulses that benefit from polarizing its ecclesiology against those of other early Christian groups. Though these early movements associated with Ignatius and the Gospel and Epistles of John both had enemies, they may have not been enemies with each other.

[50]   John Webster, "The 'Self-Organizing' Power of the Gospel: Episcopacy and Community Formation," in *Community Formation in the Early Church and the Church Today*, ed. Richard N. Longenecker (Peabody, Mass.: Hendrickson, 2002), 179–93 (here 180). Though I have leveled challenges against his understanding of Johannine ecclesiology, the tendency is also observed by Hans-Josef Klauck, who urges interpreters to take special care when making claims about ecclesiastical offices in early Christianity, carefully differentiating between the description of the historical situation and one's own theological assessment of that which is described. To maintain objectivity, we must strive "soweit als möglich sorgfältig zu trennen zwischen der *Beschreibung* der historischen Situation und ihrer theologischen *Bewertung*" (Klauck, "Gemeinde ohne Amt?" 194).

The Spirit-Paraclete and Corporate Charismatic Authority

The question to which I now turn in this second major part of the argument is how a Johannine leadership structure would accord with the role of the Spirit-Paraclete. Since anti-clerical, anti-institutional, and anti-hierarchical are labels applied to Johannine Christianity within the sectarian hermeneutic that views the Gospel and Letters of John as polemical texts of a self-isolating fringe community, I have sought to complicate those labels in the comparative study of the *Epistles* of Ignatius. But reinforcing the claims that John is opposed to the emerging leadership trends in wider streams of early Christianity are entrenched notions about Johannine pneumatology. As alluded to above, John is viewed as promoting a corporate charismatic authority that is incommensurate with episcopal leadership offices and located within an egalitarian community comprising individuals who each have direct access to the Spirit. In the eyes of some interpreters, such a combination amounts to an ecclesial model admirable yet unsustainable, and more is lost than gained.

To review, a standard take on the *Sitz im Leben* is that disagreements emerged within the "Johannine community" (perhaps over the correct interpretation of the Gospel) that resulted in a painful schism (1 John 2:18-19).[51] Pneumatology is deemed a primary factor, because the offending "secessionists" or "opponents" or "progressives" or "docetists" must have based their views on direct inspiration by the Spirit. As a charismatic egalitarian community resistant to hierarchies and formal accountability structures, the Johannine movement had no recourse for adequately addressing this sort of threat. It floundered, eventually dissipating. The departing faction was absorbed into early gnostic streams and the faithful Johannine remnant survived only by relinquishing

[51]   Though appearing throughout Johannine scholarship, this account—repeatedly referred to in this chapter and in the previous chapter—has been most convincingly and persistently articulated by Raymond Brown in multiple publications, already cited above: *Community of the Beloved Disciple*, 138–44; *Churches the Apostles Left Behind*, 102–23; and in Raymond E. Brown, *The Epistles of John: A New Translation with Introduction and Commentary*, AB 30 (New Haven, Conn.: Yale University Press, 1982), 69–115.

its anti-clerical and anti-institutional sentiments and then fading into the wider Christian church, its characteristic features now blanched to the point of extinction. Here is a summary statement from Harold Attridge:

> Disputes eventually divided the community. By the middle of the second century some representatives of the Johannine tradition achieved a respected role in the emerging 'great church', the interconnected web of believers throughout the Mediterranean that provided mutual support and maintained fellowship under the leadership of emerging episcopal authorities.[52]

We have noted that this fate is often attributed to a pathological combination of a low ecclesiology and a high pneumatology. Gary Burge poses the key question that Johannine Christianity faced, ultimately unsuccessfully: "*When text and tradition are not the basis of theological discourse, when unprecedented revelations are offered with confidence, how does one challenge a new theological teaching?*"[53]

For our purposes, this standard reading derives from John's alleged sectarian outlook, and emboldens claims today that this early Christian group was a closed social system resistant to "the other," a category that includes not only the departing opponents of 1 John 2:18-19, but also other Christian communities holding other ideas, other polities, and other traditions. I have sought to weaken this prevailing account of John's ecclesiology by arguing for a Johannine congruence with the theology underlying Ignatius' episcopal model of church leadership. Here, I take a similar approach in regard to the Johannine vision of the Spirit-Paraclete. Though the conventional reading of John's anti-institutional and anti-hierarchical pneumatology has a sturdy footing in biblical scholarship, I intend to demonstrate below that, exegetically, the ground is not exactly solid. In the following material I identify a set of overarching stereotypes, and then question some of the

---

[52]   Attridge, "Johannine Christianity," 3.
[53]   Gary M. Burge, "Spirit-Inspired Theology and Ecclesial Correction: Charting One Shift in the Development of Johannine Ecclesiology and Pneumatology," in *Communities in Dispute: Current Scholarship on the Johannine Epistles*, ed. R. Alan Culpepper and Paul N. Anderson, SBLECL 13 (Atlanta: SBL Press, 2014), 179–85 (here 184; emphases original).

established exegetical assumptions on which the conventional narrative described above is based. As I challenge these presuppositions and interpretive decisions, I will also propose alternative angles of interpretation. Since it is tempting in scholarly argumentation to construct an easily dismissible "straw man" by presenting only the more extreme positions, I will limit my interactions to a handful of notable scholars (whom I hold in high regard) whose works are influential and representative yet measured, insightful, and carefully researched.[54] As elsewhere, the purpose is not to overcorrect or to demolish longstanding arguments in an iconoclastic spirit (another temptation), but to complicate the standard model for the sake of opening new seams of understanding.

Ecclesiological Stereotypes: "Spiritual" vs. "Institutional" and "Liturgical"; "Charismatic" vs. "Episcopal" and "Hierarchical"

A brief vignette illustrates the observation I hope to make in this section.

I was studying in a café recently when I overheard a friend of mine at the adjoining table blurt out with surprise, "What does *that* mean?!" She was reading an article on university student ministry and came across a reference to a strange species of Christian: "charismatic Anglican." We are both active members of a low-church charismatic congregation in town, and to her, the idea that a liturgical and episcopal tradition could be labelled "charismatic" seemed unimaginable. Why? Because "charismatic" means "freedom in worship" (not worship proscribed by stuffy liturgy that quenches the Spirit) and involves the contributions of the wider congregation (not merely a short homily by a collared priest followed by the breaking of bread by ordained hands while a professionally trained choir sings Latin verse).

---

[54] As pointed out previously, in spite of Raymond Brown's contributions to the historical reconstruction largely adopted in the sectarian hermeneutic, he was never comfortable labelling Johannine Christianity as "sectarian": "The Gospel [of John] is not an in-group manifesto meant as a triumph over outsiders; its goal is to challenge the Johannine community itself to understand Jesus more deeply" (*Community*, 62). See also his "'Other Sheep Not of the This Fold': The Johannine Perspective on Christian Diversity the Late First Century," *JBL* 97, no. 1 (1978): 5–22.

My friend's surprised reaction to the phrase "charismatic Angli-can" laid bare a number of stereotypes pertaining to both pneuma-tology and ecclesiology from which biblical scholars are not immune. In many churchly circles, "Spirit-led" is often associated with a collec-tive freedom unhindered by scripted traditions, like the rote recita-tion of a predetermined liturgy or a prewritten prayer. "Charismatic" in today's usage often implies a congregational polity in which each member is endowed with power and authority for ministry uninter-rupted by formally appointed leadership figures like priests, deans, or bishops. "Episcopal" and "liturgical" are at times accounted as polar opposites of "Pentecostal" and "charismatic."

Though there are countless contemporary examples that con-found the syllogistic reasoning (e.g., "charismatic Anglicans"), ecclesiological trends over the past century since Azusa Street may have colored scholarly impressions of Johannine ecclesiology and pneumatology. Gary Burge, for example, directly links the Johan-nine context to that of contemporary Pentecostalism and charis-matic church-life in a recent (as well as insightful and well-written) essay on John's pneumatology.[55] He rightly finds wisdom from John's Epistles that can be applied to a contemporary church-life, yet the ecclesial contexts may not be as parallel as assumed. In similar fashion, Bruce Woll argues that John's charismatic commu-nity is plagued with "too much 'salvation,' that is to say, too many claimants to saving powers, too many successor figures, resulting in rivalry and 'charismatic competition.'"[56]

James Dunn has also envisioned Johannine spirituality as enthu-siastic in ways that seem influenced by contemporary charismatic

[55]   Burge, "Spirit-Inspired Theology." After an insightful discussion, he recalls that "I was once speaking at the Society of Pentecostal Stud-ies and mentioned this theological dilemma of 1 John to a friend there in the Assemblies of God. 'I get it exactly,' he said, 'and this is why we now require our pastors to go to seminary.' This theological and pastoral tension between inspiration and tradition is timeless" ("Spirit-Inspired Theology," 184).

[56]   D. Bruce Woll, *Johannine Christianity in Conflict: Authority, Rank, and Succession in the Farewell Discourse*, SBLDS 60 (Chico, Calif.: Scholars Press, 1981), 32. Cited in Werner Kelber, "Metaphysics and Marginality in John," in *What is John?* vol. 1: *Readers and Readings of the Fourth Gospel*, SBLSymS 3 (Atlanta: Scholars Press, 1996), 129–54 (here 133).

expressions. Taking as his primary text Jesus' remark in John 4:24 that "God is Spirit, and those who worship him must worship in Spirit and truth," he writes:

> "In Spirit" must imply "by inspiration of Spirit"—that is, charismatic worship—for in the immediate context worship in Spirit is set in pointed contrast to worship through the temple and sacred place. The worship that God seeks is not frozen to a sacred building or by loyalty to a particular tradition, but a worship which is living, the ever new response to God who is Spirit as prompted and enabled by the Spirit of God.[57]

For Dunn, attempts to formalize leadership structures in the Pastoral Epistles "testify to the loss of Pauline vitality and vision."[58] Yet the Johannine literature shows that in the later decades of the first century, "there were Christians and Christian communities where the flame still burned brightly and experience of the Spirit created a fresh vision," what Dunn refers to as "the vitality of religious experience."[59] A tradition that celebrates the Spirit is assumed to be "charismatic" in the sense of an energetic social culture free from sacred places, stodgy traditions, and official leaders. Hierarchy quenches the Spirit and saps the community of its spiritual verve (even if it more effectively preserves the community's integrity over time, as commentators like Brown would point out).

Episcopal ecclesiology is thus equated with a *diminished pneumatology*.

The operative stereotypes are 1) that the work of the Spirit is always dramatic, experiential, and spontaneous; and 2) the work of the Spirit is quenched by institutions, ritual, and liturgy. Though perhaps drawn primarily from observations and experiences of contemporary charismatic church life, these stereotypes certainly have some foundation in Scripture, namely in the writings of Luke and Paul. When the Spirit comes in Acts 2, the scene is,

[57] James D. G. Dunn, *Jesus and the Spirit: A Study of the Religious and Charismatic Experience of Jesus and the First Christians as Reflected in the New Testament* (London: SCM Press, 1975), 353–54.

[58] Dunn, *Jesus and the Spirit*, 350.

[59] Dunn, *Jesus and the Spirit*, 350.

well, "Pentecostal," as we have come to understand the term. Yet it is debatable just how paradigmatic the initial Pentecost should be for the work of the Spirit in the church since it was a unique event in salvation history. And large swaths of Christian experience today are premised on 1 Corinthians 12–14, where Paul highlights charismatic practices. The apostle's intention, however, is primarily to correct and modify those practices. Our most consulted source for understanding early Christian charismata is a passage of *corrective* teaching written precisely because those spiritual manifestations were being employed irresponsibly. Even so, Acts 2 and 1 Corinthians 12–14, along with the congregational culture of many modern-day charismatic churches, have established key assumptions shaping the church's view of Spirit-inspired Christianity—and this is also the case in biblical scholarship.

Does John promote the sort of pneumatological experiences found in 1 Corinthians 12–14 and Acts 2, and the sort of charismatic culture promoted by today's Azusa Street traditions? It is impossible to recover a clear picture of Johannine ecclesial life, but the roles and activities of the Spirit according to its literary corpus are not necessarily dramatic or ecstatic. The Spirit generates and sustains life (John 3:5-7; 6:63; 7:37-39); teaches, reveals, reminds, and guides into truth (John 14:26; 16:13; 1 John 2:20, 27); testifies on behalf of Jesus (John 15:26; 1 John 5:6); glorifies Jesus (John 16:14); exposes sin and brings conviction (John 16:8-11); affirms God's presence (1 John 3:24; 4:13); and somehow allocates forgiveness from sins through human mediation (John 20:22). The Spirit is closely linked with Jesus' words (John 6:63) and with "truth" (John 4:23-24; 1 John 5:6; the phrase "Spirit of truth" appears in John 14:17, 15:26, and 16:23). As implied by the title "Paraclete," this divine figure exhorts, comforts, and advocates.

None of these roles, functions, and attributions necessarily links Johannine pneumatology to more ecstatic forms of corporate spirituality. Convicting of sin, guiding into truth, reviving memory, sustaining life, affirming presence—these activities may be slow, tedious, and rather undramatic in the life of a Christian community. And as the *Paraclete*, the Spirit is more of a personified character in

John,[60] not so much a supernatural force or power easily instrumentalized as in some unhealthy forms of charismatic experientialism.[61]

To the immediate question at hand: are these features of Johannine pneumatology truly incompatible with formal leadership structures? It may well be imagined that those within the Johannine social matrix exhibiting those roles most exemplary of the Spirit's activities would rise into positions of authority. Teaching, admonishing, consoling, and reaffirming tradition are surely key ministry practices that would be recognizably "pneumatic" in this early Christian framework and therefore surely celebrated as leadership activities, qualities, and characteristics. In fact, many low-church, charismatic expressions of Christianity today actually operate in an episcopal polity, even if on an informal basis. Though the title "bishop" is rarely used, the roles of "pastor," "church planter," or perhaps "apostle" often carry what is in effect episcopal authority in many of today's congregations and denominations. So even if the worship culture of the Johannine Christians was akin to our modern conceptions of "charismatic," "enthusiastic," or "ecstatic," the conclusion that their spiritual revelations and experiences faced no authoritative framework for authentication is unwarranted.[62] For the argument to work that leadership roles were largely absent, this early community must be viewed not only as charismatic and experiential, but as egalitarian and individualistic.

Theological and Historical Assumptions: Individualism, Egalitarianism, Leadership, and the Spirit

In the most influential reconstructions of John's community history, a fundamental axiom is that Johannine individualism incited pneumatological confusion and egalitarianism inhibited the ecclesial

---

[60]   Brown, *Churches the Apostles Left Behind*, 106–7. See also Byers, *Ecclesiology and Theosis in the Gospel of John*, 224–34.

[61]   I have written on this elsewhere in a more popular-level book: Andrew Byers, *Faith Without Illusions: Following Jesus as a Cynic-Saint* (Downers Grove, Ill.: InterVarsity Press, 2011), 59–85.

[62]   In the historical reconstructions, John/the Elder is often viewed as a strong leader in this sense, but his leadership derives from his longstanding association with tradition and with his own charismatic personality. I discuss below how his authority may well have been more formalized.

leadership required for dealing with it. Individualism and egalitarianism work well together conceptually—as the logic goes, hierarchical structures (that may give rise to elitist leadership figures) are unnecessary if each individual member of the community is reliant on the revelatory activity of the Spirit. Problems arise, however, if one person's inspiration contradicts another's. This interlinked egalitarianism and individualism is central to Raymond Brown's assessment of the overall Johannine dilemma. His wider remarks deserve attention:

> Perhaps the most serious weakness in Johannine ecclesiology and the one most apparent in the Epistles centers on the role of the Paraclete. The thought that there is a living divine teacher in the heart of each believer—a teacher who is the ongoing presence of Jesus, preserving what he taught but interpreting it anew in each generation—is surely one of the greatest contributions made to Christianity by the Fourth Gospel. But the Jesus who sends the Paraclete never tells his followers what is to happen when believers who possess the Paraclete disagree with each other. The Johannine Epistles tell us what frequently happens: they break their *koinōnia* or communion with each other. If the Spirit is the highest and only authority and if each side appeals to him as support for its position, it is nigh impossible (particularly in a dualistic framework where all is either light or darkness) to make concessions and to work out compromises.[63]

Similarly, Dunn believes that John promotes a "a sort of *individualistic pietism*" in which each believer has direct, unmediated access to the Spirit, and thus no perceived need for mutual accountability in the life of the community.[64] In this model, revelations and recollections are matters of personal experience.

Such arguments are not without exegetical reasoning. Jesus himself provided grounds for expecting new insights:

> Yet I have many things to say to you, but you are not able to bear them now; whenever that one comes, the Spirit of truth,

---

63   Brown, *Churches the Apostles Left Behind*, 121–22.
64   Dunn, *Unity and Diversity in the New Testament*, 143 (emphases original).

> he will guide you into all the truth; for he will not speak from
> himself, but as much as he will hear he will speak, and he will
> announce to you the things that are coming. (John 16:12-13)

Though the Gospel of John envisions an ecclesial life grounded in
and guided by the Spirit-Paraclete, the references to the Spirit in the
Epistles are minimal and the Paraclete is now understood as Jesus
(1 John 2:1). The conclusion often drawn from this reticence is that
the author/Elder does not want to draw attention to this source of
revelatory authority because his opponents must have attributed
their teaching to the Spirit's guidance.[65] The call to "test the spirits"
in 1 John 4:1-3 provides further support for the scholarly understanding that the problem lies with individualistic pneumatology
(that is, that anyone can claim inspiration). The Spirit-Paraclete,
it would seem, reveals new truths and unveils "the things that are
coming" to a community of individuals who are equally connected
to the vine and who are each accorded the same status as sheep
in the Shepherd's flock. Such an egalitarianism precludes any con-
sequential interventions or correctives in corporate life since it
"obviates" the need for teachers and accords each member's contributions the same level of authority.[66] Another implicating passage for this understanding of the Johannine community experience is 1 John 2:27: "As for you the anointing (χρῖσμα) that you
received from him abides in you, and so you do not need anyone
to teach you" (NRSV). To challenge an insight or revelation is thus
to impinge on the personal integrity granted to each branch of the
vine, to each sheep within the fold. Indeed, John's supposed promo-
tion of individualism has become an established feature in Johannine scholarship.[67]

[65]   Trebilco, *Early Christians in Ephesus*, 482. From Gary M. Burge:
"The Johannine schism [the departure of the secessionists] is thus typical of a charismatic/enthusiastic schism: both sides are claiming authority
through the authenticity of their own spiritual experiences." See Gary M.
Burge, *The Anointed Community: The Holy Spirit in the Johannine Tradition* (Grand Rapids: Eerdmans, 1987), 173.

[66]   Dunn, *Unity and Diversity in the New Testament*, 128–29.

[67]   Other studies that argue for some form of Johannine individualism include C. F. D. Moule, "Individualism of the Fourth Gospel," *NovT*
5, no. 2–3 (1962): 171–90 (esp. 172). Moule's discussion on Johannine

In the model described above, revelatory catastrophe is inevitable. But does the logic obtain that the sort of "individualism" John envisions "obviates" leadership roles? And does leadership per se truly preclude a community's egalitarian nature? If the recipients of 1 John all have the Spirit-anointing (2:27) and therefore have no need of a teacher, why does the author teach through his writing?[68] Furthermore, if indeed the opponents (who feature so prominently in the sectarian models of Johannine Christianity) are claiming pneumatological inspiration, how reasonable is it to assume that this author—so unafraid to challenge his audience on difficult topics like sin and the ethical mistreatment of the poor, who is bold enough to even dictate those to whom the "elect lady" opens her doors (2 John 10-11)—would avoid offering any paraenetic clarifications for how pneumatology should actually work?[69]

---

individualism centers on eschatology. See also Brown, *Churches the Apostles Left Behind*, 84–85, 95; John F. O'Grady, "Individualism and Johannine Ecclesiology," *BTB* 5, no. 3 (1975): 227–61; Schweizer, "Concept of the Church"; Udo Schnelle, "Johanneische Ekklesiologie," *NTS* 37 (1991): 37–50 (esp. 49); Stephen S. Smalley, *John: Evangelist and Interpreter* (Exeter: Paternoster, 1978), 233–34; John P. Meier, "The Absence and Presence of the Church in John's Gospel," *Mid-Stream* 41, no. 4 (2002): 27–34; and Urban C. von Wahlde, *The Gospels and Letters of John*, 3 vols., ECC (Grand Rapids: Eerdmans, 2010), 1:541.

[68] The teaching here in 1 John 2:27 may refer to the unveiling of truths, but broadly speaking, instruction is more than this. Access to knowledge does not necessitate following through with its implications. The author may acknowledge this access yet feel the need to urge them to act on it (hence his twofold exhortation, "abide in him" in 2:27-28). Indeed, it is *because* they know the truth that he writes to them (1 John 2:21), which is very similar to Paul's own paraenetic approach: "Now concerning love of the brothers and sisters, you do not need to have anyone write to you, for you yourselves have been taught by God to love one another . . . but we urge you, beloved, to do so more and more" (1 Thess 4:9-10 NRSV; cf. 5:1-2). As George Parsenios points out, "the repetition and affirmation of things already known is a typical feature of paraenetic discourse, not because people need further instruction, but because they need to be encouraged, under difficult circumstances, to follow what they already know is the correct course of action." See George L. Parsenios, *First, Second, and Third John*, Paideia (Grand Rapids: Baker Academic, 2014), 90.

[69] It is certainly possible that the opponents claimed the inspiration of the Spirit, but nowhere is this stated. If John's opponents had indeed claimed the Spirit as their guide, the author may well have addressed this

Is the individualism and egalitarianism impregnable against some exhortations (e.g., misuse of the Spirit) and yet open to others (e.g., mistreatment of brothers and sisters)?

In an important essay, Richard Bauckham clarifies that the sort of "individualism" in view is not based on the modern Western idea of an "autonomous and atomized" self.[70] He observes that

> one ingredient of modern Western individualism is an understanding of the self as an independent and firmly bounded unit, averse to compromising its independence through committed involvement with others.[71]

Preferring instead the language of "individuality" or "individuation" over "individualism,"[72] Bauckham argues that the Gospel of John affirms the "personal coinherence" each member of the collective enjoys with Jesus, a sort of "in-one-anotherness," even though it is most certainly written from within a more collectivist perspective. This unique theme of individuation, which Bauckham believes to be underappreciated in scholarship,[73] emphasizes the access each person has to Jesus in a highly collectivist culture that may have downplayed the personal experience of faith for the sake of its corporate expressions.

Yet John simply does not imagine a social system comprising nothing more than a loose confederation of individuals, unaccountable to each other. The personal enriches the corporate, and the corporate strengthens the personal. Bauckham acknowledges that "the kind of love this Gospel describes cannot be confined to any one relationship but always overflows."[74] In fact,

---

directly. The assumption above stands if John is not someone who wishes to tackle a problem head-on, yet we see him doing just that with other matters. It could be that the charismatic authority has been abused, yet why would the author back down from providing further clarification on how his pneumatology works? It may well be that the reason the Spirit is rarely mentioned is because there is no problem with the Spirit.

70   Richard Bauckham, *Gospel of Glory: Major Themes in the Johannine Theology* (Grand Rapids: Baker Academic, 2015), 3.

71   Bauckham, *Gospel of Glory*, 12–13.

72   Bauckham, *Gospel of Glory*, 2.

73   Bauckham, *Gospel of Glory*, 2, 17.

74   Bauckham, *Gospel of Glory*, 19. It may well be intentional that Bauckham's very next chapter is entitled "Divine and Human Community" (21–41).

The Johannine image posits centered selves with open bound-aries, persons who can be part of each other without losing their self-identity. It is an image that breaks open the self-enclosed independence of the bounded self.[75]

This openness to the other, most immediately to the fellow com-munity member, seems largely overlooked in less nuanced remarks on John's purported individualism. In spite of the personal nature of Johannine spirituality, believers are unmistakably *incorporated*. Their "personal coinherence"—to go with Bauckham's helpful phrase—with Jesus is inconceivable outside their participation within a wider ecclesial body. Though Jesus calls his own sheep "by name" (John 10:3), they are part of "one flock" (John 10:16). The ecclesial connotation of "sheep" (πρόβατα) is always in the plural, yet any sheep outside the communal domain must be gathered (John 10:16; 11:52). Though the branches are directly affixed to Jesus, they collectively constitute a vine and are addressed in the plural as well as in the singular (John 15:1-6), and unable to survive outside the whole ("apart from me, you [plural] are not able to do anything," John 15:5).[76] Individual sheep are always to be integrated into a flock; individual branches are always to be integrated into the vine. Whatever is meant by "Johannine individualism," it cannot mean a sort of spiritual self-sufficiency or a socially atomized expe-rience of worship.

The most dominant ecclesial image in the Gospel of John, however, is not the vine or the flock but the family/household.[77] Though Jesus is referred to in the singular as the Son or the μονογενής, believers are only referred to in the collective, plural sense as "children of God" (1:12; 11:52), "sons of light" (12:36), "little children" (13:33), and "my brothers" (20:17). In the Epistles, it is this collective, familial language that proliferates:

[75] Bauckham, *Gospel of Glory*, 13.
[76] Singular: "every branch (πᾶν κλῆμα)"; "the one abiding in me, and I in him (ὁ μένων ἐν ἐμοὶ κἀγὼ ἐν αὐτῷ)." Plural: "you (ὑμεῖς)"; "abide in me and I in you (μείνατε ἐν ἐμοί κἀγὼ ἐν ὑμῖν)."
[77] See the studies Jan G. van der Watt, *Family of the King: Dynamics of Metaphor in the Gospel of John*, BibInt 47 (Leiden: Brill, 2000), and Mary L. Coloe, *Dwelling in the Household of God: Johannine Ecclesiology and Spiri-tuality* (Collegeville, Minn.: Liturgical Press, 2007).

My *little children* (τεκνία), I am writing these things to you so that you may not sin. But if anyone does sin, we have an advocate with the Father, Jesus Christ the righteous. (1 John 2:1)

I write to you, *children* (παιδία), because you know the Father. (1 John 2:14)

I am writing to you, *little children* (τεκνία), because your sins are forgiven on account of his name. (1 John 2:12)

Children (παιδία), it is the last hour! As you have heard that antichrist is coming, so now many antichrists have come. From this we know that it is the last hour. (1 John 2:18)

And now, *little children* (τεκνία), abide in him, so that when he is revealed we may have confidence and not be put to shame before him at his coming. (1 John 2:28)

See what love the Father has given us, that we should be called *children of God* (τέκνα θεοῦ); and that is what we are. The reason the world does not know us is that it did not know him. Beloved, we are *God's children* (τέκνα θεοῦ) now; what we will be has not yet been revealed. What we do know is this: when he is revealed, we will be like him, for we will see him as he is. (1 John 3:1-2)

Little children (τεκνία), let no one deceive you. Everyone who does what is right is righteous, just as he is righteous. (1 John 3:7)

The *children of God* (τὰ τέκνα τοῦ θεοῦ) and the children of the devil are revealed in this way: all who do not do what is right are not from God, nor are those who do not love their *brothers and sisters*. (1 John 3:10)

Little children (τεκνία), let us love, not in word or speech, but in truth and action. (1 John 3:18)

Little children (τεκνία), you are from God, and have conquered them; for the one who is in you is greater than the one who is in the world. (1 John 4:4)

By this we know that we love the *children of God* (τὰ τέκνα τοῦ θεοῦ), when we love God and obey his commandments. (1 John 5:2)

Little children (τεκνία), keep yourselves from idols. (1 John 5:21)

The elder to the elect lady and her *children* (τέκνοις), whom I love in the truth, and not only I but also all who know the truth. (2 John 1)

I was overjoyed to find some of your *children* (τέκνων) walking in the truth, just as we have been commanded by the Father. (2 John 4)

The *children* (τέκνα) of your elect sister send you their greetings. (2 John 13)

I have no greater joy than this, to hear that my *children* (τέκνα) are walking in the truth. (3 John 4)[78]

The preponderance of the terms "children" (τέκνα) and "little children" (τεκνία—always as a vocative address) is clear from the passages listed above. The term "brother" (ἀδελφός, envisioning in the plural the wider members of the community and thus translatable as "brothers and sisters" or, as in the NRSV, as "friends") is just as abundant, appearing eighteen times in the Epistles (though, incidentally, not in 2 John).[79] A related address with family connotations is "beloved" (ἀγαπητοί), appearing ten times (again, minus 2 John).[80]

The point to note here is that this dense filial language must be allowed to qualify our notions of Johannine individualism and egalitarianism. In the customary picture of the Johannine situation, each community member has direct access to Jesus through the Spirit-Paraclete *and stands above interdependence and arbitration*. The former claim seems accurate, but the latter claim goes too far. What family or household—today or in the Greco-Roman world—functions without any form of accountability or

---

[78] These passages are all from the NRSV, emphases added.
[79] 1 John 2:9-11; 3:10, 12, 13-17; 4:20-21; 5:16; 3 John 3, 5, 10.
[80] 1 John 2:7; 3:2, 21; 4:1, 7, 11; 3 John 1, 2, 5, 11.

established authority? If every participant of the Johannine fellowship were simply "brothers," "children," or "little children," then perhaps some form of non-hierarchical ecclesial chaos might ensue. But the author of 1 John presupposes a more varied composition of his audience by referring to "fathers" (πατέρες) and "young men" (νεανίσκοι), as well as to beloved children (1 John 2:12-14); and the author of 2 and 3 John designates himself with a term that is unquestionably authoritative within a family metaphor system: "the Elder." Though this author includes himself within the children of God ("that is what *we* are," 1 John 3:1, emphasis added), he can authoritatively (and surely lovingly) speak of his fellow siblings *in the possessive*:

> *My* little children (τεκνία μου), I am writing these things to you so that you may not sin. (1 John 2:1 NRSV; emphasis added)

> I have no greater joy than this, to hear that *my* children (τὰ ἐμὰ τέκνα) are walking in the truth. (3 John 4 NRSV; emphasis added)

This John is a family member. But family membership does not forestall leadership or authority. It will certainly qualify the type and style of leadership, but the familial imagery *assumes and even necessitates* leadership.

In the vine imagery there is a Gardener. In the pastoral imagery there is a Shepherd. And in the family imagery, there is a Father and a one and only Son (μονογενής). There is also an "Elder."[81] As discussed in the study on John and Ignatius above, reciprocity and participation permit human agents to inhabit certain divine roles.[82] It is clear from Jesus' appointment of Peter to the divine role of (under-)shepherd that leadership is valued in Johannine communal life (this is true even if John 21 was a later

[81] It is worth noting here that Judith Lieu, in her (admirable) characteristic reluctance to claim too much historically on the literary evidence, acknowledges that one cannot deduce from what is written whether an institutional or non-institutional idea of "elder" is in view. Judith M. Lieu, *Theology of the Johannine Epistles*, NTT (Cambridge: Cambridge University Press, 1991), 92.

[82] Note that Jesus addresses the disciples as "children (παιδία)" in John 21:5.

addition, since it indicates an inclination within the tradition to affirm pastoral authority). It is surely also the case that human figures may participate in varying degrees in the divine role of pruning the vine.[83] And although there is only one Father in the Johannine household, there is clearly someone with pen in hand who can address his audience not only as fellow children but also as "*my* children." This "John" behind the Epistles does not have his hands tied behind his back as a reluctant leadership figure. He is certainly operating within the well-established ecclesial vision of his tradition, a vision that celebrates personal access to Jesus and certainly some degree of egalitarian mutuality. But the ecclesial imagery of the family/household affords grounds for assertive accountability. When it comes to discerning the activity of the Spirit, individualism and egalitarianism may be legitimately supplemented by authoritative leadership.

Conclusion: John and Other Leaders, and the (So-Called) Failure of Johannine Christianity

I anticipate a question of protest: if indeed the author of these Epistles possesses a reasonable degree of recognizable leverage and would potentially countenance an (eventual) episcopal expansion of his leadership theology, why is he so diffident or weak in exercising his authority?

It is in the conflict with Diotrephes that the Elder's authority, which many understand to be more personal than formal, seems limited and unrecognized:

> 3 John shows that the problem for the elder is precisely that Diotrephes is in no sense structurally under the elder's authority. . . .

---

[83] The divine extension (and withholding) of forgiveness is also a divine action that is to be administered through the disciples as agents of the Spirit (John 20:22). If the disciples who receive this commission are representative of all believers, it is another instance of the egalitarian vision. If the disciples in this scene are to be understood as representative leadership figures, then we have an instance of a priestly, perhaps even sacerdotal, vision of Christian ministry. My tendency is to assume the former, affirming that a broad egalitarian vision does not necessitate a leaderless polity.

In the situation revealed by 3 Jn, Diotrephes seems to have chosen to ignore this personal authority of the elder. Given Diotrephes' rejection of his personal authority, the elder shows that he is unable to appeal to his possession of any other form of authority in his dispute with Diotrephes, precisely because he has no such supra-local authority apart from his already-rejected personal authority.[84]

The Elder is deemed as powerless. As John Painter points out, rather than "when" I come, he writes "if" I come.[85]

I have argued that ecclesial leadership is amenable to some form of Johannine individualism and egalitarianism. Yet many interpreters assume that the author of the Epistles, unadorned with any formalized leadership role, is reluctant to assert his authority, which is merely personal. Rather than dictating commands in the first-person singular, he places himself not above or outside the community but within it, opting for a voice in the first-person plural. Though Paul Trebilco grants that "there is some sense of the authority of the author" and "that the author wrote the letter to the community seems in itself to be an act of leadership," he nonetheless argues that the locus of authority is the anointed community.[86] Again from Burge: "In this same situation one would have expected Paul to respond with an authoritative 'I' (e.g., Galatians). But in the Johannine church the prominence of the Paraclete has relativized the authority of any single teacher."[87]

Could the Elder's approach not be a matter of leadership *style*?

Every Christian leader must exercise authority within an upturned value system amidst a community of equals, of brothers and sisters, a community in which the highest becomes lowest and washes the feet of her subjects, in which office does not determine status or worth, and amidst a kingdom in which the first are last and the last first, and the greatest is the child, the servant, and the

---

[84] Trebilco, *Early Christians in Ephesus*, 483–84.

[85] Painter, *1, 2, and 3 John*, 376. For Martin Hengel, however, the writer's "if I come" does not express an empty threat but "announces a firm purpose" (*Johannine Question*, 37).

[86] Painter, *1, 2, and 3 John*, 476 and 481, respectively.

[87] Burge, *Anointed Community*, 173.

least significant. Peter may have been deemed the Rock with connotations of episcopal power in Matthew 16:18-20, but Jesus flatly
charged his disciples in Matthew 23:8-12 not to be called "Rabbi" or
"Teacher," but "brother." Paul was conscious of his leadership clout,
but in his personal letter to Philemon his preference was to appeal
to friendship, not to apostolic authority. Though the Pastoral Epistles are cited as examples of the move toward the formal leadership
structures of early catholicism, the Pauline author nonetheless urges
the *episkopos* to be "gentle, not quarrelsome" (1 Tim 3:3). The ideal
leader of these later epistles—writings regularly set in contrast to
the Johannine Epistles—is to be "kindly to everyone, an apt teacher,
patient, correcting opponents with gentleness" (2 Tim 2:24). Titus
is told that the *episkopos* (who may be synonymous with "elder" in
1:5) "must not be arrogant or quick-tempered" (1:7). The author of
1 Peter, presumably supportive of the Petrine leadership tradition
that many scholars view as conflicting with its Johannine counterpart, presents himself as an "elder" (1 Pet 5:1) as well as an (under-)
shepherd (1 Pet 5:2), yet promotes a "holy" and "royal priesthood"
of all believers (1 Pet 2:5, 9), and charges fellow leaders, "Do not
lord it over those in your charge" (1 Pet 5:3).[88]

Even Ignatius, with his clear program of fortifying an episcopal
ecclesiology throughout Asian cities, writes with florid deference
"as a humble sacrifice" (Ign. *Eph.* 8.1) and "not as though I were
someone important" (Ign. *Eph.* 3.1).[89] As much ink has been spilt
comparing the antipodal leadership styles of Ignatius and the Elder,
Ignatius seems to embody the leadership "weakness" many interpreters detect in the Johannine Epistles when he writes of the Tral-
lian bishop "whose gentleness is his power" (Ign. *Tra.* 3.2); indeed,
the great Syrian prisoner claims that he "needs gentleness, by which
the ruler of this age (ὁ ἄρχων τοῦ αἰῶνος τούτου[90]) is destroyed"
(Ign. *Tra.* 4.2). Ignatius commends the same leadership demeanor
to Polycarp, his episcopal protégé: "If you love good disciples, it is
no credit to you; rather *with gentleness* bring the more troublesome

---

[88]   Citations above are from the NRSV.
[89]   Ignatius refers to Jesus as "our only teacher" (*Mag.* 9.1)
[90]   Note the Johannine ring to this designation. See, e.g., ὁ ἄρχων τοῦ
κόσμου τούτου (John 12:31; 16:11); ὁ τοῦ κόσμου ἄρχων (John 14:30).

ones into submission" (Ign. *Pol.* 2.1; emphases added). Ignatius may write as a formally recognized church official, but he also writes "as the very least" of his own congregation, of whom he is "not worthy to be considered a member" (Ign. *Tra.* 13.1; see also Ign. *Smyr.* 11.1). His own personal struggle with exercising authority within the values of the Christ he serves is evident in his remark that "I do not give orders like Peter and Paul: they were apostles, I am a convict; they were free, but I am even now still a slave" (Ign. *Rom.* 4.3).

In my reading, John does not seem to be a weak figure drained of authority by the Johannine refusal to conform to emerging episcopal forms of church governance. He may well employ a rhetorical stance that appeals more than it commands, but that merely places him in good company among the early Christian leadership figures he is so often pitted against in modern scholarship. And if he seems less harsh than, say, Paul's labelling of deviants as "anathema" or delivery of miscreants over to Satan, perhaps it is because he is less *sectarian*.

Did Johannine Christianity "Fail"?

There are many arguments in today's sectarian hermeneutic that are inconsistent or might fare better with alternative conclusions. One glaring inconsistency is to claim that this early Christian group advanced a low, anti-hierarchical and anti-clerical ecclesiology while also declaring that the Beloved Disciple commanded enough heft to compete with Peter, the exemplar of episcopal authority in the incipient Great Church. The argument that Johannine Christianity failed, fading from the historical scene because it was so sectarian it could not survive the test of time, can also be turned on its head.[91] Perhaps, as the standard reading goes, this movement dug in its theological heels, bleeding some members off to proto-gnostic bands while inflexibly refusing to abandon an ecclesial ship that eventually sank into history. But perhaps Johannine believers, led

---

[91]   Francis Moloney believes that Johannine Christianity failed, "but their failure was not because they closed the doors and became an early Christian sect" but because "the command to make God known to the world by loving as Jesus had loved them was easier to talk about than to live." See Francis J. Moloney, *Love in the Gospel of John: An Exegetical, Theological, and Literary Study* (Grand Rapids: Baker Academic, 2013), 210.

by the Spirit-Paraclete who would show them new things and the things that are to come, recognized the pluriform depth of meaning in their texts, celebrated the opportunity to wash the feet of other sheep not in their fold, and happily streamed into the broader traditions of the growing church. The lack of evidence of a distinctive Johannine community persisting deep into the second century may not be a sign of failure. It may simply be the strongest evidence available that this early stream was *distinctive* but not *sectarian*.

5

The Other Disciple's
Theology of the "Other"

The edifice challenged throughout these chapters is the "sectarian hermeneutic" in Johannine studies, an influential interpretive frame in which the New Testament writings attributed to "John" are read as the product of an insular community internally fractured and externally adversarial. This communal network certainly experienced internal problems, and there is no denying its determination to remain distinctive from the surrounding environs. But is it hermeneutically correct to perceive only "Do not cross" banners interlaced throughout its social history and embedded within its literature?

In the confidence that there is a more complicated story to tell about Johannine Christianity, the task now turns to the constructive work of theological synthesis. While being honest about the sharp edges of this literary corpus, I hope to demonstrate here its capacity to resource readers in a secular age that tends to accentuate alterity to the point of agonistic extremes and at times attacks diversity as energetically as it claims to cherish it. The narrative and epistolary modes of writing are conducive for many theological and pastoral tasks, yet John's Gospel and Letters are not designed to produce a tidy policy in response to our modern-day questions. The question at the forefront of this chapter asks how we might read this tradition today in light of the difference and alterity within our present-day pluralistic societies. In what follows, I hope to offer a reply that is exegetically responsible, theologically rich, and culturally translatable.

We begin "in the beginning."

Perichoretic Otherness and the Incarnation: "The Word became flesh . . ."

When the Fourth Evangelist opens his Gospel, he introduces us to two interrelated divine figures, God and the Logos. They are co-identified:

> In the beginning was the Logos . . .[1]

> the Logos was God . . .

and simultaneously differentiated:

> the Logos was with God. . . .

> This one was in the beginning with God.[2]

Their identities cannot be homogenized, yet in their heterogenous co-relation, they are not set at odds. They are *other* while nonetheless "one," as later passages will indicate (10:30; 17:11, 21-23). This unity-in-plurality and plurality-in-unity express an otherness that does not exclude or antagonize. As John's story unfolds, another divine figure emerges as co-identifiable with God and the Logos.[3] The cumulative yet subtle characterization of the Spirit-Paraclete is such that the dyadic otherness of divinity in the Prologue seems to

---

[1]   The Logos' co-identification with God occurs here because readers and auditors familiar with the Scripture of Israel would expect "in the beginning θεός," not "λόγος."

[2]   Differentiation is expressed through the preposition translated here as "with" (πρός), indicating two entities who are appreciably distinct.

[3]   For a theological account of the Spirit's role in maintaining particularity and unity in the relations between Father and Son, see Colin E. Gunton, *The One, the Three and the Many: God, Creation and the Culture of Modernity* (Cambridge: Cambridge University Press, 1993), 205-6, 215.

expand into triadic (Trinitarian, we could say) otherness in which the three entities mutually co-inhere, a dynamic later theologians would call "perichoresis."[4] Jürgen Moltmann brings his theology of divine space to bear on a Trinitarian reading of Johannine perichoresis:

> The unity of Jesus, the Son of the Father, and God, the Father of Jesus, is not an exclusive and closed unity like a circle or a triangle, often used in the tradition as symbols of the divine Trinity. It is a wide open, inviting, and integrating unity. The perichoretic unity of the divine Persons and Spaces is so wide open that the whole world can find room and rest and the fullness of eternal life within it. All creatures can enter into God to find their freedom and living-space and home in the Trinity. The divine Trinity is not "open" because it is imperfect, but by virtue of graciously overflowing love ... the Trinity is an open and living and uniting environment for the whole creation redeemed and renewed in God.[5]

What is important to note for our purposes here is that within this perichoretic otherness, the Father and Son (and Spirit) are distinct while unified, a "co-inherence without coalescence."[6] They are "other" without being "othered."

Steeped in Israel's scriptural traditions, this Johannine notion of divine plurality (though not without precedence) seeks to reconfigure conventional Jewish theology. It is not, however, the only controversial innovation of the Fourth Gospel's Prologue. Just as astonishing as the coordination of the Logos and the Theos (and eventually the Spirit) is the idea that, within their relational space,

---

[4]   Gunton's succinct phrasing is helpful: "A perichoretic unity is a unity of a plural rather than unitary kind" (*One, the Three and the Many*, 212).

[5]   Jürgen Moltmann, "God in the World—The World in God: Perichoresis in Trinity and Eschatology," in *The Gospel of John and Christian Theology*, ed. Richard Bauckham and Carl Mosser (Grand Rapids: Eerdmans, 2008); 369–81 (here, 375–76).

[6]   This quote is taken from Miroslav Volf's compression of George L. Prestige's explanation of perichoresis in *God in Patristic Thought* (London: SPCK, 1956), 298 (cited in Miroslav Volf, *After Our Likeness: The Church as the Image of the Trinity* [Grand Rapids: Eerdmans, 1998], 209, n. 84).

they invite the presence of the mortal "other." Perichoretic plurality in unity is not exclusively inward in focus but inclusively outward, oriented toward humanity. The relational extension that opens divine perichoresis to human beings is the Incarnation: "The Logos became flesh and dwelled among us" (1:14).

There are two fundamental events of de-othering in the Incarnation. One is internal to the Person of Christ. To use the later language of Chalcedon, Jesus is "the same perfect in divinity and also perfect in humanity, the same truly God and truly a human being composed of rational soul and body." As the confession continues, beholden in part to the Fourth Gospel, Jesus is to

> be acknowledged in two natures, without confusion or change, without division or separation. The distinction between the natures was never abolished by their union but rather the character proper to each of the two natures was preserved as they came together in one person and hypostasis. He is not split or divided into two persons, but he is one and the same only begotten Son, God the Word, the Lord Jesus Christ.[7]

In this creedal reformulation of Johannine ideas in later theological idiom, varied antitheses are not dissolved, but held together coextensively (synthetically) in the divine and human Son. In his very person, the (Johannine) Christ embodies *harmonious alterity*. Different natures are not subsumed; instead, they coinhere. Jesus within himself embodies *an identity of non-othered otherness*.[8]

The second de-othering event of the Incarnation is external and intimated in another Chalcedonian line that presents Jesus as "the same one in being with the Father as to the divinity and one in being with us as to the humanity." As stated in the Introduction, the Incarnation of Jesus is a radical act of de-othering in which the

---

[7] Heinrich Denzinger et al., eds., *Compendium of Creeds, Definitions, and Declarations on Matters of Faith and Morals*, 43rd ed. (San Francisco: Ignatius Press, 2012). I am using above Ian A. McFarland's slightly altered translation in *The Word Made Flesh: A Theology of the Incarnation* (Louisville: Westminster John Knox, 2019), 2–3.

[8] Moltmann points out that even within the very person of Jesus there persists "the mutual penetration of two heterogenous natures, the divine and the human" ("God in the World," 373).

divine Other becomes an-Other, *another* among human beings. He is not Käsemann's and Baur's aloof deity striding across the earth, nor Meeks' divine stranger enshrouded in indecipherable mystery. The Logos is not like the title character in Albert Camus' *The Outsider* (*L'Etranger*), who stands apart from the pains and sufferings of the world he has entered.[9] No, the Divine Other weeps outside Lazarus' grave and strides across Judean, Galilean, and even Samaritan soil to befriend strangers, console friends, and join the celebrations of a wedding in Cana. The motif of christological descent and ascent does not reinforce divine estrangement; it intersects cosmic partitions. Jesus strides not over the earth like an untouchable other, but across borders emblazoned with "Do not cross."

When this divine Other becomes flesh, fleshly beings become divine: in receiving this incarnate Other, they are given authority to become "children of God . . . born not out of bloodlines and not out of the will of the flesh, and not out of the design of a husband, but ἐκ θεοῦ (out of God)" (1:12, 13). This inclusivity of the mortal other is expressed through the oneness motif as Jesus prays to the Father that his disciples "may be one, just as we are one" (17:22). Again, this oneness is not homogenized sameness. These divine mortals become individual participants within the perichoretic otherness but retain a distinctive corporate identity.[10] In Johannine oneness, alterity and unity coinhere: God alone is Father, Jesus is the Son—the μονογενής—and human beings who believe in him are "sons of light" or "children of God." Kinship language articulates

---

[9]   The story is largely a trial narrative, but of someone who feels no regret and finds himself disconnected from ethical realities (or at least the perception of ethical realities by others). See Albert Camus, *The Outsider*, trans. Joseph Laredo (Harmondsworth, England: Penguin, 1981 [1942]).

[10]   Miroslav Volf provides an insightful account (focused on John's Gospel) of how human beings participate within the divine interrelationality without sharing in the interiority of the divine persons reserved for the Father, Son, and Spirit (*After Our Likeness*, 208–13). Human perichoresis differs from divine perichoresis since "Human persons are always external to one another *as subjects*" (211; emphases original). But since the Son dwells in believers through the Spirit, humans are caught up into the inter-divine communion, the Spirit serving as the relational connecting point between the divine communion and the human communion of the church (213).

differentiation within a corporate unity. Drawing on Trinitarian theology as a resource for addressing the fragmentation in contemporary culture, Colin Gunton observed two opposite approaches, both of which are unsatisfactory: "The individualist teaches that we are what we are in separation from our neighbor, the collectivist that we are so involved with others in society that we lose particularity."[11] In Johannine perichoresis, filiation resists homogeneity yet nonetheless ensures social cohesion. Plurality thrives within the unity of Father, Son, and the children of God (and the Spirit). Diversity among is not an adversity to overcome.

The Incarnation's act of de-othering is a cornerstone in Christian theology and the bedrock premise for its promise of salvation. As the patristic adage goes, "that which is not assumed is not healed."[12] The categorical distinctiveness of our humanity constitutes no barrier for divine rescue. Ian McFarland eloquently expresses the point: "It is precisely as creatures who are other than God that we are saved because God, in a love beyond telling, has willed not to be other than us."[13] By becoming flesh, the Logos became not only relatable, tangible, and approachable, but also killable. And the horrific violence of the cross is one of the means by which divinity and (sinful) humanity are de-othered. In *Exclusion and Embrace*, Miroslav Volf is reflecting on John's Gospel when he writes,

> That same love that sustains nonself-enclosed identities in the Trinity seeks to make space "in God" for humanity. Humanity is, however, not just the other of God, but the beloved other who has become an enemy. When God sets out to embrace the enemy, the result is the cross. On the cross the dancing circle of self-giving and mutually indwelling divine persons opens up for the enemy; in the agony of the passion the movement stops for a brief moment and a fissure appears so that sinful humanity can join in (see John 17:21). We, the others—we, the enemies—are embraced by the divine persons who love us with

[11] Gunton, *One, the Three and the Many*, 169. These options are, of course, presented in their most extreme forms. Most of us are not entirely collectivists or entirely individualists. See Gunton's wider discussion on perichoresis, 163–73.

[12] See Gregory of Nazianzus, *Ep.* 101.

[13] McFarland, *Word Made Flesh*, 14.

the same love with which they love each other and therefore make space for us within their own eternal embrace.[14]

Inscribed into the narrative of the Fourth Gospel is divine discontent: God longs to end the estranged otherness of humanity: "By becoming flesh, the Word intimately united itself precisely to that which has alienated itself from God."[15] To that end, nothing is withheld. The furthest lengths are traversed. The highest fortifications are scaled. John perceives that lines once signposted with "Do Not Cross" are made permeable in the Christ-event. Divinity and humanity, the heavenly and the earthly, above and below, flesh and spirit—these contrasted pairings are opened to one other in the Incarnation of the Logos and in the filiation of believers. In this way "God loved the world" (John 3:16), by bridging the deepest chasms and demolishing the highest walls that together lay the foundations for acts of othering. John presents his readers with *an alterity that loves*, both within and without.

The idea and model of perichoretic alterity—in which otherness persists without othering and generates the loving pursuit of the mortal other by the divine Other—is perhaps the greatest gift Johannine theology offers to societies beleaguered by division. We do not have to be "same" to be "one." As much as it may incite exclusion, diversity can invite embrace since God himself exists in a plural unity, a unified plurality, and is presented in a posture of openness to "the other." If the Johannine vision of triadic divinity is foundationally open to otherness, then surely Christians—ancient and contemporary—are unfaithful to Johannine theology if they view difference and otherness as intrinsically negative.

Yet there is an undeniable Johannine theology of *negative othering*.

The Johannine Negative Other: "The Light Shines in the Darkness"

Otherness may obtain in a perichoretic harmony into which human others are invited, but the Fourth Gospel is clear from the start that there is a foundational alterity that cannot be united—Light shines

---

[14]   Miroslav Volf, *Exclusion and Embrace: A Theological Exploration of Identity, Otherness, and Reconciliation* (Nashville: Abingdon, 1996), 128–29.

[15]   Miroslav Volf, "Johannine Dualism and Contemporary Pluralism," in *The Gospel of John and Christian Theology*, ed. Richard Bauckham and Carl Mosser (Grand Rapids: Eerdmans, 2008), 19–50 (here 23).

in the Darkness, but the Darkness does not comprehend or overcome it (1:5).[16] The difference between the two is essentialized at
the cosmic plane and fundamentally antagonistic.[17] Whereas flesh
and spirit, above and below, and humanity and divinity are pairings
that may be bridged or interlinked, Light and Darkness can never
coinhere. There is no possible unity between the Light/Dark antithesis, only duality. A movement from Darkness into Light is rendered possible by the Incarnation, but human beings may choose to
remain in the former.

When the Logos enters this cosmos, humanity and divinity may be potentially de-othered, but a rupture also occurs.
Those human beings who receive the Logos with faith are in the
minority: the Logos came to his own, and his own did not receive
him. For John, those rejecting the divine Other cast themselves
into a trajectory toward cosmic Darkness. Humanity is splin-
tered apart into those who believe, and those who do not.[18] In the
double-edged dynamic of reception/rejection, the Incarnation de-
others, yet also reifies otherness.

[16]   From Ruth Sheridan: "Everything negative and dark in the Gospel
of John is displaced onto the 'other' in accordance with the cosmological
and theological dualism at work in the Gospel." See Ruth Sheridan, "Identity, Alterity, and the Gospel of John," *BibInt* 22 (2014): 188–209 (here 201).
[17]   Though I am comfortable with the term "duality," I am avoided
the term "dualism," a religious and philosophical concept that has been
regularly used to describe Johannine metaphysics. A sharp binarism
has contributed to the sectarian hermeneutic because it divides human
beings into foundational polarities that cannot be bridged. A number of
significant challenges have emerged against the attribution of dualism to
John. Though these texts feature contrasts between abstract terms and
ideas, John is operating out of a monistic theological stream that cannot
accommodate the sort of dualistic worldview common in gnostic texts. For
robust challenges to the notion of Johannine dualism, see Douglas Estes,
"Dualism or Paradox? A New 'Light' on the Gospel of John," *JTS* 71, no. 1
(2020): 90–118; Volf, "Johannine Dualism and Contemporary Pluralism";
Stephen C. Barton, "Johannine Dualism and Contemporary Pluralism," in
Bauckham and Mosser, *Gospel of John and Christian Theology*, 3–18. These
studies were in many respects anticipated by C. K. Barrett, *Essays on John*
(London: SPCK, 1982), 98–115.
[18]   Bultmann referred to this phenomenon as a "dualism of decision."
See Rudolf Bultmann, *Theology of the New Testament*, trans. Kendrick Grobel (Waco, Tex.: Baylor University Press, 2007 [1955, 1951]), 2:76–77.

As the Logos remains an "Other" within the world, believers who are incorporated into John's triadic perichoresis participate in Jesus' divine alterity through the Spirit. They are children of God who are in the world but not of it (John 17:11, 14-16). Characterizing their otherness is the presence of the Paraclete whom the world cannot receive (John 14:16-17; 1 John 3:24), a resistance to that world's temptations (1 John 2:15-17), and loving action toward one another (John 13:34-35; 1 John 3). The distinctiveness between the children of God and the rest of humanity is outlined in no uncertain terms:

> The children of God and the children of the devil are revealed in this way: all who do not do what is right are not from God, nor are those who do not love their brothers and sisters. (1 John 3:10)

> Whoever has the Son has life; whoever does not have the Son of God does not have life (1 John 5:12)

> We know that we are God's children, and that the whole world lies under the power of the evil one (1 John 5:19).

There are branches that abide in Jesus, and there are those who do not. The latter are cast off and burned (John 15:7).

It is significant to note, however, that this division within humanity *is not ethnically determined*. Race is no divider in Johannine othering. Ethnic othering is a mode of boundary construction unacceptable in the world the Logos has entered. Geographical borders matter no longer. What matters is *cosmic alignment*, an alignment determined by belief or unbelief in Jesus.

So, John offers a means by which all humanity might be unified, yet not all avail themselves of this particularized means. All interhuman barriers dissolve in this new social reality except for one's stance toward the Logos. The standard differences that tend to disrupt, complicate, and burst communal ties—race, culture, ethnicity, gender[19]—shed their power (at least theoretically) to demarcate, disrupt, and divide. Johannine Christianity resources humankind

---

[19] Many interpreters of John have pointed out that women are presented favorably and feature as potential leadership figures. See, e.g., Sandra M. Schneiders, *Written That You May Believe: Encountering Jesus in the Fourth Gospel*, rev. ed. (New York: Crossroad, 2003 [1999]), 93–114, 233–54.

with a vision of difference and solidarity that subverts our standard modes of othering. But it undeniably creates a new means of dividing human beings into two distinct groups.

The actual allocation of human beings into these divisions, however, *is not necessarily straightforward*. John's profile of the negative "other" is more ambiguous than his sharp dualities suggest.[20] In spite of the clarity of division between Life and Death, Light and Darkness, the Johannine literature allows that identifying cosmic alignment on the human plane is imprecise, and perhaps at times impossible. Though "the Jews" seem clearly aligned with evil forces at several points, their overall characterization is more equivocal—some believe, some comfort the friends of Jesus, some are simply bystanders representing the potential for belief or unbelief—and virtually every Gospel character is Jewish by implication, regardless of whether their specific depictions are negative, positive, or even neutral.[21]

[20]   After writing this section, I discovered that Volf offers a similar account of John's "shades of gray" in "Johannine Dualism and Contemporary Pluralism," 43–45. I am also grateful to David Lamb for allowing me to read a paper relevant to this theme: David A. Lamb, "The Boundaries of Love: 'Us and Them' Language in 1 John" (paper presented at the International Colloquium: Love, Boundaries, and Sacred Texts, University of Chester, May 2, 2019). Lamb points out that the hard lines drawn in 1 John are often more amorphous than acknowledged. On the "us and them" boundaries between the Johannine believers and the "secessionists," he helpfully points to discussions about the ambiguity of the distinctions in Judith M. Lieu, *I, II, & III John: A Commentary*, NTL (Louisville: Westminster John Knox, 2008) and in Craig R. Koester, "The Antichrist Theme in the Johannine Epistles and Its Role in Christian Tradition," in *Communities in Dispute: Current Scholarship on the Johannine Epistles*, ed. R. Alan Culpepper and Paul N. Anderson, SBLECL 13 (Atlanta: SBL Press, 2014), 187–96 (esp. 194–95).

[21]   Again, from Ruth Sheridan: "The danger of an uncritical or 'compliant' reading (following Reinhartz's terminology) of the Gospel of John, and of an empathetic engagement only with those positive characters who express faith in Jesus, is that it may lead to the reader adopting a faith identity that routinely identifies all Jews as 'others'" ("Identity," 206). In one sense I agree; but as argued, John concurrently "others" the rhetorical construct of "the Jews" while he ambiguates who may or may not belong to that generic categorization. For Sheridan, although "the Jews" are indeed presented positively in some respects, "the theological coherence of the Gospel of John tends to blend these subtleties into one mix, with its overarching insistence on belief in Jesus as Son of God and

Bracketing what many scholars call "the book of signs" are two clear statements by the evangelist that no one believes in Jesus, one in the Prologue ("he came to his own, and his own did not receive him," 1:11) and the other in John 12 ("but having done so many signs before them they were not believing in him," 12:37); yet both ostensibly unambivalent statements are immediately followed, almost confusingly, by accounts of belief—"but as many as received him, he gave them the authority to become children of God" (1:12) and, though God hardens hearts and blinds eyes as Isaiah predicted, "yet nevertheless (ὅμως μέντοι) many out of the rulers believed in him" (12:42).[22] The evangelist simultaneously defines and blurs.[23] The literal "others (ἄλλοι)" in the Fourth Gospel carry the common function of serving as members of the crowd who express different views or ask certain questions about Jesus, views and questions that can be either positive toward him or negative.[24] These "others" brim with indeterminate potential.

Though the practice of sin vividly distinguishes unbelievers from the children of God, the author of 1 John betrays that the reality on the ground is less clear-cut, since he continually urges his

Messiah" ("Identity," 208). I would suggest that John wants his audience to resist a "mix" and to recognize a composite portrayal of "the Jews" that complicates unambiguous othering. Alicia Myers shows how this works in John through a rhetorical analysis. See Alicia D. Myers, "Just Opponents? Ambiguity, Empathy, and the Jews in the Gospel of John," in *Johannine Ethics: The Moral World of the Gospel and Epistles of John*, ed. Christopher W. Skinner and Sherri Brown (Minneapolis: Fortress, 2017), 159–76.

22   Along with Isaiah 6, the Johannine narrator references Isaiah 53:1, a line from a wider prophecy bearing universal language. See Carlos Raúl Sosa Siliezar, *Savior of the World: A Theology of the Universal Gospel* (Waco, Tex.: Baylor University Press, 2019), 80–82, who also cites Mary L. Coloe, "Gentiles in the Gospel of John: Narrative Possibilities—12:12-43," in *Attitudes to Gentiles in Ancient Judaism and Early Christianity*, ed. David C. Sim and James S. McLaren, LNTS 499 (London: T&T Clark, 2013), 209–13.

23   *Pace* the more sectarian interpretation offered by Jaime Clark-Soles, "Scripture Cannot Be Broken: The Social Function of the Use of Scripture in the Fourth Gospel," in *Abiding Words: The Use of Scripture in the Gospel of John*, ed. Alicia D. Myers and Bruce G. Schuchard, SBLRBS 81 (Atlanta: SBL Press, 2015), 95–117 (here 103–8).

24   See John 7:12, 41; 9:9, 16; 10:21; 12:29.

readers not to sin and provides the consolation that, if they do, Jesus is the atoning sacrifice. The disciples mouth appropriate christological titles in the Gospel's call narrative, but the unfolding account demonstrates that their alignment with Jesus stands on the edge of a blade—some will fall away, many will misunderstand, and others will generate no small suspense over the integrity of their belief. Even in the intimate setting of the Farewell Discourse, Judas' dark mission is entirely lost on the other disciples, demonstrating that, at times, one cannot identify on which side of the cosmic line someone may stand, even when they are willfully and dramatically committed to malicious ends. Satan's entrance into their compatriot—"one out of the twelve" (6:71)—was a fateful event of instantiated cosmic alignment that was absolutely imperceptible (13:2, 27-30). Nicodemus approaches Jesus "by night," but his three narrative appearances chart a trajectory from cautious interest to what may well be a guarded loyalty, with his full trajectory left unresolved. From the brief reference to the faction that left the Johannine social network in 1 John 2:18-20, it seems as though their actual group allegiance (or lack thereof) was only manifest in their departure. The point is this: in spite of the definitive nature of John's metaphysical dualities, identifying the actual cosmic alignment of groups and individuals at a given point is far from straightforward. An ambiguity abounds that obfuscates labelling and invites a range of possible movements from Death and Darkness into Life and Light.

Yet negative othering in the Johannine literature is usually unambiguous the more directly groups or individuals align themselves with that which is antagonistically "other" on the cosmic plane. For John, Death, Darkness, and the Devil constitute a disfigured trinity atop the pantheon of negative alterity. Collectively, they are associated with murder, falsehood, and violent opposition to Jesus. Those human figures and groups who exhibit these activities, values, and inclinations are most readily identified as misaligned and, in the contemporized language I have chosen to work with, "other." In the Epistles, these include "antichrists" (1 John 2:18, 22; 4:3; 2 John 7), the "murderer (ἀνθρωποκτόνος)" (1 John 3:15), "deceivers" (2 John 7), and "liars" (1 John 1:10; 2:4, 22; 4:20; 5:10). Three of these potential roles for human players are directly linked to cosmic evil, and that link is strongly implied in the designation "deceiver."

> **Antichrist**: every spirit that does not confess Jesus is not from God. And *this is the spirit of the antichrist*, of which you have heard that it is coming; and now it is already in the world. (1 John 4:3)

> **Murder**: We must not be like Cain who was *from the evil one* and *murdered* his brother. (1 John 3:12a)

> **Murder and Lying**: You are from your father the devil, and you choose to do your father's desires. *He was a murderer from the beginning* and does not stand in the truth, because there is no truth in him. When he *lies*, he speaks according to his own nature, for *he is a liar and the father of lies*. (John 8:44)

> **Deceivers/Deceiver**: Many deceivers (πλάνοι) have gone out into the world, those who do not confess that Jesus Christ has come in the flesh; any such person is the deceiver (ὁ πλάνος) and the antichrist![25] (2 John 7)

In the Gospel, the negative others include "the Jews" when they participate in murderous intent (John 8:44) and, in the Shepherd Discourse, the "thief (κλέπτης)" and "bandit (λῃστής)" (John 10:1, 8, 10). These two figures enter the sheepfold by "another way (ἀλλαχόθεν)" (10:1) and are collectively referred to as the ἀλλότριος, a term the NRSV translates as "stranger" (10:5). Prefixed with the Greek for "other (ἄλλος)," the ἀλλότριος is portrayed as breaking and entering, accessing the sheepfold by illegitimate means (ἀλλαχόθεν) and committed to the diabolical work of stealing, killing, and destroying (John 10:10).

The pattern coming into view here is that John's negative human others are primarily *leaders*, specifically, those *who exercise authority and power aligned with evil and operate in falsehood and injustice*.

In Israel's prophetic tradition, the harshest divine rhetoric is frequently deployed against the powerful who exploit, mislead, and misguide God's people (e.g., Jeremiah 23:1-6 and Ezekiel 34 and

---

[25] Passages here are taken from the NRSV, with emphases added.

37, texts underlying the shepherd language in John 10:1-16). John surely envisions himself as operating within this rhetorical stream, even if with his own signature. Though the Johannine literature is not normally mined for material on ecclesial leadership, "John" is programmatically criticizing authority and power shaped by the world and influenced by the devil, the world's ruler. "The Jews," persistently (even if not consistently) implicated as the ruling elite, partner with the evil one by their antipathy toward Jesus the royal Shepherd who sacrificially cares for and protects God's people. Judas serves as Satan's agent in securing Jesus' arrest by Jewish (and Roman) authorities. The composite figure of the ἀλλότριος holds a leadership vocation which presumes the following of sheep (John 10:5). The antichrists seek to lead astray the children by wayward teaching. In summary, the negative other for John is cosmically aligned with Death, Darkness, and the Devil to mislead, misguide, and mistreat God's people from a position of power.

There are many "others" in John. Though the perichoretic alterity of the triadic divine identity embraces otherness without negative othering, human beings who reject the Logos and align with the cosmic triad of Death, Darkness, and the Devil are delineated as outsiders, especially those so aligned who hold leadership responsibility over God's people. It is *cosmic misalignment* and *misguided leadership*—not ethnicity, background, gender, or social standing—that determine negative alterity for John. Though only a small minority within John's Gospel receive the Logos, only a small fraction of groups or individuals are directly cast as the *negative* other. And as with Nicodemus, "a ruler of the Jews" (John 3:1), the prospect of entering the perichoretic alterity of the divine family is held open throughout the Gospel narrative.

It is John's negative othering that many readers of this Gospel and Letters find deserving of the label "sectarian." Yet once it is acknowledged that ethnic othering is not a Johannine program, as argued above and in more detail in chapter 2, the polemical targets are not that controversial even for our modern audiences. Our own society decries falsehood, violence, and leadership that is abusive and self-serving, against all of which sharp rhetoric is frequently arrayed. The Johannine idea of cosmic darkness is of course controversial in a secular society that demystifies evil, often reducing it to nothing more than a survivalist instinct addressable by better education, perhaps appropriate medical care, and surely improved government services. Such a view is perhaps the sanitized idea found in freshly printed textbooks, but on the ground and in the streets (no matter on which side of the proverbial "tracks"), we have reasons to believe strongly in the concept of cosmic evil. Secularization has in effect ensured that we identify evil as solely a human problem. When we call something "evil" today, we are normally referring to the practices or ideas of "other" human individuals, human groups, or human institutions and systems.

Perhaps John is on to something. He is honest about evil but locates its ultimate source beyond the human domain.[26] If evil is always human, our (post)modern tendency is to demonize not demons but one another. John is clear that Death, Darkness, and the Devil are the foundational forces of evil. As human beings we may align with them, finding ourselves as unwitting agents of their influences (like "the Jews") or as willing hosts ready to enact their agendas (like Judas Iscariot). But John's ultimate polemical targets are supernatural powers, not human beings, whose collective sin the Lamb of God has come to remove. Since secularism has epistemologically evicted transcendental reality and anchored itself within an immanent frame,[27] we have no one else to target—to demonize—*except one another.*

In spite of reservations about the supernatural,[28] twenty-first-century societies are able to agree with John that lying, killing, and misleading are worthy of some form of negative labelling. What is much more controversial than John's idea of Darkness is his idea

[26]   See Andrew J. Byers, "Abide in Me: A Johannine Theology of Resilience," in *Biblical and Theological Visions of Resilience: Pastoral and Clinical Insights*, ed. Christopher C. H. Cook and Nathan H. White, New Critical Thinking in Religion, Theology and Biblical Studies (London: Routledge, 2019), 70–82.

[27]   I am drawing here on Charles Taylor, *A Secular Age* (Cambridge, Mass.: Belknap, 2007).

[28]   For an energetic (and atheistic) exploration of naturalism and evil, see Michael Ruse, "Naturalism, Evil, and God," in *The Cambridge Companion to the Problem of Evil*, ed. Chad Meister and Paul K. Moser (New York: Cambridge University Press, 2017), 249–66.

of *Light*: the Johannine divider is Jesus. John cannot be responsibly used to accommodate divisions within humanity on the basis of racial, cultic, or geographical othering. The labels "Samaritan," "Jew," "Gentile," "Greek," and "Roman" are welcome as long as they are not deployed as means of elevating one group over another. The boundary line John has scored into human society (and he is joined in this by the other New Testament writers) is *christological*. The reception of Jesus the Logos made flesh is the means out of Darkness and into Light. John is not a theologian who can be pressed into the service of a soteriological universalism. His writings are unmistakably particularistic: Jesus is the articular way, truth, and life. Branches that do not abide in him are eventually cast off. It is an uncomfortable position to hold within pluralistic societies that claim tolerance as a chief virtue. As social commentators regularly point out, though, our contemporary label of "tolerant" is at times little more than a self-congratulatory mode of being selectively intolerant. Like John, we have our own boundary lines and means of negative othering. What John may be able to offer us is a model of how to engage the other in such a way that our convictions are upheld without the violence that so often accompanies the tensions of diversity. To that model we now turn.

John's Missional Disposition toward the Other: Testimony, Invitation, and Resistance

In spite of Johannine Christianity's putative sectarianism, in no way does John envision Christ-followers as perpetrators of violence against those identified as negative others. The Johannine stance toward the other is "missional" in that believers are enlisted in a divine program of engaging the world. This missional orientation is variegated and entails three dispositions or modes of practice: *testimony*, *invitation*, and, in certain contexts, *resistance*.

The missional mode of *testimony* is the initial, and one could say the default, Johannine stance toward a world of "others." As an extramural means of engagement, a testimonial approach encompasses the important Johannine concepts of declaration and confession[29]

---

[29]   On declaration, see John 4:25; 5:15; 8:26, 38; 16:13-15; 1 John 1:1-5. On confession (of christological truth), see John 1:20; 9:22; 12:42; 1 John 2:23; 4:2-3, 15; 2 John 7.

and by necessity employs an intentional rhetoric of persuasion.[30] The theme of witness-bearing appears immediately in the Prologue with the introduction of John the Baptist as the one who "came as a witness (μαρτυρίαν) to bear witness (μαρτυρήσῃ) to the light" (1:7), a vocation that sustains throughout, even as he fades from the narrative stage (3:30). The Baptist serves as the first witness called to the stand in the Johannine trial motif, a cosmic drama in which God and his divine agent are arraigned to the makeshift court of God's nominal people.[31] Jesus will serve as a witness (7:7; 8:13-18; 18:37), as well as the Father (5:37; 8:18) and the Spirit (15:26; 1 John 5:6-7). Faithful believers are also assigned this missional vocation: "You also are to testify" (15:27 NRSV; cf. 1 John 1:2; 4:14). The Gospel itself is a testimonial product of the "other" disciple (20:35; 21:24).

As a mode of engaging with the world, testimony presupposes conflict as a range of perspectives stand in contention. To bear witness in a trial in support of a defendant is to identify a stance and contend for it. Though a courtroom arena anticipates a forthcoming judgment, the very exercise of giving testimony anticipates *acceptance*. A trial is a discursive context pregnant with potential for differing verdicts. When a hearing is in session, there is dialogue and debate as competing ideas and claims are presented and weighed. As a missional disposition and practice, testimony is dialogical and interactive. John implores his faithful readers to enter this courtroom drama, consider the claims, and then (through the power of the Spirit-Advocate) join those taking the stand in support of Jesus who, "by absorbing the negative verdict of death . . . also becomes the source of the positive verdict of life."[32]

The mode of *testimony* is not the mode of *judgment*. A judgment certainly awaits the end of any trial, but Johannine testimony engages a world opposed to its co-Creator Logos and seeks open debate that may lead to an alternative view, and thus not to judgment but to embrace. As Andrew Lincoln writes,

---

[30]   For a recent overview of John's rhetorical style and intent, see Adele Reinhartz, *Cast Out of the Covenant: Jews and Anti-Judaism in the Gospel of John* (Lanham, Md.: Fortress, 2018), xxiii–xxxi.

[31]   See especially Andrew T. Lincoln, *Truth on Trial: The Lawsuit Motif in the Fourth Gospel* (Peabody, Mass.: Hendrickson, 2000).

[32]   Lincoln, *Truth on Trial*, 215.

the primary goal of the process of judgment is not condemnation. Its overall purpose is the reversal of alienation and death and the establishment of well-being and life. Jesus' mission statement—"I have come that they may have life and have it in abundance" (10.10) is in complete harmony with the preceding mission statement about judging—"I came into this world for judgement, so that those who do not see might see and those who see might become blind" (9.39), because the goal of the judging is the positive verdict of life. Only where there is wilful refusal to receive this life and its light is there the secondary outcome of a judgment of death and blindness.[33]

John is uncompromising in his christological convictions, but his default mode of engaging outsiders is not one of insular retreat or distanced condemnation. The testimonial/confessional tack presents the world with the crisis of christological claims with the hope that "the other" might accept the particulars of the case in this cosmic trial. And this leads to a second mode of missional engagement: *invitation*.

"Come and see" is the language of John's *invitational* approach to the world of outsiders and "others." When John the Baptist's testimony evokes curiosity in two of his disciples, they approach Jesus directly. To their query, "Rabbi . . . where are you staying (μένεις)?" the response is "come and you will see" (1:39). The phrase is taken up elsewhere. Philip issues the same invitation to Nathanael ("come and see," 1:46), and the Samaritan woman to her village ("come see," 4:29).[34] As a divine and royal shepherd, Jesus "calls (φωνεῖ) his own sheep by name" (10:3), and his invitation extends to those beyond his immediate fold (10:16). This approach is evident in the Elder's praise of Gaius for welcoming the "strangers" (3 John 5)—though they are not exactly outsiders since they are believers, it is clear that invitation and hospitality are features of Johannine Christianity and its missional ethos. The appeal to "come and see" holds out hope

[33]   Andrew T. Lincoln, *The Gospel According to Saint John*, BNTC (Peabody, Mass.: Hendrickson, 2005), 62.

[34]   1:39: ἔρχεσηε καὶ ὄψεσηε; 1:46: ἔρχου καὶ ἴδε; 4:29: δεῦτε ἴδετε. It is perhaps worth noting that Mary says ἔρχου καὶ ἴδε to Jesus in 11:34.

for an acceptance of John's Christology, but it is not coercive or forceful. Inviting an individual or a group to "come and see" signals a comfort with uncertain outcomes and manifests an expectation that the invited will need time to weigh and consider that which they encounter. A journey is anticipated. As Richard Hays points out, after the solemn reflections on Jewish unbelief anchored in Isaiah's theology of divinely-imposed blindness (John 12:37--40, Isa 53:1 and 6:10), the dramatic curtain of John 12 closes in the mode of "*appeal* to the hearers to trust Jesus as the one sent by the Father."[35] And as Hays reminds us, the narrative arc of Isaiah's message eventually undercuts the blindness of eyes and hardness of hearts by pointing to new creation and restoration.[36]

In addition to testimony and invitation must be added *resistance* as a mode of John's engagement with the world. Bearing faithful witness may generate a pool of interested parties open to the invitation to come and see, but it also generates a cadre of opponents. Since opposition to Jesus is understood as fundamentally linked to the powers of Darkness, Johannine resistance is ultimately directed toward the ambiguous but ominous cosmic domain of "the world" (1 John 2:15-17). Resistance is particularized toward those discussed above who hold some kind of leadership authority or influence over Johannine believers or potential believers: the thief, the bandit, and the ἀλλότριος who seek illegitimate access to the sheep; "the Jews" who would deploy religious authority to restrict the parameters of Johannine belonging and soteriology and seek Jesus' death; the "deceivers" and "antichrists" who deny essential christological claims and guide astray; and Diotrephes who wields unsanctioned religious authority that excludes others.

There are two other points to note about the Johannine mode of resistance. One is that active resistance is not necessarily insular *retreat*. In the sectarian hermeneutic, believers in this tradition can be easily caricatured as a closed in-group content with isolating themselves from the world. Retreating from the surrounding culture is one way to resist its influences, but

---

[35] Richard B. Hays, *Echoes of Scripture in the Gospels* (Waco, Tex.: Baylor University Press, 2016), 307 (emphases original).

[36] Hays, *Echoes of Scripture in the Gospels*, 308.

there are signs that Johannine resistance has an outward orientation and a missional purpose.[37] Though highly criticized for its emphasis on loving one another (without the specific charge to love one's enemies or the world),[38] the call to intramural love has extramural effects as it displays Johannine convictions to those beyond the communal walls. A sectarian hermeneutical lens moors itself to John's polemical statements about "the world" to the disregard of the positive statements, like this one by Jesus in John 3:17: "For God did not send the Son into the world that he might judge the world, but in order that the world may be saved through him." In John 17, the oneness of Johannine Christians has a missional purpose—"so that the world may believe that you have sent me" (17:21) and "so that the world may know that you have sent me and have loved them [the disciples] even as you have loved me" (17:23). Commenting on Jesus' dual claims in that prayer ending the "Mission Discourse," that believers are not of the world yet sent into it just as Jesus was sent, Michael Gorman argues that

> withdrawal from the world, then, is not an option for Jesus' disciples, for it would not be "just as" Jesus; it would be the opposite of their master's life-narrative of being sent into the world (v. 18). Retreat from the world would mean the cessation of mission, a failure to follow Jesus in bearing public testimony to the life-giving truth in word and deed, and it would contradict the very purpose of the disciples' election.[39]

Similarly, Marianne Meye Thompson writes that "If Jesus' own mission is the model for the disciples' mission, then that mission will lead

[37]   "John's Gospel echoes the voice of the divine Shepherd who seeks to lead his people beyond a gloomy picture of the church huddled fearfully together, and into a grace-filled life offered to the whole world" (Hays, *Echoes of Scripture in the Gospels*, 343).

[38]   See, e.g., Wayne A. Meeks, "The Ethics of the Fourth Evangelist," in *Exploring the Gospel of John: In Honor of D. Moody Smith*, ed. R. Alan Culpepper and C. Clifton Black (Louisville: Westminster John Knox, 1996), 317–26.

[39]   Michael J. Gorman, *Abide and Go: Missional Theosis in the Gospel of John* (Eugene, Ore.: Cascade, 2018), 118. "Mission Discourse" is his preferred label of what we regularly call the "Farewell Discourse."

them into deep engagement with, not withdrawal from, the world."[40] The Johannine concern with the internal health of believers demands a *missional* resistance, one that protects communal integrity from worldly influences while maintaining the modes of testimony and invitation. Even so, *resistance against* is not *retreat from.*[41]

The second point is that Johannine resistance is *nonviolent.* For these early Christians, *resistance against* is not *violence towards.*[42] For John, murder is a diabolical atrocity. When under physical threat, Jesus' words to his disciples in the garden were "put your sword back in its sheath." *There are no unsheathed swords in Johannine Christianity.* No violent recourse is justifiable.[43] Resistance for John is not fighting back but retaining one's testimony as death sentences are decreed. Resistance is not retributive: Jesus washes the feet of Judas Iscariot and serves him bread. The collapse of the guards in the garden merely accentuates his divine restraint. He refuses to reciprocate the unjust assault before the high priest, and before Pilate and the soldiers of Rome he does not summon armed supporters or even the divine armies presumably at his disposal (18:36). How does Jesus confront his enemies? He may voice protests at accusations leveled against him and he may attribute murderous intent to evil, but he ultimately yields to their physical and political might. He dies. And he dies for them, for the others, to remove the sins of the world.

It is true that these writings speak of victory and conquering, but it is never through triumphalistic means. Jesus' moment of glorification is his apparent defeat on the cross (John 12:31; 16:33), his succumbing to the murderous appetite of the evil one. The means

[40]   Marianne Meye Thompson, *John: A Commentary*, NTL (Louisville: Westminster John Knox, 2015), 352 (cited in Gorman, *Abide and Go*, 118).

[41]   A popular development on this general theme is found in Rod Dreher, *The Benedict Option: A Strategy for Christians in a Post-Christian Nation* (New York: Sentinel, 2018 [2017]).

[42]   Gorman, *Abide and Go*, 167–69.

[43]   "Johannine Christianity presents a challenge to the world's violence and injustice, its oppression, greed, and divisiveness. Among those who profess the kingship of Jesus, the world's idolatrous chauvinisms—of nation, race, gender, or otherwise—are dissolved" (David K. Rensberger, *Johannine Faith and the Liberating Community* [Philadelphia: Westminster, 1988], 150).

by which believers conquer the world are not unsheathed weapons but their faith (1 John 5:3-5; cf. 2:13-14; 4:4). With all the ink spilt detailing John's sectarianism, there is rarely discussion about John's nonviolent ethos. The only violence envisioned toward the other is a *cosmic* violence, exacted not on Jews or "the Jews," wayward church leaders, or itinerant heretics but on Death, Darkness, and the Devil (1 John 3:8). John deals with human otherness not by eliminating it, but by testifying with courage, inviting with hospitality, and, when opposed, by resisting without violence.

Missional Self-Othering in Johannine Faith ("In" but Not "Of")

Finally, Johannine Christianity is not so much invested in othering outsiders but *in ensuring the otherness of its insiders*. The charge of sectarianism is drawn primarily from what is implied in the Gospel and Letters of John, not by what is directly stated. Though there are indeed calls to resist the world and negative labelling, it is the repeated emphasis on internal social dynamics that lead to comments like this one from Robert Gundry:

> Just as Jesus the Word of God spoke God's Word to the world . . . so Jesus' disciples are to do. But they are not to love the unbelieving world any more than Jesus did. . . . It is enough to love one another and dangerous to love worldlings.[44]

Yet the Johannine literature's internal focus is more intended to maintain an intramural otherness than it is to other outright those beyond its social walls. Admittedly, the very idea of otherness is inescapably double-edged, but the sharper side of this (sheathed) Johannine blade is arrayed inward.

This tradition embraces otherness for itself; alterity is a Johannine vocation. The catchphrase "*in* but not *of* the world" derives from Jesus' prayer in John 17, urging a fundamental distinctiveness that nonetheless coinhabits the *oikumene* with all others. The modes of engaging this world—testimony, invitation, and resistance—are

[44] Robert H. Gundry, *Jesus the Word according to John the Sectarian: A Paleofundamentalist Manifesto for Contemporary Evangelicalism, Especially Its Elites, in North America* (Grand Rapids: Eerdmans, 2002), 61 (cited in Gorman, *Abide and Go*, 157).

meaningless unless the community that adopts their practices and dispositions is itself "other." Only that which is Other can extend any help to the world since "that which is born out of the flesh is flesh" (John 3:6) and "the one who is out of the earth is out of the earth and speaks out of the earth" (John 3:31). Craig Koester writes that "Jesus encounters the world as someone 'other,' who can speak to the world precisely because he is different . . ." and that this missional otherness extends to Johannine believers: "Separation from the world is the basis for engagement with the world."[45]

John is stunningly clear that there are bounded markers between Light and Dark, Above and Below, Spirit and Flesh. More than othering those over the lines, however, he is concerned with bringing readers into a Johannine otherness that is aligned with cosmic goodness and beauty, that participates within the open interrelation of triadic divinity, that pledges allegiance to a kingdom not of this world. Alterity is certainly negative at times in these writings, but weighted with much greater significance is the programmatic construction of a missional self-otherness that testifies and invites as energetically as it resists. For this tradition, there is exceptional clarity on a conviction common throughout early Christianity: society, culture, and the wider cosmic sphere are ultimately incapable of self-healing and self-rescue. A community that only offers a recycled or rearranged version of human ingenuity or earth-bound wisdom or worldly competence will ultimately have very little to offer. It takes a community that is alien, strange, and "other" to offer something new, durable, and from beyond our self-fashioned enclosures.

In but not *of:* John identifies distinctions between his fellowship of Christ-believers and those beyond this fold while recognizing a social location of embeddedness among them within the wider world (that is, a "nested identity" that is missional[46]). But his writing invests more in the maintenance of his own flock's otherness

---

[45]   Craig R. Koester, *The Word of Life: A Theology of John's Gospel* (Grand Rapids: Eerdmans, 2008), 209.

[46]   Andrew Benko offers a helpful discussion on "nested identities" in *Race in John's Gospel: An Ethno-Conscious Approach* (Lanham, Md.: Fortress, 2019), 58–62.

than in the negative "othering" of outsiders. This mode of boundary construction may well be deemed sectarian if intra-otherness were designed to malign or injure those detached from their social sphere. The stance is missional, not antagonistic, because Johannine alterity is *for* the world, not *against* it, just as it is *in* the world and not *of* it.

Conclusion: John as Both "Other" and "Beloved"

We have considered a divine alterity that loves. We close identifying a correlative human alterity that is loved. Just as Jesus embodies within his own person the coexistence of divinity and humanity in which otherness flourishes, the Fourth Evangelist casts himself as one who embodies otherness alongside being loved—he is "the other disciple, whom Jesus loved" (20:2). In this self-presentation he embraces otherness, particularly an otherness from Peter (20:2-4, 8; and possibly 18:15-16). Yet his alterity is not deemed as negative or ostracized or antagonized. He is other and also "beloved" (13:23; 19:26; 21:7, 20). The author behind this construct was of course unversed in the contemporary sociological and psychological ideas of otherness, but there is clear evidence of a social vision that calls for a positive otherness that avoids othering. The other disciple, whom Jesus loved, is perhaps early Christianity's greatest theologian for a world full of others; this is not least because he seems to have known himself what it means to be loved while also being "other."

Conclusion

The Johannine Voice: Sectarian or Prophetic?

I opened this book with a brief consideration of a photograph portraying a contemporary scene of divisive otherness. A Black police officer stands on one side of a fence, its galvanized steel bars interlaced with barricade tape bearing the words "Do Not Cross." On the other side of the barrier are White protestors whose right to free speech and assembly are, ironically, being guarded by the officer of color. The protestor clutching the pole of a Confederate flag in one hand has in the other a placard reading "Jews Are Satan's Children," a slogan directly attributed to passages in John's Gospel. This picture visually seizes the fraction of a moment on a hot day in Virginia when "others" are starkly arrayed as antagonists. The divides cut racially (White, Black, Jewish), geographically (the Secessionist South and the North as its implied enemy), and physically (with the interlocking fence panel).

"Do Not Cross."

Though still controversial, the Fourth Evangelist verbally crafts a different sort of picture with a different sort of Johannine placard. This one reads "The King of the Jews" in the universal languages of the day, and it is positioned over the head of a disrobed Jewish victim of injustice who chose nonviolent resistance and died sacrificially as a Lamb for the sins not just of Jews, Greeks, Whites, Samaritans, or Blacks, but of "the world." The descending and ascending of this Lamb-King punctures cosmic boundaries and seeks to eradicate traditional barricades that are figuratively and literally inscribed with "Do Not Cross." New fences are certainly erected, but not without a Gate that can open to "the other." When the Elder concludes his epistles to the "elect lady" and the "beloved Gaius," he acknowledges the limitations of paper, pen, and ink for his communicative task. He would prefer interactive discourse: στόμα πρὸς στόμα. That phrase is "mouth to mouth" in the Greek, though rendered more elegantly by the NRSV and other translations as "face to face."[1] The Johannine theology of excess discussed in chapter 3 relieves the pressure of ancient and contemporary writers to produce a closed and conclusive text. Writing prompts discourse beyond the page. In this closing chapter, I offer a review of the preceding material, revisit the foundational coordinates of the sectarian hermeneutic, and offer final reflections about reading "John" in our present day. The hope is that this study will lead to many interactions "face to face," and not without the joy of fruitful discourse (2 John 12). If my inconclusive study generates further conversations on how we may need to rethink our ideas about Johannine Christianity, then I will be pleased. But first, I offer a summary of what pen has put to paper thus far.

A Review

A brief etiological sketch of the "sectarian hermeneutic" was provided in chapter 1. Diversity has been customarily construed as adversarial in the influential history-of-religion school and in the Bauer thesis that have shaped the backdrop of scholarly assumptions and questions about Christian origins. In the lingering shadows of these conflict models, major interpreters such as Wayne Meeks, Ernst Käsemann, and James Charlesworth pitted Johannine Christianity against the mainstream of the first-century church. Digging into the texts for the prize of historical artifacts, interpreters crafted *Sitzen im Leben* of the "historical Johannine community." Reconstructions like those of J. Louis Martyn and Raymond Brown established, even if inadvertently, the received wisdom of today that the Epistles and Gospel of John were penned by antagonized

---

[1]   2 John 12; 3 John 14.

and antagonizing leaders of an embattled minority group within early Judaism and early Christianity. Such proposals have now been taken up by scholars who draw on the sociological phenomena of sects or employ more formally social-scientific methodologies, collectively reinforcing standard readings of this ancient literature as products of a sect or "anti-community" entrenched not only against the Jewish social life out of which it emerged but also against the wider Christian movement into which it entered. Much was affirmed in this series of developments, but not without calling for reconsiderations.

Chapter 2, "John and Other Jews," explored what has come to be understood as an irresolvable question in Gospel scholarship: "Why would a Jewish text portray Jews who negatively call other Jews, 'the Jews'?" The answer ventured is that John's polemical use of οἱ Ἰουδαῖοι subverts the ethnicizing of soteriology and emplots the vision of a divinely generated, not racially or ethnically determined, ecclesial identity. John's primary target is an understanding of covenant membership limited to the less mutable categories of bloodline and ancestral descent and, on the whole, embodied within the narrative by a collective group of Jewish leaders affiliated with Jerusalem. Labeling them "the Jews" is a rhetorical move that ironically grants this group their prized self-identification, one they assume is requisite for belonging to "Israel." After briefly considering contemporary approaches to race and ethnicity in New Testament studies, the chapter outlined the Johannine ecclesiological vision of divine participation (what later theologians would call "theosis") and showed that the Fourth Evangelist was not writing to attack or undermine Jewish ethnicity but to invite readers to relativize race, deracialize soteriology, and resocialize into a family sourced "from above" and made "one" with God. Rather than casting a vision of anti-Jewishness or anti-Semitism, John wrote to invite his audience into a salvation that extends beyond Jews, Samaritans, Romans, and Greeks to the "world" for whose sins the (Jewish) Lamb of God was slain.

Focus shifted to "John and Other Christians" in chapter 3. The Fourth Gospel's manifest differences from the Synoptic Gospels in style, language, and theological emphases have reinforced the notion that Johannine Christianity stood in opposition to the developing Christian mainstream. However, John did not necessarily "other" alternative Gospels and their writers; in fact, he seems to have written in acknowledgement of their existence and offered his own composition not as a replacement or substitution but as a supplemental (and certainly authoritative) account. Though Johannine Christianity is viewed as fractious and combative, the oneness motif is not necessarily a polemical ploy to unite a community so divisive it tends to other its own others. Moreover, the import of both the secessionists in 1 John 2:18-19 and Diotrephes in 3 John are often over-dramatized in historical reconstructions without regard to the fact that the Elder also urged an openness to "strangers."

Chapter 4 considered John and other Christian traditions of ecclesial life. Since the differences between Johannine Christianity and what may have been emerging as a mainstream movement are often attributed to disagreements over leadership theology, this chapter offered alternative readings of John's ecclesial vision of both episcopal and charismatic authority. Though the Gospel and Letters of John are widely understood as the products of a "low church" community averse to leadership hierarchies, the later episcopal ecclesiology of Ignatius of Antioch bears consonance with certain Johannine convictions. Ignatius envisioned the office of bishop as deriving from *participatory reciprocity*, a dynamic demonstrated in the narrative coordination of Peter and the Beloved Disciple, who were shown as less at odds than scholarly trends avow. Even if the traditions behind the Gospel and Epistles of John had promoted an egalitarianism disinclined toward formal leadership structures, the Johannine themes of reciprocity and participation may have contributed to mainstream episcopal models of church order that became established in second-century Christianity and beyond.

I also questioned in that chapter the conventional understanding that John's alleged emphasis on charismatic authority invalidated hierarchical modes of leadership. In modern and contemporary ecclesiology, "spiritual" is viewed as incompatible with "institutional" and "liturgical"; similarly, "charismatic" is seen as antithetical to "episcopal" and "hierarchical." Perhaps under the influence of these stereotypes, the Fourth Gospel's emphasis on the Paraclete has often been viewed as a reaction against the wider ecclesiastical structures promoting ordered worship under clerical authority. The assumed rationale is that no episcopal authority or hierarchy is required for a community comprising individuals who are each guided by the Spirit of Truth. Such individualism, paired with an egalitarian and charismatic polity, has been judged as the source of Johannine Christianity's demise—without clerical leadership, a community that places all its truck in individual access to a Spirit who will reveal new things is a prescription for organizational disaster. Yet John's model of church is discernible through a range of images that assume leadership figures: flocks have shepherds, vines have gardeners, and households have parents. Johannine Christianity's nuanced tensions may have made it not only porous and durable in the midst of social change, but also capable of assimilation into wider movements. The apparent absence of an historical Johannine community persisting well into the second century may not be a sign that it "failed" as some have claimed; its apparent amalgamation into the so-called mainstream may actually have been indicative of its openness to others.

Chapter 5 outlined a Johannine theology of alterity and difference. Though John's material has been exploited to dangerous ends throughout Christendom's checkered timeline, there are theological gifts for thinking creatively and constructively about otherness. Today's readers are addressed in the Fourth Gospel's prologue by a striking vision of intra-divine alterity in which it is possible to be "other" without being "othered." This "perichoretic otherness" comprises the Father, Son, and Spirit, who coinhabit a fellowship without becoming compressed into a homogenized unit. As the divine Other becomes flesh in the Logos, this unity-in-plurality opens inclusively toward human beings. Such a vision bears enormous import on contemporary thinking about alterity, much of which is surely unexplored.

Even so, there is a Johannine program of negative othering that cannot be ignored. Many conventional means of exclusion are no longer applicable, but John is clear that Darkness and Light are permanently incompatible. Cosmic darkness is real, and a chasm is gashed among human beings over the one definitive line of partition:

Christology. Reception or rejection of Christ determines one's placement within this scheme. Emphasis lies on the opening capacity of the Gate, who is Jesus, yet an honest reading acknowledges that the Gate is also a means of closure. Still, there is ambiguity. The Johannine boundary line is definite, and the christological point of ingress and egress is fixed, but the evangelist often leaves a cloud over one's position in relation to them. The negative other is more clearly identified, however, with those in communal leadership aligned with cosmic evil and its practices of murder, lying, and abuse of power. The obscurity of standing for most characters, which at times includes Jesus' disciples, leaves the world ripe with potential for a range of reactions to Jesus while the clarity of John's sketch of evil forces justifies critique of those misusing power. The promoted disposition toward the wider sphere of the world, however, is testimonial and invitational, as well as resistant. This chapter ended considering the missional self-othering John envisages for his audience. More than othering outsiders, Johannine Christianity promotes the otherness of its insiders. Only something "other" can save.

Is John's Theology of the Other *Sectarian*?

Having presented so many alternative readings and made some attempt at articulating a Johannine theology of "the other," still the question remains: Is this early (Jewish-)Christian tradition sectarian?[2]

Many would agree that "sect" and "sectarian" are unfortunate terms. Though heuristically important in sociology and anthropology, their connotations—no matter how many qualifications and redefinitions we may provide in the footnotes—are problematic for confessional readers of John, potentially misleading for newcomers to his texts, and limited in their capacity to account for more positive social dynamics among early Christian groups. David

---

[2]   Though he is honest about the negative aspects of "Johannine sectarianism," David Rensberger additionally finds positive dimensions that may prove helpful for a church called to a countercultural vocation in our secular world. See the chapter "Sect, World, and Mission: Johannine Christianity Today," in David K. Rensberger, *Johannine Faith and the Liberating Community* (Philadelphia: Westminster, 1988), 135–54.

Rensberger has expressed with seasoned insight the difficulty of working with this terminology:

> Part of the problem may be that we are used to thinking of sects as deviant, narrow, even deranged—in other words, wrong. A sect is a fringe group, and we cannot seem to help taking "fringe" to mean "*lunatic* fringe." Sectarian theology, then, is by definition alien, dangerous, uncomfortable. It is liable not to be civilized enough to be conservative or broad-minded enough to be liberal, and not to be moderate in any sense at all. But what happens if we find a sect that is not wrong but right? Or, conversely, what happens if the "right" theology turns out to have been espoused originally by a sect?[3]

Rensberger notes that "John's general theological contentiousness is not properly understood when it is considered in terms of later institutional and dogmatic Christianity rather than in terms of a sect fighting for its existence *against* religious institutions."[4] He even suggests that

> for a disestablished church considering its place in society no longer officially Christian, John's sectarianism offers an authentic place to stand. The Johannine Christians did not seek to gain control of the levers of their society but instead offered a critique and an alternative vision.[5]

Because he is sympathetic to marginal and marginalized communities, Rensberger's remarks offer a helpfully tempered understanding of Johannine sectarianism. Whether or not we currently possess the technical registry to redefine our terms for early Christian groups, the Johannine theology of alterity and difference outlined above should modify the usage, perhaps altering the largely negative

---

[3]   David K. Rensberger, "Sectarianism and Theological Interpretation in John," in *"What Is John?" Volume II: Literary and Social Readings of the Fourth Gospel*, ed. Fernando F. Segovia, SBLSymS 7 (Atlanta: SBL Press, 1998), 139–156; 140. Similarly, see the discussion on sectarianism in John W. Pryor, *John: Evangelist of the Covenant People: The Narrative & Themes of the Fourth Gospel* (Downers Grove, Ill.: InterVarsity Press, 1992), 164–67.

[4]   Rensberger, "Sectarianism and Theological Interpretation in John," 141.

[5]   Rensberger, "Sectarianism and Theological Interpretation in John," 156.

"sectarian hermeneutic." Are John's writings really the final product of a raw social calculus of vigorous clashes between incompatible "others"? Is there a theological vision that justifies sectarian othering or undermines it?

To address these interrelated questions, I reproduce the list of five reasons identified in chapter 1 as the coordinates of the sectarian hermeneutic. Johannine Christianity is viewed as comprising an anti-Jewish and anti-mainstream anti-community whose collective voice operates in an anti-language for the following reasons, some of which I have addressed in more detail than others throughout this book. After listing the points, however, I will provide brief reflections, correctives, or nuances drawn from the foregoing chapters:

1. *Difference*: John's Gospel is distinct from the Synoptics. When read in relation to the other three, this "other" Gospel seems out of place among Matthew, Mark, and Luke, suggesting that Johannine Gospel writing was a competitive act.

John is indeed different. Yet the case has been made that diversity does not always generate enmity. The perichoretic alterity of the Father, Son, and Spirit-Paraclete that opens to include the mortal other of humankind represents a tremendous conceptual feat in thinking about difference. Though it is impossible to discern with historical certainty just how Johannine Christians read and applied their own texts, the literary and theological significance of the Fourth Gospel's Prologue suggests that this network of early believers was resourced with a sophisticated frame of thinking about otherness. There are even reasons to believe that the evangelist is alert to the existence of other Gospels and situates his alongside theirs rather than seeking to supplant them. The Gospel's concluding acknowledgment that many *other* books might be written is a subtle but astonishing anticipation of later canonical decisions that led to the Fourfold Gospel. Finally, it is curious that in a contemporary society where we are keen to promote diversity that we also find perpetuated the disparaging of John's social group due to difference. "Different" does not necessarily mean "sectarian." It may just mean "different."

2. *Cosmological Dualism*: John erects boundaries and partitions humanity into two groups corresponding to the unbridgeable otherness of Light and Darkness. Human beings who are "from above" and "not of this world" are contrasted with those "from below" and "of this world."

Though Johannine theology was capable of complex accommodations for alterity, unequivocal clarity marked the cosmic register. Light and Darkness, Above and Below, Life and Death are pairings that are never compatible, though Jesus makes possible a passage between the latter two. Human beings, however, as individuals and as groups, are variously aligned with these dualities along a more ambiguous scale, beclouded in part by the sequence of narrative (and actual) time. A careful reading of John's material warns against overconfident judgments as to how others are aligned. "Rabbi, who sinned, this man or his parents?" Jesus' reply is "neither" (John 9:2-3). But clarity emerges among those in leadership who mislead, misguide, or seek to enact violence against the reconfigured people of God—such authorities and power-wielding activities are associated with the negative other precisely because they represent a cosmic alignment with the powers of evil. Even so, human alignments are contingent and reversible. The world is a domain to be resisted, yet Johannine believers envision themselves as sent into it just as Jesus was sent. Invitational and testimonial modes of missional engagement hold on to the prospect of re-alignments.

3. *Harsh Polemics*: The Gospel's occasional sharp rhetoric seems to justify antagonism toward those on the wrong side of the dualistic divide.

It is this feature of Johannine Christianity I find the most difficult to accommodate in the argument that John is not abetting sectarianism. Though the case was made in chapter 2 that the language targeting "the Jews" is part of a rhetorical program to prevent race from barring soteriological access and social inclusion, the use of ethnic terminology is rightly disturbing for modern audiences. Though racist language must always be condemned, polemical ferocity is unfortunately the order of the day in our own public discourse and broadcast loudly across our social media channels. There is within many academic circles an impulse to defend the ethnic slurs of minority voices reacting against white privilege, yet it is difficult to extend the same sympathies when the reversal of power dynamics between Jews and Christians has left the latter in the more dominant political positions for so many centuries. Still, the rhetoric found in John's Gospel and Letters must be read not within our own Western twenty-first-century contexts in which every mode of discourse is increasingly racialized (when justifiable and when not so justifiable). John's language must be situated within its own rhetorical environs and their indigenous conventions of polemic.[6] Perhaps even more important is recognizing first the rhetorical purposes behind John's use of "the Jews," "the antichrists," "liars," and "deceivers," and second the indeterminacy associated with each negative term.

> 4. *Insular Ethics*: The love commands in both the Gospel and the Epistles are often decried because their explicit orientation is toward "one another," with no corollary imperatives calling for a love of the neighbor or outsider.

One of the great frustrations of working with ancient texts is dealing with what they withhold and omit. If only Paul could have added one or two more lines of explanation in Romans 9–11, if only Mark had tidied up his ending and said just a bit more about the man who fled Gethsemane naked, and if only John had dropped in at

---

[6] And as Luke Timothy Johnson has pointed out, "by the measure of Hellenistic conventions, and certainly by the measure of contemporary Jewish polemic, the NT's slander against fellow Jews is remarkably mild." See Luke T. Johnson, "The New Testament's Anti-Jewish Slander and the Conventions of Ancient Polemic," *JBL* 108, no. 3 (1989): 419–41. He also writes that "If Socrates was suspect because of his 'demon' and sophists are 'evil-spirited' and the brothers of Joseph are driven by evil-spirits, and all dwellers on earth have evil spirits and the sons of the pit are children of Belial, should we be surprised to find that Samaritans have demons, or that Jesus has a demon, or that his opponents have the devil as their father, or that when he betrays Jesus, Judas is said to have Satan enter his heart?" (440–41).

least a word or two about loving enemies and neighbors. Historical-critical work is regularly eluded by such details in its literary artifacts. As discussed above, however, the Gospels and Letters of John provision readers with the example of Christ's nonviolence toward his enemies.[7] How did the Elder deal with his enemy Diotrephes? Though often criticized for lacking real authority, perhaps he resisted a more hard-lined approach because he was a peaceable shepherd rather than a tight-fisted sectarian leader eager to quell all forms of dissent. How are Johannine believers to engage with their enemies? These writings supply enough theological wisdom to venture the ethical claim that love for one another was not love *only* for one another.[8] A missional resisting of the world's temptations is not necessarily a refusal to love the world's inhabitants. As outsiders invited into the divine interrelations, as agents sent by Jesus who gave his very flesh "for the life of the world" (John 6:51) in service of the God who loves the world (John 3:16), it is not a leap to envision the Johannine Christians as decent neighbors committed to loving even those who would threaten and injure them just as their Lord had been injured and threatened.[9] Francis Moloney points

[7]   See Paul N. Anderson, "Anti-Semitism and Religious Violence as Flawed Interpretations of the Gospel of John," in *John and Judaism: A Contested Relationship in Context*, ed. R. Alan Culpepper and Paul N. Anderson, RBS 87 (Atlanta: SBL Press, 2017), 265–311 (esp. 273–75).

[8]   Cornelis Bennema writes, "Johannine ethics is primarily about *imitating Jesus* (and God). At the heart of the believers' dynamic Spirit-led relationship with the Father and Son we find not a list of do's and don'ts but mimesis as a creative, cognitive and mnemonic process that directs the believer's conduct and character." He also allows "scope for creating *new forms of mimesis* from Jesus' teaching or personal example." As such, Johannine ethics is premised not on a cloning of patterned behavior or a rote repetition of commands, but a "creative, cognitive and volitional act." See Cornelis Bennema, *Mimesis in the Johannine Literature*, LNTS 498 (London: T&T Clark, 2017), 201–2 (emphases original).

[9]   For other arguments that John's internal love commands do not imply antipathy to outsiders, see Pryor, *John*, 163; Bennema, *Mimesis in the Johannine Literature*, 120–23; Michael J. Gorman, *Abide and Go: Missional Theosis in the Gospel of John* (Eugene, Ore.: Cascade, 2018), 156–78; and Christopher W. Skinner, "Love One Another: The Love Command in the Farewell Discourse," in *Johannine Ethics: The Moral World of the Gospel and Epistles of John*, ed. Christopher W. Skinner and Sherri Brown (Minneapolis: Fortress, 2017), 25–42.

out that "nowhere in John does Jesus request that the disciples love God"[10]—the absence of an ethical command or statement cannot therefore be interpreted as authorial opposition to those ideas or exhortations. Once more from Volf:

> Jesus gave his life for the salvation of those who murdered him and whose sins he was so uncompromisingly castigating. In this, John does not differ markedly from what the rest of the New Testament says both about Jesus' death on the cross and about how Christians should treat their enemies. The narrative of John as a whole offers one large affirmation of what I take to be one of the extraordinary features of early Christianity: a combination of moral clarity that does not shy away from calling evildoers by their proper name and of deep compassion toward them that is willing to sacrifice one's own life on their behalf.[11]

5. *Charismatic Authority*: Since the Spirit-Paraclete is portrayed (at least in the Gospel) as an extradiegetic character who will guide believers after Jesus' ascension, it is often assumed that Johannine Christianity is unaccountable to ecclesial structures and hierarchies that soon developed within the broader traditions of the early church (to which a low-church "Johannine community" would have been opposed).

The arguments in chapter 4 will hopefully gain some ground in removing the overlay of contemporary stereotypes of charismatic and Pentecostal ecclesiology over John's writings (and perhaps they will also help in undermining those contemporary stereotypes). A high pneumatology does not necessarily demand a low ecclesiology, and vice versa. Though John or the Elder is often viewed as a charismatic leader, the case could also be made that his role and authority are akin to the episcopal model of leadership that

---

[10]   Francis J. Moloney, *Love in the Gospel of John: An Exegetical, Theological, and Literary Study* (Grand Rapids: Baker Academic, 2013), 2.

[11]   Miroslav Volf, "Johannine Dualism and Contemporary Pluralism," in *The Gospel of John and Christian Theology*, ed. Richard Bauckham and Carl Mosser (Grand Rapids: Eerdmans, 2008), 19–50 (here 34).

was under development in early Christianity. The leading figure of Johannine Christianity certainly expected compliance, and the theological traditions and former sayings of Jesus were marshalled as authoritative, even if the Spirit-Paraclete was expected to reveal new insights. Some have claimed that this early Christian movement failed because its congregational polity and charismatic pneumatology put it at sectarian odds with mainstream Christianity. What if the reason a Johannine Church did not formally emerge is because its ecclesiology and theology of leadership were not so incompatible with other strands of tradition? The "failure" may well be because John was *not* sectarian, but open to "the other" in a diverse world of different expressions of Christian faith. And perhaps the Spirit-Paraclete served as a helpful guide in the process of embracing other models.

Was Johannine Christianity sectarian?[12] It was surely a minority group amidst the wider movements of Jewish faith and emerging Christianity. According to whatever set of models may be at play in sociological studies, that description may warrant the designation "sect." But that does not mean its outlook was "sectarian" in a way that was violent toward others or antagonistic to all outsiders. The Johannine voice is a *marginal* voice full of conviction, but that does not mean it is an adversarial voice with a belligerent tone. Historical access to the details of this network's intramural and extramural life are severely limited, but its core theological convictions certainly bear the potential for a radical openness to "the other," even as it has redefined negative otherness in cosmic terms. Descriptive terminology is largely determined by methodological frameworks, and "sectarian" may work within those modes of inquiry. But within a Christian theological reading, there is a different term that readily comes to mind for a marginal voice full of conviction yet oriented toward mission: *prophetic.*

---

[12] As repeatedly stated, Raymond Brown did not view the Johannine community as a sect. See his reflections presented in the 1977 SBL presidential address in Raymond E. Brown, "'Other Sheep Not of the This Fold': The Johannine Perspective on Christian Diversity the Late First Century," *JBL* 97, no. 1 (1978): 5–22.

Final Reflections:
Reading John's Prophetic Voice in a Pluralistic Age of Others

Read within a theological frame, John's prophetic voice lodges protests and airs claims that bear relevance for the church today, and perhaps even for those beyond the pews and outside the ecclesial walls. In juxtaposition with the list above enumerating the coordinates of the sectarian hermeneutic, I close with another list. Below are key ideas for contemporary reflection drawn from this study with the conviction that John is best labeled as *prophetic* rather than *sectarian*.

1. *One can be "other" without being "othered," different without being homogenized.* Though John engaged in negative labeling, the Incarnation stands at his theological core. The triune interrelations that make space for the mortal other prompt an imaginative rethinking of how we relate to difference and alterity today.

2. *Since cosmic evil is real, we should demonize the demonic before we demonize each other.* John is serious about the existence of evil, and willing to co-identify human partners with its operations. But this cosmology points ultimately to the darker entities behind the scenes. Co-identification must accompany a discernment between "the ruler of this world" and those within the "world" to which a Johannine response entails testimony and invitation as well as resistance. And since cosmic evil is real, we must resist those dark forces that would enlist us (especially when we are in positions of leadership) for its agendas.

3. *Johannine resistance is not violent or retributive.* These writings are not to be coopted for the disfigured trinity of Death, Darkness, and the Devil. Any vindication of violence against the other cannot be legitimately premised on Johannine ideas. If verses are placed on placards, they do not belong in Far-Right propaganda. Their use should echo the meaning of the placard nailed above Jesus' cross broadcasting universal access to the atonement of sins through the victim of the Lamb slain for the sin of the world.

4. *Johannine boundary walls have a Gate (for both exit and entry).* Johannine Christianity erects partitions, but these enclosures are accessible to outsiders and even permeable for insiders who choose to leave. Though the Gate is fixed, there is a way in as well as a way

out. The christological porosity of the boundary wall honors voli-
tion and human agency while maintaining both a protective as well
as a corrective function for those within its defined fold. But across
the gate is posted the invitation, "Come and see."

5. *Since a theology of excess underwrites Johannine reception,
these texts should be read canonically.* John commends his Gospel
as authoritative and certainly envisions doctrinal boundaries. But
the significance of Jesus cannot be exhausted. "Other" books will
obtain. The recognition of these additional works and Gaius' openness to strangers invite interactivity with the "other books" of the
Christian canon. John would not have anticipated the textual construct of the Fourfold Gospel or a codex in which his Epistles were
bound several pages away from his narrative of Jesus. Even so, his
compositions may be coordinated with others just as Peter and the
Beloved Disciple persist in a healthy tension of varying witnesses to
Jesus. Though John's expression of Christianity has its distinguish-
ing colors, what he demands for orthodoxy does not raise the bar
higher than the bar set by his New Testament colleagues. The claim
that Jesus is divine and came in the flesh is not a lot to demand for
an early Christian confession. Though scholarly engagement with
these texts may deconstruct the canonical tension (and rightly so,
in certain respects), many of the anxieties about Johannine Christianity are resolved within the church because its texts are situated
within a broader canon.

These five ideas are all summed up in the final item of the list,
which will serve as the basis of my concluding reflection:

6. *Only Something—or Someone—Other can save.* Such a claim
often comes only from a prophetic voice on the margins, since the
powerbrokers of the dominant culture insist on their own soteriological efficacy.[13] Controlling forces are threatened by unsanctioned
outliers proffering an alien vision of human flourishing. Some read
the Johannine literature as if it arose out of and not prior to the

---

[13] I have in mind here the model of prophetic ministry in Walter
Brueggemann, *The Prophetic Imagination,* 2nd ed. (Minneapolis: Fortress,
2001 [1978]). Another helpful work on prophetic ministry for today is
Luke Timothy Johnson, *Prophetic Jesus, Prophetic Church: The Challenge of
Luke-Acts to Contemporary Christians* (Grand Rapids: Eerdmans, 2011).

hegemonic influence of Christendom. In such a reading, the Fourth Evangelist and the Elder come across as the privileged voices of Eurocentric theology and Roman political elitism. Alternatively, many are reading these texts as the output of a backwards sect that is divisive, ever dividing, and *contra mundum*.

As repeatedly affirmed, John's is certainly a marginal voice. But in a day when marginalized groups are receiving a belated hearing, the message of Johannine Christianity deserves renewed amplification. Bursting into the soundscape of our own cultural moment, after long periods of muffled silence, are angry cries for justice and outbursts of lament too long delayed. Oppression and powerlessness within today's wider world governed by unassailable authorities are experiences John and his network of early Christian believers would have understood. And like many minority groups who decry the behavior of the cultural elites, John is courageous enough to name evil.

He is not fooled, however, by a false hope in human power or human capacity. John looks to the divine "Other" for aid, rescue, and transformation. "Behold the Lamb," cries the prophet. Look at him—look at Jesus, the Logos, the Light, the otherworldly King, who stands as a ladder between heaven and earth and dissolves divine and human relational barriers in his own flesh, who invalidates boundaries that are ethnic, territorial, and cultic. From this evangelist we find that God himself exists in triadic interrelation between the Father, Son, and Spirit, a harmonious alterity of divine persons that opens to the mortal other to form a new type of human community.

Though his vision for a new society within a hostile world encompasses degrees of plurality, John is nonetheless no pluralist. His vision of human flourishing is met only in the particularity of Jesus. What many readers find wrong with John is not so much that he is presumably anti-Jewish or sectarian, but that he is explicitly *Christian*. Of course, contemporary Western societies are not very pluralistic, either. Liberalism and conservatism alike are increasingly uncompromising in their negative constructions of "the other." The claims are becoming ironically absolutist. While the Right fabricates its own convenient realities, many voices on the Left that once called for tolerance now sponsor campaigns of "canceling" the ideologically opposed other.[14]

The ancient movement of Johannine Christianity emerged in a world of absolutist claims. It made its own with the conviction that the divine Other, who created diversity and comprises it within his own being, loves the world that misunderstands and resists his rescue. There is no compromise in the particularity of this vision. There is, however, an invitational openness to the other. Moreover, evil is not squarely placed on human shoulders, but distributed across a cosmic plane to which secular optics are largely blind. Human beings may be agents of violent and deceitful operations in the world, but our indignation must be directed toward more complex powers and not simply toward one another. Finally, this ancient and marginal voice envisions something that has become all too alien within our own dominant cultures in the West: the de-othering power of forgiveness. If the Incarnation of the Lamb who takes away the sin of the world is a radical *divine* act of de-othering, then this is the ultimate *human* act of de-othering: "if you forgive the sins of any, they are forgiven them" (John 20:22). To thrive in human society, we need some account of an alterity that loves more than it threatens. The surprising voice of the disciple who was "other" yet "beloved," though at times coarse with honesty about evil and malpractice, is worthy of a judicious and responsible fresh hearing.

---

[14]   Many progressive elites are recognizing the dangerous turn public discourse has taken in a way that undermines cherished principles of Liberalism. See, e.g., "A Letter on Justice and Open Debate," *Harper's Magazine*, July 7, 2020, https://harpers.org/a-letter-on-justice-and-open-debate/ (last accessed July 24, 2020); Isaac Chotiner, "Thomas Chatterton Williams on Race, Identity, and Cancel Culture," *New Yorker*, July 22, 2020, https://www.newyorker.com/news/q-and-a/thomas-chatterton-williams-on-race-identity-and-cancel-culture (last accessed July 24, 2020); and "The New Ideology of Race and What's Wrong with It," *Economist*, July 9, 2020, https://www.economist.com/leaders/2020/07/09/the-new-ideology-of-race (last accessed July 24, 2020).

Bibliography

Allen, Garrick V. "Rewriting and the Gospels." *JSNT* 41, no. 1 (2018): 58–69.

Allison, Dale C. *The Historical Christ and the Theological Jesus*. Grand Rapids: Eerdmans, 2009.

Anderson, Paul N. "Anti-Semitism and Religious Violence as Flawed Interpretations of the Gospel of John." Pages 265–311 in *John and Judaism: A Contested Relationship in Context*. Edited by R. Alan Culpepper and Paul N. Anderson. RBS 87. Atlanta: SBL Press, 2017.

Appold, Mark L. *The Oneness Motif of the Fourth Gospel: Motif Analysis and Exegetical Probe into the Fourth Gospel*. WUNT 2/1. Tübingen: Mohr, 1976.

Ashton, John. "The Identity and Function of the Ἰουδαῖοι in the Fourth Gospel." *NovT* 27 (1985): 40–75.

Attridge, Harold W. *Essays on John and Hebrews*. Grand Rapids: Baker Academic. 2010.

———. "John and Other Gospels." Pages 45–62 in *The Oxford Handbook of Johannine Studies*. Edited by Judith M. Lieu and Martinus C. de Boer. Oxford: Oxford University Press, 2018.

Baker, Coleman A. "A Narrative-Identity Model for Biblical Interpretation: The Role of Memory and Narrative in Social Identity Formation." Pages 105–18 in *T&T Clark Handbook to Social Identity in the New Testament*. Edited by J. Brian Tucker and Coleman A. Baker. London: T&T Clark, 2014.

Barclay, John M. G. "Ἰουδαῖος: Ethnicity and Translation." Pages 46–58 in *Ethnicity, Race, Religion: Identities and Ideologies in Early Jewish and Christian Texts, and in Modern Biblical Interpretation*. Edited by Katherine M. Hockey and David G. Horrell. London: T&T Clark, 2018.

———. *Jews in the Mediterranean Diaspora: From Alexander to Trajan (323 BCE–117 CE)*. Berkeley: University of California Press, 1996.

———. "Universalism and Particularism: Twin Components of Both Judaism and Early Christianity." Pages 207–24 in *A Vision for the Church: Studies in Early Christian Ecclesiology in Honour of J. P. M. Sweet*. Edited by Marcus Bockmuehl and Michael B. Thompson. Edinburgh: T&T Clark, 1997.

Baron, Lori. "The Shema in John's Gospel and Jewish Restoration Eschatology." Pages 165–73 in *John and Judaism: A Contested Relationship in Context*. Edited by R. Alan Culpepper and Paul N. Anderson. RBS 87. Atlanta: SBL Press, 2017.

———. "The Shema in Mark and John and the Parting of the Ways." Pages 187–210 in *The Ways That Often Parted: Essays in Honor of Joel Marcus*. Edited by Lori Baron, Jill Hicks-Keeton, and Matthew Thiessen. SBLECL 24. Atlanta: SBL Press, 2018.

Barrett, C. K. *Essays on John*. London: SPCK, 1982.

———. *The Gospel According to St John: An Introduction with Commentary and Notes on the Greek Text*. 2nd ed. London: SPCK, 1978 (1955).

———. *The Gospel of John and Judaism*. Translated by D. Moody Smith. Philadelphia: Fortress, 1975 (1970).

Barth, Fredrik. *Ethnic Groups and Boundaries: The Social Organization of Culture Difference*. Long Grove, Ill.: Waveland Press, 1998.

Barton, Stephen C. "Can We Identify the Gospel Audiences?" Pages 173–94 in *The Gospels for All Christians: Rethinking the Gospel Audiences*. Edited by Richard Bauckham. Grand Rapids: Eerdmans, 1998.

———. "Christian Community in the Light of the Gospel of John." Pages 279–301 in *Christology, Controversy and Community: New Testament Essays in Honour of David R. Catchpole*. Edited by David G. Horrell and Christopher M. Tuckett. NovTSup 99. Leiden: Brill, 2000.

———. "Early Christianity and the Sociology of the Sect." Pages 140–62 in *The Open Text: New Directions for Biblical Studies?* Edited by Francis Watson. London: SCM Press, 1993.

———. "Johannine Dualism and Contemporary Pluralism." Pages 3–18 in *The Gospel of John and Christian Theology*. Edited by Richard Bauckham and Carl Mosser. Grand Rapids: Eerdmans, 2008.

Bauckham, Richard. "For Whom Were Gospels Written?" Pages 9–48 in *The Gospels for All Christians: Rethinking the Gospel Audiences*. Edited by Richard Bauckham. Grand Rapids: Eerdmans, 1998.

———. *Gospel of Glory: Major Themes in the Johannine Theology*. Grand Rapids: Baker Academic, 2015.

———. *Jesus and the Eyewitnesses: The Gospels as Eyewitness Testimony*. 2nd ed. Grand Rapids: Eerdmans, 2017 (2006).

———. "Papias and Polycrates on the Origin of the Fourth Gospel." *JTS* 44 (1993): 24–69.

——. *The Testimony of the Beloved Disciple: Narrative, History, and Theology in the Gospel of John.* Grand Rapids: Baker Academic, 2007.

Bauer, Walter. *Das Johannesevangelium.* HNT 6/3. Tübingen: J. C. B. Mohr, 1933 (1925).

——. *Orthodoxy and Heresy in Earliest Christianity.* Edited by Robert A. Kraft and Gerhard Krodel. Translated by the Philadelphia Seminar on Christian Origins. Philadelphia: Fortress, 1971 (1934).

——. *Rechtgläubigkeit und Ketzerei im ältesten Christentum.* 2. Auflage. BHT 10. Tübingen: Mohr Siebeck, 1963 (1934).

Baur, Ferdinand C. *The Church History of the First Three Centuries.* Translated by Allan Menzies. 2 vols. 3rd ed. London: Williams and Norgate, 1878.

——. "Die Christuspartie in der korinthischen Gemeinde, der Gegensatz des petrinischen und paulinischen Christenthums in der ältesten Kirche, der Apostel Petrus in Rom." *TZT* 4 (1831): 61–206.

Becker, Eve-Marie, Helen K. Bond, and Catrin H. Williams, eds. *John's Transformation of Mark.* London: T&T Clark, 2020.

Benko, Andrew. *Race in John's Gospel: Toward an Ethnos-Conscious Approach.* Lanham, Md.: Fortress, 2019.

Bennema, Cornelis. *Encountering Jesus: Character Studies in the Gospel of John.* Milton Keynes: Paternoster, 2009.

——. "The Identity and Composition of Οι Ιουδαιοι in the Gospel of John." *TynBul* 60, no. 2 (2009): 239–63.

——. *Mimesis in the Johannine Literature.* LNTS 498. London: T&T Clark, 2017.

Berger, Klaus. *Theologiegeschichte des Urchristentums: Theologie des Neuen Testaments.* Tübingen: Francke, 1994.

Berger, Peter, and Thomas Luckmann. *The Social Construction of Reality: A Treatise in the Sociology of Knowledge.* New York: Doubleday, 1967.

Beutler, Johannes. *A Commentary on the Gospel of John.* Translated by Michael Tait. Grand Rapids: Eerdmans, 2017 (2013).

Bieringer, Reimund, Didier Pollefeyt, and Frederique Vandecasteele-Vanneuville. "Wrestling with Johannine Anti-Judaism: A Hermeneutical Framework for the Analysis of the Current Debate." Pages 3–37 in *Anti-Judaism and the Fourth Gospel.* Edited by Reimund Bieringer, Didier Pollefeyt, and Frederique Vandecasteele-Vanneuville. Louisville: Westminster John Knox, 2001.

Black, C. Clifton. "The Johannine Epistles and the Question of Early Catholicism." *NovT* 28, no. 2 (1986): 131–58.

Blaine, Bradford B., Jr. *Peter in the Gospel of John: The Making of an Authentic Disciple.* SBLABib 27. Atlanta: SBL Press, 2007.

Blenkinsopp, Joseph. "Presbyter to Priest: Ministry in the Early Church." *Worship* 41, no. 7 (1967): 428–38.

Blumhofer, Mark. *The Gospel of John and the Future of Israel.* SNTSMS 177. Cambridge: Cambridge University Press, 2019.

Bockmuehl, Markus. *Simon Peter in Scripture and Memory: The New Testament Apostle in the Early Church.* Grand Rapids: Baker Academic, 2012.

Bornkamm, Günther. "Die eucharistische Rede im Johannes-Evangelium." *ZNW* 47 (1956): 161–69.

Bornkamm, Günther, Gerhard Barth, and Heinz Joachim Held. *Tradition and Interpretation in Matthew.* Translated by Percy Scott. 2nd and enlarged ed. London: SCM, 1982.

Boyce, Travis D. and Winsome M. Chunnu. "'I Want to Get Rid of My Fear': An Introduction." Pages 3–16 in *Historicizing Fear: Ignorance, Vilification, and Othering.* Edited by Travis D. Boyce and Winsome M. Chunnu. Louisville: University Press of Colorado, 2019.

Brant, Jo-Ann. *John.* Paideia. Grand Rapids: Baker Academic, 2011.

Brent, Allen. *Cultural Episcopacy and Ecumenism: Representative Ministry in Church History from the Age of Ignatius of Antioch to the Reformation with Special Reference to Contemporary Ecumenism.* SCM 6. Leiden: Brill, 1992.

———. *Ignatius of Antioch: A Martyr Bishop and the Origins of Episcopacy.* New York: T&T Clark, 2007.

———. *Ignatius of Antioch and the Second Sophistic: A Study of Early Christian Transformation of Pagan Culture.* STAC 36. Tübingen: Mohr Siebeck, 2006.

———. "Ignatius and Polycarp: The Transformation of New Testament Traditions in the Context of the Mystery Cults." Pages 325–49 in *Trajectories through the New Testament and the Apostolic Fathers.* Edited by Andrew F. Gregory and Christopher M. Tucker. Oxford: Oxford University Press, 2007.

———. *The Imperial Cult and the Development of Church Order: Concepts and Images of Authority in Paganism and Early Christianity before the Age of Cyprian.* VCS 45. Leiden: Brill, 1999.

Bron, Lajos. "Othering, an Analysis." *Transcience* 6, no. 1 (2015): 69–90.

Brooke, Alan. *A Critical and Exegetical Commentary on the Johannine Epistles.* ICC. Edinburgh: T&T Clark, 1912.

Brown, Sherri. "The Greeks: Jesus' Hour and the Weight of the World." Pages 397–402 in *Character Studies in the Fourth Gospel: Narrative Approaches to Seventy Figures in John.* Edited by Steven A. Hunt, D. Francois Tolmie, and Ruben Zimmermann. WUNT 314. Tübingen: Mohr Siebeck, 2013.

Brown, Raymond E. *The Churches the Apostles Left Behind.* New York: Paulist Press, 1984.

———. *The Community of the Beloved Disciple: The Life, Loves, and Hates of an Individual Church in New Testament Times.* New York: Paulist Press, 1979.

———. *The Epistles of John: A New Translation with Introduction and Commentary.* AB 30. New Haven, Conn.: Yale University Press, 1982.

———. *The Gospel According to John: Introduction, Translation, and Notes.* 2 vols. AB 29, 29A. Garden City, N.Y.: Doubleday, 1966, 1970.

———. "'Other Sheep Not of the This Fold': The Johannine Perspective on Christian Diversity the Late First Century." *JBL* 97, no. 1 (1978): 5–22.

Brown, Raymond E., and John P. Meier. *Antioch & Rome: New Testament Cradles of Catholic Christianity.* Mahwah, N.J.: Paulist Press, 2004 (1983).

Brueggemann, Walter. *The Prophetic Imagination.* 2nd ed. Minneapolis: Fortress, 2001 (1978).

Buell, Denise Kimber. "Early Christian Universalism and Modern Forms of Racism." Pages 109–31 in *The Origins of Racism in the West.* Edited by Miriam Eliav-Feldon, Benjamin Isaac, and Joseph Ziegler. Cambridge: Cambridge University Press, 2009.

———. *Why This New Race: Ethnic Reasoning in Early Christianity.* New York: Columbia University Press, 2005.

Bultmann, Rudolf. *Die Geschichte der synoptischen Tradition.* Göttingen: Vandenhoeck & Ruprecht, 1921. ET: *The History of the Synoptic Tradition.* Translated by John Marsh. Rev. ed. Oxford: Blackwell, 1972 (1921).

———. *The Gospel of John: A Commentary.* Translated by George R. Beasley-Murray, R. W. N. Hoare, and J. K. Riches. Philadelphia: Westminster, 1971.

———. *The Johannine Epistles: A Commentary on the Johannine Epistles.* Translated by R. Philip O'Hara, with Lane C. McGaughy and Robert W. Funk. Hermeneia. Philadelphia: Fortress, 1973 (1967).

———. *Theology of the New Testament.* Translated by Kendrick Grobel. Waco, Tex.: Baylor University Press, 2007 (1955, 1951).

Burge, Gary M. *The Anointed Community: The Holy Spirit in the Johannine Tradition.* Grand Rapids: Eerdmans, 1987.

———. "Spirit-Inspired Theology and Ecclesial Correction: Charting One Shift in the Development of Johannine Ecclesiology and Pneumatology." Pages 179–85 in *Communities in Dispute: Current Scholarship on the Johannine Epistles.* Edited by R. Alan Culpepper and Paul N. Anderson. SBLECL 13. Atlanta: SBL Press, 2014.

Burke, Patrick. "The Monarchial Episcopate at the End of the First Century." *JES* 7 (1970): 499–518.

Byers, Andrew J. "Abide in Me: A Johannine Theology of Resilience." Pages 70–82 in *Biblical and Theological Visions of Resilience: Pastoral and Clinical Insights*. Edited by Christopher C. H. Cook and Nathan H. White. New Critical Thinking in Religion, Theology and Biblical Studies. London: Routledge, 2019.

———. *Ecclesiology and Theosis in the Gospel of John*. SNTSMS 166. Cambridge: Cambridge University Press, 2017.

———. *Faith Without Illusions: Following Jesus as a Cynic-Saint*. Downers Grove, Ill.: InterVarsity Press, 2011.

———. "Johannine Bishops? The Fourth Evangelist, John the Elder, and the Episcopal Ecclesiology of Ignatius of Antioch." *NovT* 60 (2018): 121–39.

———. Review of *Cast Out of the Covenant*, by Adele Reinhartz. *RBL* 6 (2019).

———. "Theosis and 'the Jews': Divine and Ethnic Identity in the Fourth Gospel." Tyndale Fellowship Conference New Testament Lecture, Tyndale House, Cambridge, June 27, 2018.

Byrskog, Samuel. "A Century with the *Sitz im Leben*: From Form-Critical Setting to Gospel Community and Beyond." *ZNW* 98 (2001): 1–27.

Campbell, Joan Cecilia. *Kinship Relations in the Gospel of John*. CBQMS 42. Washington, D.C.: Catholic Biblical Association of America, 2007.

Campenhausen, Hans von. *Ecclesiastical Authority and Spiritual Power in the Church of the First Three Centuries*. Translated by J. A. Baker. Peabody, Mass.: Hendrickson, 1997.

Camus, Albert. *The Outsider*. Translated by Joseph Laredo. Harmondsworth, England: Penguin, 1981 (1942).

Carson, D. A. *The Gospel According to John*. PNTC. Grand Rapids: Eerdmans, 1991.

Carter, Warren. "The Prologue and John's Gospel: Function, Symbol and the Definitive Word." *JSNT* 39 (1990): 35–58.

Charlesworth, James H. *The Beloved Disciple: Whose Witness Validates the Gospel of John?* Valley Forge, Penn.: Trinity Press International, 1995.

Chotiner, Isaac. "Thomas Chatterton Williams on Race, Identity, and Cancel Culture." *New Yorker*, July 22, 2020. https://www.newyorker.com/news/q-and-a/thomas-chatterton-williams-on-race-identity-and-cancel-culture.

Cirafesi, Wally W. "The Johannine Community Hypothesis (1868–Present): Past and Present Approaches and a New Way Forward." *CurBR* 12 (2014): 173–93.

———. "The 'Johannine Community' in (More) Current Research: A Critical Appraisal of Recent Methods and Models." *Neot* 48 (2014): 341–64.

Clark-Soles, Jaime. "Scripture Cannot be Broken: The Social Function of the Use of Scripture in the Fourth Gospel." Pages 95–117 in *Abiding Words: The Use of Scripture in the Gospel of John*. Edited by Alicia D. Myers and Bruce G. Schuchard. SBLRBS 81. Atlanta: SBL Press, 2015.

Coloe, Mary L. *Dwelling in the Household of God: Johannine Ecclesiology and Spirituality*. Collegeville, Minn.: Liturgical Press, 2007.

———. "Gentiles in the Gospel of John: Narrative Possibilities—12:12-43." Pages 209-13 in *Attitudes to Gentiles in Ancient Judaism and Early Christianity*. Edited by David C. Sim and James S. McLaren. LNTS 499. London: T&T Clark, 2013.

Coloe, Mary L., and Tom Thatcher, eds. *John, Qumran, and the Dead Sea Scrolls: Sixty Years of Discovery and Debate*. SBLEJL 32. Atlanta: SBL Press, 2011.

Conway, Colleen M. *Men and Women in the Fourth Gospel: Gender and Johannine Characterization*. SBLDS 167. Atlanta: Society of Biblical Literature, 1999.

Conzelmann, Hans. *The Theology of St. Luke*. Translated by Geoffrey Buswell. New York: Harper & Brothers, 1960.

Corsar, Elizabeth J. B. "John's Use of Mark: A Study in Light of Ancient Compositional Practices." PhD diss., University of Edinburgh, 2018.

Coutts, Joshua. *The Divine Name in the Gospel of John: Significance and Impetus*. WUNT 447. Tübingen: Mohr Siebeck, 2017.

Cullmann, Oscar. *The Johannine Circle: Its Place in Judaism, among the Disciples of Jesus and in Early Christianity; A Study in the Origin of John's Gospel*. Translated by John Bowden. London: SCM Press, 1976 (1975).

———. "A New Approach to the Interpretation of the Fourth Gospel—I." *ExpTim*, 71, no. 1 (1959): 8-12.

Culpepper, R. Alan. *The Johannine School: An Evaluation of the Johannine School Hypothesis Based on an Investigation of the Nature of Ancient Schools*. Missoula, Mont.: Scholars Press, 1975.

Culpepper, R. Alan, and Paul N. Anderson, eds. *Communities in Dispute: Current Scholarship on the Johannine Epistles*. SBLECL 13. Atlanta: SBL Press, 2014.

De Boer, Martinus C. "The Depiction of 'the Jews' in John's Gospel: Matters of Behavior and Identity." Pages 141-57 in *Anti-Judaism and the Fourth Gospel*. Edited by Reimund Bieringer, Didier Pollefeyt, and Frederique Vandecasteele-Vanneuville. Louisville: Westminster John Knox, 2001.

Denaux, Adelbert, ed. *John and the Synoptics*. BETL 101. Leuven: Leuven University Press, 1992.

Denzinger, Heinrich, et al., eds. *Compendium of Creeds, Definitions, and Declarations on Matters of Faith and Morals*. 43rd ed. San Francisco: Ignatius Press, 2012.

Dibelius, Martin. *Die Formgeschichte der synoptischen des Evangeliums*. Tübingen: J. C. B. Mohr, 1919. ET: *From Tradition to Gospel*. Translated by Bertram Lee Woolf. London: James Clarke, 1971 (1919).

Dobelli, Rolf. *Stop Reading the News: A Manifesto for a Happier, Calmer, and Wiser Life.* Translated by Caroline Waight. London: Sceptre, 2020 (2019).

Dodd, C. H. *Historical Tradition in the Fourth Gospel.* Cambridge: Cambridge University Press, 1963.

———. *The Interpretation of the Fourth Gospel.* Cambridge: Cambridge University Press, 1953.

Donaldson, Terence L. *Jews and Anti-Judaism in the New Testament: Decision Points and Divergent Interpretations.* Waco, Tex.: Baylor University Press, 2010.

Donfried, Karl Paul. "Ecclesiastical Authority in 2–3 John." Pages 325–33 in *L'Evangile de Jean: Sources, Rédaction, Théologie.* Edited by Marinus de Jonge. BETL XLIV. Leuven: Leuven University Press, 1977.

Dreher, Rod. *The Benedict Option: A Strategy for Christians in a Post-Christian Nation.* New York: Sentinel, 2018 (2017).

Dunn, James D. G. *Jesus and the Spirit: A Study of the Religious and Charismatic Experience of Jesus and the First Christians as Reflected in the New Testament.* London: SCM Press, 1975.

———. *Unity and Diversity in the New Testament: An Inquiry into the Character of Earliest Christianity.* 3rd ed. London: SCM Press, 2010 (1997).

Edwards, Ruth B. *The Johannine Epistles.* New Testament Guides. Sheffield: Sheffield Academic Press, 1996.

Eriksen, Thomas Hylland and Marek Jakoubek, eds. *Ethnic Groups and Boundaries Today: A Legacy of Fifty Years.* Research in Migration and Ethnic Relations Series. London: Routledge, 2019.

Esler, Philip F. *The First Christians in Their Social Worlds: Social-Scientific Approaches to New Testament Interpretation.* London: Routledge, 1994.

———. "From *Ioudaioi* to Children of God: The Development of a Non-Ethnic Group Identity in the Gospel of John." Pages 106–37 in *In Other Words: Essays on Social-Science Methods and the New Testament in Honor of Jerome H. Neyrey.* Edited by Anselm C. Hagedorn, Zeba A. Crook, and Eric Stewart. Sheffield: Sheffield University Press, 2007.

———. "Introduction: Models, Context, and Kerygma in New Testament Interpretation." Pages 1–20 in *Modelling Early Christianity: Social-Scientific Studies of the New Testament in Its Context.* Edited by Philip F. Esler. London: Routledge, 1995.

Estes, Douglas. "Dualism or Paradox? A New 'Light' on the Gospel of John." *JTS* 71, no. 1 (2020): 90–118.

Eusebius. *Ecclesiastical History.* Vol. 1: *Books 1–5.* Translated by Kirsopp Lake. Loeb Classical Library 153. Cambridge, Mass.: Harvard University Press, 1926.

Eve, Eric. *Writing the Gospels: Composition and Memory*. London: SPCK, 2016.

Falk, Daniel K. "Sabbath." Pages 1174–76 in *The Eerdmans Dictionary of Early Judaism*. Edited by John J. Collins and Daniel C. Harlow. Grand Rapids: Eerdmans, 2010.

Farelly, Nicolas. *The Disciples in the Fourth Gospel: A Narrative Analysis of Their Faith and Understanding*. WUNT 290. Tübingen: Mohr Siebeck, 2010.

Foster, Paul. "The Epistles of Ignatius of Antioch and the Writings that Later Formed the New Testament." Pages 159–85 in *The Reception of the New Testament in the Apostolic Fathers*. Edited by Andrew F. Gregory and Christopher M. Tuckett. Oxford: Oxford University Press, 2005.

Frankfurter, David. "'Jews or Not': Reconstructing the 'Other' in Revelation 2:9 and 3:9." *HTR* 94, no. 4 (2001): 403–25.

Freeman, Mark. *The Priority of the Other: Thinking and Living Beyond the Self*. Oxford: Oxford University Press, 2013.

Frey, Jörg. *The Glory of the Crucified One: Christology and Theology in the Gospel of John*. BMSEC. Waco, Tex.: Baylor University Press, 2018.

Fuglseth, Kåro Sigvald. *Johannine Sectarianism in Perspective: A Sociological, Historical, and Comparative Analysis of Temple and Social Relationships in the Gospel of John, Philo and Qumran*. NovTSup 119. Leiden: Brill, 2005.

Gerdmar, Anders. "Baur and the Creation of the Judaism-Hellenism Dichotomy." Pages 107–28 in *Ferdinand Christian Baur und die Geschichte des frühen Christentums*. Edited by Martin Bauspieß, Christof Landmesser, and David Lincicum. WUNT 333. Tübingen: Mohr Siebeck, 2014.

———. *Roots of Theological Anti-Semitism: German Biblical Interpretation and the Jews, from Herder and Semler to Kittel and Bultmann*. SJHC 20. London: Brill, 2009.

Gieschen, Charles A. "The Divine Name that the Son Shares with the Father in the Gospel of John." Pages 387–410 in *Reading the Gospel of John's Christology as Jewish Messianism: Royal, Prophetic, and Divine Messiahs*. Edited by Benjamin E. Reynolds and Gabriele Boccaccini. AJEC 106. Leiden: Brill, 2018.

Gingrich, Andre. "Conceptualizing Identities: Anthropological Alternatives to Essentialising Difference and Moralizing about the Other." Pages 3–17 in *Grammars of Identity/Alterity—A Structuralist Approach*. Edited by G. Bauman and Andre Gingrich. Oxford: Berghahn, 2004.

Gorman, Michael J. *Abide and Go: Missional Theosis in the Gospel of John*. Eugene, Ore.: Cascade, 2018.

————. "John: The Nonsectarian, Missional Gospel." *Canadian-American Theological Review* 7 (2018): 138–62.

Grant, Robert M. "Scripture and Tradition in St. Ignatius of Antioch." *CBQ* 25, no. 3 (1963): 322–35.

Green, Joel B. *The Gospel of Luke*. NICNT. Grand Rapids: Eerdmans, 1997.

Griffith, Terry. *Keep Yourselves from Idols: A New Look at 1 John*. JSNT-Sup 233. Sheffield: Sheffield Academic Press, 2002.

————. "A Non-Polemical Reading of 1 John: Sin, Christology and the Limits of Johannine Christianity." *TynBul* 49, no. 2 (1998): 253–76.

Gruen, Erich S. *Ethnicity in the Ancient World—Did It Matter?* Berlin: De Gruyter, 2020.

————. "Judaism in the Diaspora." Pages 77–96 in *The Eerdmans Dictionary of Early Judaism*. Edited by John J. Collins and Daniel C. Harlow. Grand Rapids: Eerdmans, 2010.

————. *Rethinking the Other in Antiquity*. Princeton: Princeton University Press, 2011.

Gundry, Robert H. *Jesus the Word according to John the Sectarian: A Paleofundamentalist Manifesto for Contemporary Evangelicalism, Especially Its Elites, in North America*. Grand Rapids: Eerdmans, 2002.

Gunton, Colin E. *The One, the Three and the Many: God, Creation and the Culture of Modernity*. Cambridge: Cambridge University Press, 1993.

Han, Horst. *Tradition und Neuinterpretation im ersten Johannesbrief*. Zürich: Theologische Verlag Zürich, 2009.

Hakola, Raimo. *Identity Matters: John, the Jews and Jewishness*. NovTSup 118. Leiden: Brill, 2005.

————. *Reconsidering Johannine Christianity: A Social Identity Approach*. BibleWorld. London: Routledge, 2015.

Halliday, Michael A. K. *Language as Social Semiotic: The Social Interpretation of Meaning*. London: Arnold, 1978.

Harland, Philip A. *Dynamics of Identity in the World of the Early Christians: Associations, Judeans, and Cultural Minorities*. London: T&T Clark, 2009.

Harnack, Adolf von. "Über den dritten Johannesbrief." *TU* 15, no. 3 (1897): 3–27.

Harris, Elizabeth. *Prologue and Gospel: The Theology of the Fourth Evangelist*. JSNTSup 107. Sheffield: Sheffield University Press, 1994.

Harris, Horton. *The Tübingen School*. Oxford: Clarendon Press, 1975.

Hartog, Paul A., ed. *Orthodoxy and Heresy in Early Christian Contexts: Reconsidering the Bauer Thesis*. Eugene, Ore.: Pickwick, 2015.

Hayes, Christine E. *Gentile Impurities and Jewish Identities: Intermarriage and Conversion from the Bible to the Talmud*. Oxford: Oxford University Press, 2002.

Hays, Richard B. *Echoes of Scripture in the Gospels*. Waco, Tex.: Baylor University Press, 2016.

———. *The Moral Vision of the New Testament: Community, Cross, New Creation: A Contemporary Introduction to New Testament Ethics*. New York: HarperCollins, 1996.

Hegel, Georg Wilhelm Fredrich. *The Phenomenology of Spirit*. Edited and translated by Terry Pinkard and Michael Baur. Cambridge: Cambridge University Press, 2018.

Hengel, Martin. *The Johannine Question*. Translated by John Bowden. London: SCM Press, 1989.

———. *Judaism and Hellenism: Studies in Their Encounter in Palestine during the Early Hellenistic Period*. Philadelphia: Fortress, 1974 (1973).

———. "The Prologue of the Gospel of John as the Gateway to Christological Truth." Pages 265–94 in *The Gospel of John and Christian Theology*. Edited by Richard Bauckham and Carl Mosser. Grand Rapids: Eerdmans, 2008.

Heschel, Susannah. *The Aryan Jesus: Christian Theologians and the Bible in Nazi Germany*. Princeton: Princeton University Press, 2008.

Hill, Charles E. *The Johannine Corpus in the Early Church*. Oxford: Oxford University Press, 2004.

———. "'The Orthodox Gospel': The Reception of John in the Great Church Prior to Irenaeus." Pages 233–300 in *The Legacy of John: Second-Century Reception of the Fourth Gospel*. Edited by Tuomas Rasimus. NovTSup 132. Leiden: Brill, 2010.

Holmes, Michael W., ed. *The Apostolic Fathers: Greek Texts and English Translations*. 3rd ed. Grand Rapids: Baker Academic, 2007.

Hooker, Morna D. "Beginnings and Endings." Pages 184–202 in *The Written Gospel*. Edited by Markus Bockmuehl and D.A. Hagner. Cambridge: Cambridge University Press, 2005.

Horrell, David G. *Ethnicity and Inclusion: Religion, Race, and Whiteness in Constructions of Jewish and Christian Identities*. Grand Rapids: Eerdmans, 2020.

———. Introduction. Pages 1–20 in *Ethnicity, Race, Religion: Identities and Ideologies in Early Jewish and Christian Texts, and in Modern Biblical Interpretation*. Edited by Katherine M. Hockey and David G. Horrell. London: T&T Clark, 2018.

———. "Whither Social-Scientific Approaches to New Testament Interpretation? Reflections on Contested Methodologies and the Future." Pages 6–20 in *After the First Urban Christians: The Social-Scientific Study of Pauline Christianity Twenty-Five Years Later*. Edited by Todd D. Still and David G. Horrell. London: T&T Clark, 2009.

Hoskyns, Edwin. *The Fourth Gospel*. Edited by Francis Noel Davey. 2nd rev. ed. London: Faber and Faber, 1947.

Hutchinson, John and Anthony D. Smith. Introduction. Pages 3–15 in *Ethnicity*. Edited by John Hutchinson and Anthony D. Smith. Oxford Readers. Oxford: Oxford University Press, 1996.

Isherwood, Lisa and David Harris. *Radical Otherness: Sociological and Theological Approaches*. London: Routledge, 2013.

Jensen, Alexander. *John's Gospel as Witness: The Development of the Early Christian Language of Faith*. Aldershot: Ashgate, 2004.

Jensen, Sune Qvotrup. "Othering, Identity Formation and Agency." *Qualitative Studies* 2, no. 2 (2011): 63–78.

Jobes, Karen H. *1, 2, & 3 John*. ZECNT. Grand Rapids: Zondervan, 2014.

Johnson, Luke T. "On Finding the Lukan Community: A Cautious Cautionary Essay." Pages 87–100 in *Society for Biblical Literature 1979 Seminar Papers*. Edited by Paul J. Achtemeier. Missoula, Mont.: Scholars Press, 1979.

———. "The New Testament's Anti-Jewish Slander and the Conventions of Ancient Polemic." *JBL* 108 (1989): 419–41.

———. *Prophetic Jesus, Prophetic Church: The Challenge of Luke-Acts to Contemporary Christians*. Grand Rapids: Eerdmans, 2011.

Käsemann, Ernst. "Ketzer und Zeuge: Zum johanneischen Verfasserproblem." *ZTK* 48 (1951): 292–311.

———. *The Testament of Jesus According to John 17*. Translated by Gerhard Krodel. Philadelphia: Fortress, 1978 (1966).

Katz, Andrew. "The Story Behind the Viral Photo of the Officer and the KKK." *Time Magazine*, August 14 [16], 2017. https://time.com/4899668/charlottesville-virginia-protest-officer-kkk-photo/.

Katz, Steven T. "Issues in the Separation of Judaism and Christianity after 70 CE: A Reconsideration." *JBL* 103 (1984): 43–76.

Keith, Chris. *The Gospel as Manuscript: An Early History of the Jesus Tradition as Material Artifact*. New York: Oxford University Press, 2020.

Keener, Craig S. *The Gospel of John: A Commentary*. 2 vols. Peabody, Mass.: Hendrickson, 2003.

Kelber, Werner. "Metaphysics and Marginality in John." Pages 129–54 in *What Is John?* Vol. 1: *Readers and Readings of the Fourth Gospel*. SBLSymS 3. Atlanta: Scholars Press, 1996.

Kierspel, Lars. *The Jews and the World in the Fourth Gospel*. WUNT 2/220. Tübingen: Mohr Siebeck, 2006.

Kimelman, Reuven. "*Birkat Ha-Minim* and the Lack of Evidence for an Anti-Christian Prayer in Late Antiquity." Pages 226–44 in *Aspects of Judaism in the Greco-Roman World*. Edited by E. P. Sanders, Albert I. Baumgarten, and Alan Mendelson. Vol. 2 of *Jewish and Christian Self-Definition*. Philadelphia: Fortress, 1981.

Klauck, Hans-Josef. "Gemeinde ohne Amt? Erfahrungen mit der Kirche in den johanneischen Schriften." *BZ* 29, no. 2 (1985): 193–220.

Klink, Edward W., III. *The Sheep of the Fold: The Audience and Origin of the Gospel of John*. SNTSMS 141. Cambridge: Cambridge University Press, 2007.

Koester, Craig R. "The Antichrist Theme in the Johannine Epistles and Its Role in Christian Tradition." Pages 187–96 in *Communities in Dispute: Current Scholarship on the Johannine Epistles*. Edited by R. Alan Culpepper and Paul N. Anderson. SBLECL 13. Atlanta: SBL Press, 2014.

———. *The Word of Life: A Theology of John's Gospel*. Grand Rapids: Eerdmans, 2008.

Koester, Helmut. "History and Cult in the Gospel of John and in Ignatius of Antioch." *JTC* 1 (1965): 111–23.

Kok, Kobus. "As the Father Has Sent Me, I Send You: Towards a Missional-Incarnational Ethos in John 4." Pages 168–93 in *Moral Language in the New Testament: The Interrelatedness of Language and Ethics in Early Christian Writings*. Edited by Ruben Zimmerman and Jan G. van der Watt. WUNT 2/296. Tübingen: Mohr Siebeck, 2010.

Köstenberger, Andreas J. and Michael J. Kruger. *The Heresy of Orthodoxy: How Contemporary Culture's Fascinations with Diversity Has Reshaped Our Understanding of Early Christianity*. Wheaton, Ill.: Crossway, 2010.

Kraft, Robert A. "The Reception of the Book" (appendix 2). Pages 286–316 in *Orthodoxy and Heresy in Earliest Christianity*. Translated by David Steinmetz, et al. Philadelphia: Fortress, 1971 (1934).

Kuecker, Aaron. "Ethnicity and Social Identity." Pages 59–77 in *T&T Clark Handbook to Social Identity in the New Testament*. Edited by J. Brian Tucker and Coleman A. Baker. London: T&T Clark, 2014.

———. *The Spirit and the "Other": Social Identity, Ethnicity and Intergroup Reconciliation in Luke-Acts*. LNTS 444. London: T&T Clark, 2011.

Kysar, Robert. *John: The Maverick Gospel*. 3rd ed. Louisville: Westminster John Knox, 2007, 1993 (1976).

———. "The Whence and Whither of the Johannine Community." Pages 65–81 in *Life in Abundance: Studies of John's Gospel in Tribute to Raymond E. Brown*. Edited by John R. Donahue. Collegeville, Minn.: Liturgical Press, 2005.

Labahn, Michael, and Manfred Lang. "Johannes und die Synoptiker: Positionen und Impulse seit 1990." Pages 443–515 in *Kontexte des Johannesevangeliums: Das vierte Evangelium in religions- und traditionsgeschichtlicher Perspektive*. Edited by Jörg Frey and Udo Schnelle. WUNT 175. Tübingen: Mohr Siebeck, 2004.

Lacan, Jacques. *The Seminar of Jacques Lacan*. Book 2: *The Ego in Freud's Theory and in the Technique of Psychoanalysis, 1954–1955*. New York: W. W. Norton, 1988.

Lamb, David A. "The Boundaries of Love: 'Us and Them' Language in 1 John." Paper presented at the International Colloquium: Love, Boundaries, and Sacred Texts. University of Chester, May 2, 2019.

———. *Text, Context, and the Johannine Community: A Sociolinguistic Analysis of the Johannine Writings*. LNTS 477. London: T&T Clark, 2014.

"A Letter on Justice and Open Debate." *Harper's Magazine*, July 7, 2020. https://harpers.org/a-letter-on-justice-and-open-debate/.

Levinas, Emmanuel. *Time and the Other: Lectures in Paris at the College Philosophique, 1946–1947*. Translated by Richard A. Cohen. Pittsburgh: Duquesne University Press, 1990.

———. *Totality and Infinity: An Essay on Exteriority*. Translated by Alphonso Lingis. Pittsburgh: Duquesne University Press, 1969.

Levine, Amy-Jill. "Reflections on Reflections: Jesus, Judaism, and Jewish-Christian Relations." *SCJR* 8 (2013): 1–13.

Lieu, Judith M. *I, II, & III John: A Commentary*. NTL. Louisville: Westminster John Knox, 2008.

———. "The Audience of the Johannine Letters." Pages 123–40 in *Communities in Dispute: Current Scholarship on the Johannine Epistles*. Edited by R. Alan Culpepper and Paul N. Anderson. SBLECL 13. Atlanta: SBL Press, 2014.

———. "Authority to Become Children of God: A Study of 1 John.'" *NovT* 23, no. 3 (1981): 210–28.

———. *Christian Identity in the Jewish and Graeco-Roman World*. Oxford: Oxford University Press, 2004.

———. "The Johannine Literature and the Canon." Pages 396–415 in *The Oxford Handbook of Johannine Studies*. Edited by Judith M. Lieu and Martinus C. de Boer. Oxford: Oxford University Press, 2018.

———. *Theology of the Johannine Epistles*. NTT. Cambridge: Cambridge University Press, 1991.

———. "Us or You? Persuasion and Identity in 1 John." *JBL* 127, no. 4 (2008): 805–19.

Lincoln, Andrew T. *The Gospel According to Saint John*. BNTC. London: Continuum, 2005.

———. "John 21." Pages 209–22 in *From Paul to Josephus: Literary Receptions of Jesus in the First Century CE*. Edited by Helen K. Bond. Vol. 1 of *The Reception of Jesus in the First Three Centuries*. Edited by Chris Keith, et al. London: T&T Clark, forthcoming.

———. *Truth on Trial: The Lawsuit Motif in the Fourth Gospel*. Peabody, Mass.: Hendrickson, 2000.

Ling, Timothy J. M. *The Judaean Poor in the Fourth Gospel*. SNTSMS 136. Cambridge: Cambridge University Press, 2009.

Lowe, Malcolm. "Who Were the Ἰουδαῖοι?" *NovT* 18 (1976): 101–30.

Malherbe, Abraham J. "The Inhospitality of Diotrephes." Pages 69–82 in *Light from the Gentiles: Hellenistic Philosophy and Early Christianity: Collected Essays, 1959–2012*. Edited by Carl R. Holladay, et al. NovTSup 150. Leiden: Brill, 2014 (1977).

Malina, Bruce J. *The Gospel of John in Sociolinguistic Perspective*. 48th Colloquy of the Center for Hermeneutical Studies. Berkley, Calif.: Center for Hermeneutical Studies, 1985.

———. "John's: The Maverick Christian Group: The Evidence of Sociolinguistics." *BThB* 24 (1994): 167–82.

———. "Rhetorical Criticism and Social-Scientific Criticism: Why Won't Romanticism Leave Us Alone?" Pages 5–21 in *The Social World of the New Testament: Insights and Models*. Edited by Jerome H. Neyrey and Eric C. Stewart. Peabody, Mass.: Hendrickson, 2008.

Malina, Bruce J., and Richard L. Rohrbaugh. *Social-Science Commentary on the Gospel of John*. Minneapolis: Fortress, 1998.

Marcus, Joel. "*Birkat Ha-Minim* Revisited." *NTS* 55, no. 4 (2009): 523–51.

Markschies, Christoph. *Christian Theology and Its Institutions: Prolegomena to a History of Early Christian Theology*. Translated by Wayne Coppins. BMSEC. Waco, Tex.: Baylor University Press, 2015.

Martyn, J. Louis. *History and Theology in the Fourth Gospel*. 3rd ed. Louisville: Westminster John Knox Press, 2003 (1968).

Marxsen, Willi. *Mark the Evangelist: Studies on the Redactional History of the Gospel*. Translated by James Boyce, Donald Juel, and William Poehlmann. Nashville: Abingdon, 1969.

Maurer, Christian. *Ignatius von Antiochien und das Johannesevangelium*. Zürich: Zwingli-Verlag, 1949.

McFarland, Ian A. *The Word Made Flesh: A Theology of the Incarnation*. Louisville: Westminster John Knox, 2019.

Meeks, Wayne A. "'Am I a Jew?' Johannine Christianity and Judaism." Pages 163–86 in *Christianity, Judaism and other Greco-Roman Cults: Studies for Morton Smith at Sixty*. Edited by J. Neusner. Leiden: Brill, 1975.

———. "Breaking Away: Three New Testament Pictures of Christianity's Separation from the Jewish Communities." Pages 93–115 in *"To See Ourselves as Others See Us": Christians, Jews, "Others" in Late Antiquity*. Edited by Jacob Neusner and Ernest S. Frerichs. Chico, Calif.: Scholars Press, 1985.

———. "The Ethics of the Fourth Evangelist." Pages 317–26 in *Exploring the Gospel of John: In Honor of D. Moody Smith*. Edited by R. Alan Culpepper and C. Clifton Black. Louisville: Westminster John Knox, 1996.

———. *First Urban Christians: The Social World of the Apostle Paul*. 2nd ed. New Haven, Conn.: Yale University Press, 2003 (1983).

———. "The Man from Heaven in Johannine Sectarianism." *JBL* 91, no. 1 (1972): 44–72.

Meier, John P. "The Absence and Presence of the Church in John's Gospel." *Mid-Stream* 41, no. 4 (2002): 27–34.

Méndez, Hugo. "Did the Johannine Community Exist?" *JSNT* 42, no. 3 (2020): 350–74.

Michaels, J. Ramsey. *The Gospel of John*. NICNT. Grand Rapids: Eerdmans, 2010.

Milbank, John. *Theology and Social Theory: Beyond Secular Reasoning*. 2nd ed. Oxford: Blackwell, 2006 (1990).

Mitchell, Margaret M. "'Diotrephes Does Not Receive Us': The Lexicographical and Social Context of 3 John 9-10." *JBL* 117, no. 2 (1998): 299–320.

Moessner, David P. "The Appeal and Power of Poetics (Luke 1:1-4): Luke's Superior Credentials (παρακολουθηκότι), Narrative Sequence (καθεξῆς), and Firmness of Understanding (ἡ ἀσφάλεια) for the Reader." Pages 84–123 in *Jesus and the Heritage of Israel*, edited by David P. Moessner. Harrisburg: Trinity Press International, 1999.

———. "Dionysius's Narrative 'Arrangement' (οἰκονομία) as the Hermeneutical Key to Luke's Re-Vision of the 'Many.'" Pages 149–64 in *Paul, Luke and the Graeco-Roman World: Essays in Honour of Alexander J. M. Wedderburn*. Edited by Alf Christophersen et al. JSNTSup 217. Sheffield: Sheffield University Press, 2002.

Moloney, Francis J. *Love in the Gospel of John: An Exegetical, Theological, and Literary Study*. Grand Rapids: Baker Academic, 2013.

Moltmann, Jürgen. "God in the World—The World in God: Perichoresis in Trinity and Eschatology." Pages 369–81 in *The Gospel of John and Christian Theology*. Edited by Richard Bauckham and Carl Mosser. Grand Rapids: Eerdmans, 2008.

Moule, C. F. D. "Individualism of the Fourth Gospel." *NovT* 5, no. 2–3 (1962): 171–90.

Motyer, Stephen. *Your Father the Devil? A New Approach to John and 'the Jews.'* Paternoster Biblical Monographs. Milton Keynes: Paternoster, 1997.

Myers, Alicia D. "Just Opponents? Ambiguity, Empathy, and the Jews in the Gospel of John." Pages 159–76 in *Johannine Ethics: The Moral World of the Gospel and Epistles of John*. Edited by Christopher W. Skinner and Sherri Brown. Minneapolis: Fortress, 2017.

Nagel, Titus. *Die Rezeption des Johannesevangeliums im 2. Jahrhundert: Studien zur vorirenäischen Aneignung und Auslegung des vierten Evangeliums in christlicher und christlich-gnostischer Literatur*. ABG 2. Leipzig: Evangelische Verlagsanstalt, 2000.

Naumann, Gerd. "Grammars of Identity/Alterity: A Structural Approach." Pages 18–50 in *Grammars of Identity/Alterity—A*

Structuralist Approach. Edited by G. Bauman and Andre Gingrich. Oxford: Berghahn, 2004.

Neirynck, Frans. "John and the Synoptics." Pages 73–106 in *L'Évangile de Jean: Sources, redaction, théologie.* Edited by Marinus de Jonge. BETL 44. Leuven: Leuven University Press, 1977.

"The New Ideology of Race and What's Wrong with It." *Economist,* July 9, 2020. https://www.economist.com/leaders/2020/07/09/the-new-ideology-of-race.

Neyrey, Jerome H. *The Gospel of John in Cultural and Rhetorical Perspective.* Grand Rapids: Eerdmans, 2009.

———. *An Ideology of Revolt: John's Christology in Social-Science Perspective.* Philadelphia: Fortress, 1988.

Nicklas, Tobias. "Creating the Other: The 'Jews' in the Gospel of John: Past and Future Lines of Scholarship." Pages 49–66 in *Perceiving the Other in Ancient Judaism and Early Christianity.* Edited by Michal Bar-Asher Siegal, Wolfgang Grünstädl, and Matthew Thiessen. WUNT 1/394. Tübingen: Mohr Siebeck, 2017.

———. "Jesus and Judaism: Inside or Outside? *The Gospel of John,* the *Egerton Gospel,* and the Spectrum of Ancient Christian Voices." Pages 125–41 in *Connecting Gospels: Beyond the Canonical/Non-Canonical Divide.* Edited by Francis Watson and Sarah Parkhouse. Oxford: Oxford University Press, 2018.

Niehoff, Maren R. *Philo on Jewish Identity and Culture.* TSAJ 86. Tübingen: Mohr Siebeck, 2020.

Nongbri, Brent. *Before Religion: A History of a Modern Concept.* New Haven, Conn. and London: Yale University Press, 2013.

North, Wendy E. S. "'The Jews' in John's Gospel: Observations and Inferences." Pages 207–26 in *Judaism, Jewish Identities and the Gospel Tradition: Essays in Honour of Maurice Casey.* Edited by James Crossley. London: Equinox, 2010.

———. *What John Knew and What John Wrote: A Study in John and the Synoptics.* Interpreting Johannine Literature. Lanham, Md.: Fortress, 2020.

Numada, Jonathan. "The Repetition of History? A Select Survey of Scholarly Understandings of Johannine Anti-Judaism from Baur until the End of the Weimar Republic." Pages 261–84 in *The Origins of John's Gospel.* Edited by Stanley E. Porter and Hughson T. Ong. JOST 2. Leiden: Brill, 2015.

O'Grady, John F. "Individualism and Johannine Ecclesiology." *BTB* 5, no. 3 (1975): 227–61.

———. "The Prologue and Chapter 17 of the Gospel of John." Pages 215–28 in *What We Have Heard From the Beginning: The Past, Present, and Future of Johannine Studies.* Edited by Tom Thatcher. Waco, Tex.: Baylor University Press, 2007.

Painter, John C. *1, 2, and 3 John*. SP 18. Collegeville, Minn.: The Liturgical Press, 2002.

———. "Johannine Symbols: A Case Study in Epistemology." *JTSA* 27 (1979): 26–41.

———. "The Opponents in 1 John." *NTS* 32 (1986): 48–71.

Parsenios, George L. *First, Second, and Third John*. Paideia. Grand Rapids: Baker Academic, 2014.

Parsons, Mikeal C. "A Neglected ΕΓΩ ΕΙΜΙ Saying in the Fourth Gospel? Another Look at John 9:9." Pages 145–80 in *Perspectives on John: Method and Interpretation in the Fourth Gospel*. Edited by Robert B. Sloan and Mikeal C. Parsons. NABPR Special Studies Series 11. Lampeter: Edwin Mellen Press, 1993.

Penwell, Stewart. *Jesus the Samaritan: Ethnic Labelling in the Gospel of John*. BibInt 170. Leiden: Brill, 2019.

Perkins, Pheme. "Erasure of 'the Jews' in the Farewell Discourses and Johannine Epistles." Pages 3–20 in *The Gospel of John and Jewish-Christian Relations*. Edited by Adele Reinhartz. Lanham, Md.: Fortress, 2018.

———. *The Johannine Epistles*. New Testament Message 21. Wilmington, Del.: Glazier, 1979.

———. *Peter: Apostle for the Whole Church*. Studies on Personalities of the New Testament. Minneapolis: Fortress, 2000.

Prestige, George L. *God in Patristic Thought*. London: SPCK, 1956.

Pryor, John W. "Jesus and Israel in the Fourth Gospel—John 1:11." *NovT* 32, no. 3 (1990): 201–18.

———. *John: Evangelist of the Covenant People: The Narrative & Themes of the Fourth Gospel*. Downers Grove, Ill.: InterVarsity Press, 1992.

Quast, Kevin. *Peter and the Beloved Disciple: Figures for a Community in Crisis*. JSNTSup 32. Sheffield: Sheffield Academic, 1989.

Rasimus, Tuomas. Introduction. Pages 1–16 in *The Legacy of John: Second-Century Reception of the Fourth Gospel*. Edited by Tuomas Rasimus. NovTSup 132. Leiden: Brill, 2010.

Regev, Eyal. "Were the Early Christians Sectarians?" *JBL* 130, no. 4 (2011): 771–93.

Reinhartz, Adele. *Befriending the Beloved Disciple: A Jewish Reading of the Gospel of John*. London: Continuum, 2001.

———. *Cast Out of the Covenant: Jews and Anti-Judaism in the Gospel of John*. Lanham, Md.: Fortress, 2018.

———. "'Jews' and Jews in the Fourth Gospel." Pages 213–27 in *Anti-Judaism and the Fourth Gospel*. Edited by Reimund Bieringer, Didier Pollefeyt, and Frederique Vandecasteele-Vanneuville. Louisville: Westminster John Knox, 2001.

———. "The Johannine Community and Its Jewish Neighbors: A Reappraisal." Pages 111–38 in *What is John?* Vol. 2: *Literary and Social*

Readings of the Fourth Gospel. Edited by Fernando Segovia. SBLSymS 3. Atlanta: Scholars Press, 1998.

———. *The Word in the World: The Cosmological Tale in the Fourth Gospel.* SBLMS 45. Atlanta: Scholars Press, 1992.

Rensberger, David K. *Johannine Faith and the Liberating Community.* Philadelphia: Westminster, 1988.

———. "Sectarianism and Theological Interpretation in John." Pages 139–156 in *"What Is John?"* Vol. 2: *Literary and Social Readings of the Fourth Gospel.* Edited by Fernando F. Segovia. SBLSymS 7. Atlanta: SBL Press, 1998.

Rissi, Mathias. "Die 'Juden' im Johannesevangelium." Pages 2099–141 in *ANRW* II.26/3. Berlin: De Gruyter, 1996.

Roberts, Richard H. "Theology and the Social Sciences." Pages 704–19 in *The Modern Theologians: An Introduction to Christian Theology in the Twentieth Century.* Edited by David F. Ford. 2nd ed. Oxford: Blackwell, 1997.

Robinson, Thomas A. *The Bauer Thesis Examined: The Geography of Heresy in the Early Christian Church.* Lewiston, N.Y.: Edwin Mellen Press, 1988.

———. *Ignatius and the Parting of the Ways: Early Jewish Relations.* Peabody, Mass.: Hendrikson, 2009.

Runesson, Anders. "Judging Gentiles in the Gospel of Matthew: Between 'Othering' and Inclusion." Pages 133–51 in *Jesus, Matthew's Gospel and Early Christianity: Studies in Memory of Graham N. Stanton.* Edited by Daniel M. Gurtner, Joel Willitts, and Richard A. Burridge. LNTS 435. London: T&T Clark, 2011.

Ruse, Michael. "Naturalism, Evil, and God." Pages 249–66 in *The Cambridge Companion to the Problem of Evil.* Edited by Chad Meister and Paul K. Moser. New York: Cambridge University Press, 2017.

Russell, Letty M. "Encountering the 'Other' in a World of Difference and Danger." *HTR* 99, no. 4 (2006): 457–68.

Sacks, Jonathan. *The Dignity of Difference: How to Avoid the Clash of Civilizations.* Rev. ed. London: Bloomsbury, 2003 (2002).

Said, Edward. *Orientalism.* London: Penguin Books, 1978.

Sanders, J. N. *The Fourth Gospel in the Early Church: Its Origin & Influence on Christian Theology up to Irenaeus.* Cambridge: Cambridge University Press, 1943.

Schmid, Hansjörg. *Gegner im 1. Johannesbrief? Zu Konstruktion und Selbsreferenz im johanneischen Sinnsystem.* BWANT 159. Stuttgart: Kohlhammer, 2002.

———. "How to Read the First Epistle of John Non-Polemically." *Biblica* 85, no. 1 (2004): 24–41.

Schmidt, Karl. *Der Rahmen der Geschichte Jesu.* Berlin: Trowittzsch & Sohn, 1919.

Schnackenburg, Rudolf. *The Johannine Epistles: A Commentary*. Translated by Reginald Fuller and Ilse Fuller. New York: Crossroad, 1992 (1965).

Schneiders, Sandra M. *Written That You May Believe: Encountering Jesus in the Fourth Gospel*. Rev. ed. New York: Crossroad, 2003 (1999).

Schnelle, Udo. "Johanneische Ekklesiologie." *NTS* 37 (1991): 37–50.

Schoedel, William R. *Ignatius of Antioch: A Commentary on the Letters of Ignatius of Antioch*. Hermeneia. Philadelphia: Fortress, 1985.

Schwartz, Regina M. *The Curse of Cain: The Violent Legacy of Monotheism*. Chicago: University of Chicago Press, 1997.

Schweizer, Eduard. "The Concept of the Church in the Gospel and Epistles of St John." Pages 230–45 in *New Testament Essays: Studies in Memory of Thomas Walter Manson, 1893–1958*. Edited by A. J. B. Higgins. Manchester: Manchester University Press, 1959.

Scruggs, Robin. "The Earliest Christian Communities as Sectarian Movement." Pages 1–23 in vol. 2 of *Christianity, Judaism and Other Greco-Roman Cults: Studies for Morton Smith at Sixty*. Edited by Jacob Neusner. SJLA 12. Leiden: Brill, 1975.

Segovia, Fernando F. "Inclusion and Exclusion in John 17: An Intercultural Reading." Pages 183–209 in *"What is John?"* Vol. 2: *Literary and Social Readings of the Fourth Gospel*. Edited by Fernando F. Segovia. SBLSS 7. Atlanta: Scholars Press, 1998.

———. "The Love and Hatred of Jesus and Johannine Sectarianism." *CBQ* 43, no. 2 (1981): 258–72.

Sheridan, Ruth. "Identity, Alterity, and the Gospel of John." *BibInt* 22 (2014): 188–209.

———. "Issues in the Translation of οἱ Ἰουδαῖοι in the Fourth Gospel." *JBL* 132, no. 3 (2013): 671–95.

———. "Johannine Sectarianism: A Category Now Defunct?" Pages 142–66 in *The Origins of John's Gospel*. Edited by Stanley E. Porter and Hughson T. Ong. Vol. 2 of *Johannine Studies*. Edited by Stanley E. Porter. Leiden: Brill, 2015.

Siegal, Michal Bar-Asher, Wolfgang Grünstädl, and Matthew Thiessen, eds. *Perceiving the Other in Ancient Judaism and Early Christianity*. WUNT 394. Tübingen: Mohr Siebeck, 2017.

Silberstein, Laurence J. and Robert L. Cohn, eds. *The Other in Jewish Thought and History: Constructions of Jewish Culture and Identity*. New York: New York University Press, 1994.

Sim, David C. "Matthew's Use of Mark: Did Matthew Intend to Supplement or to Replace His Primary Source?" *NTS* 57 (2011): 176–92.

Simuţ, Corneliu C. F. C. *Baur's Synthesis of Böhme and Hegel: Redefining Christian Theology as a Gnostic Philosophy of Religion*. PRWR 4. Leiden: Brill, 2015.

Skinner, Christopher W. "Introduction: (How) Can We Talk About Johannine Ethics? Looking Back and Moving Forward." Pages xvii–xxxvi in *Johannine Ethics: The Moral World of the Gospel and Epistles of John*. Edited by Christopher W. Skinner and Sherri Brown. Minneapolis: Fortress, 2017.

———. "Love One Another: The Love Command in the Farewell Discourse." Pages 25–42 in *Johannine Ethics: The Moral World of the Gospel and Epistles of John*. Edited by Christopher W. Skinner and Sherri Brown. Minneapolis: Fortress, 2017.

Slee, Michelle. *The Church in Antioch in the First Century CE: Communion and Conflict*. JSNTSup 244. London: Sheffield University Press, 2003.

Smalley, Stephen S. *John: Evangelist and Interpreter*. Exeter: Paternoster, 1978.

Smith, D. Moody. *Johannine Christianity: Essays on Its Setting, Sources, and Theology*. Columbia: University of South Carolina Press, 1984.

———. *John among the Synoptics: The Relationship in Twentieth-Century Research*. 2nd ed. Columbia: University of South Carolina Press, 2001 (1992).

———. *The Theology of the Gospel of John*. NTT. Cambridge: Cambridge University Press, 1995.

Smith, Wilfred Cantwell. *The Meaning and End of Religion*. Minneapolis: Fortress, 1991 (1962).

Smith, Jonathan Z. "Differential Equations: On Constructing the Other." Pages 230–50 in *Relating Religion: Essays on the Study of Religion*. Chicago: University of Chicago Press, 2004.

———. "Religion, Religions, Religious." Pages 269–84 in *Critical Terms for Religious Studies*. Edited by Mark C. Taylor. Chicago: University of Chicago Press, 1998.

———. "What a Difference a Difference Makes." Pages 251–302 in *Relating Religion: Essays on the Study of Religion*. Chicago: University of Chicago Press, 2004.

Smith, P. Gardner. *Saint John and the Synoptic Gospels*. Cambridge: Cambridge University Press, 2011 (1938).

Snyder, Graydon F. "John 13:16 and the Anti-Petrinism of the Johannine Tradition." BR 16 (1971): 5–15.

Sosa Siliezar, Carlos Raúl. *Savior of the World: A Theology of the Universal Gospel*. Waco, Tex.: Baylor University Press, 2019.

Spencer, Hawes, and Matt Stevens. "23 Arrested and Tear Gas Deployed After a K.K.K. Rally in Virginia." *New York Times*, July 8, 2017. https://www.nytimes.com/2017/07/08/us/kkk-rally-charlottesville-robert-e-lee-statue.html.

Spina, Frank Anthony. *The Faith of the Outsider: Exclusion and Inclusion in the Biblical Story*. Grand Rapids: Eerdmans, 2005.

Spivak, G. C. "The Rani of Sirmur: An Essay in Reading the Archives." *History and Theory* 24, no. 3 (1985): 247–72.

Stanton, Graham N. "Aspects of Early Christian-Jewish Polemic and Apologetic." *NTS* 31 (1985): 377–92.

Stark, Rodney and William S. Bainbridge. *A Theory of Religion*. New Brunswick: Rutgers University Press, 1996 (1987).

Stewart, Alistair C. *The Original Bishops: Office and Order in the First Christian Communities*. Grand Rapids: Baker Academic, 2014.

Stowers, Stanley K. "The Social Sciences and the Study of Early Christianity." Pages 149–81 in vol. 5 of *Approaches to Ancient Judaism: Theory and Practice*. Edited by W. S. Green. Missoula, Mont.: Scholars Press, 1985.

Streeter, B. H. *The Primitive Church*. New York: Macmillan, 1929.

Streett, Daniel R. *"They Went out from Us": The Identity of the Opponents in First John*. BZNW 177. Berlin: De Gruyter, 2011.

Sullivan, Francis A. *From Apostles to Bishops: The Development of the Episcopacy in the Early Church*. New York: Newman Press, 2001.

Taylor, Charles. *A Secular Age*. Cambridge, Mass.: Belknap, 2007.

Thatcher, Tom. "John and the Jews: Recent Research and Future Questions." Pages 3–38 in *John and Judaism: A Contested Relationship in Context*. Edited by R. Alan Culpepper and Paul N. Anderson. RBS 87. Atlanta: SBL Press, 2017.

———. "The Semiotics of History: C. H. Dodd on the Origins and Character of the Fourth Gospel." Pages 1–28 in *Engaging with C. H. Dodd on the Gospel of John: Sixty Years of Tradition and Interpretation*. Edited by Tom Thatcher and Catrin H. Williams. Cambridge: Cambridge University Press, 2013.

———. *Why John WROTE a Gospel: Jesus—Memory—History*. Louisville: Westminster John Knox, 2006.

Thiessen, Matthew. *Contesting Conversion: Genealogy, Circumcision, and Identity in Ancient Judaism and Christianity*. Oxford University Press, 2011.

Thompson, Marianne Meye. *John: A Commentary*. NTL. Louisville: Westminster John Knox, 2015.

Trebilco, Paul. *The Early Christians in Ephesus from Paul to Ignatius*. WUNT 166. Tübingen: Mohr Siebeck, 2004.

———. *Outsider Designations and Boundary Construction in the New Testament: Early Christian Communities and the Formation of Group Identity*. Cambridge: Cambridge University Press, 2017.

———. *Self-Designations and Group Identity in the New Testament*. Cambridge: Cambridge University Press, 2012.

Trevett, Christine. *A Study of Ignatius of Antioch in Syria and Asia*. SBEC 29. Lampeter: Edwin Mellen, 1992.

Troeltsch, Ernst. *The Social Teaching of the Christian Churches*. Library of Theological Ethics. 2 vols. Louisville: Westminster John Knox Press, 2009, 2010 (1931, 1911).

Uebele, Wolfram. *"Viele Verführer sind in die Welt ausgegangen": Die Gegner in den Briefen des Ignatius von Antiochien und in den Johannesbriefen.* BWANT 151. Stuttgart: Kohlhammer, 2001.

Van der Watt, Jan G. *Family of the King: Dynamics of Metaphor in the Gospel of John.* BibInt 47. Leiden: Brill, 2000.

Vlassopoulos, Kostas. *Greeks and Barbarians.* Cambridge: Cambridge University Press, 2013.

Volf, Miroslav. *After Our Likeness: The Church as the Image of the Trinity.* Grand Rapids: Eerdmans, 1998.

———. *Exclusion and Embrace: A Theological Exploration of Identity, Otherness, and Reconciliation.* Nashville: Abingdon, 1996.

———. "Johannine Dualism and Contemporary Pluralism." Pages 19–50 in *The Gospel of John and Christian Theology.* Edited by Richard Bauckham and Carl Mosser. Grand Rapids: Eerdmans, 2008.

Wagner, Jochen. *Die Anfänge des Amtes in der Kirche: Presbyter und Episkopen in der frühchristlichen Literatur.* TANZ 53. Tübingen: Francke, 2011.

Wahlde, Urban C. von. *The Gospels and Letters of John.* 3 vols. ECC. Grand Rapids: Eerdmans, 2010.

———. "The Jews in the Gospel of John: Fifteen Years of Research [1983–1998]." *EThL* 76 (2000): 30–55.

———. "The Johannine 'Jews': A Critical Survey." *NTS* 28 (1982): 33–60.

Warren, Meredith J. C. *My Flesh Is Meat Indeed: A Nonsacramental Reading of John 6:51-58.* Minneapolis: Fortress, 2015.

Watson, Francis. *The Fourfold Gospel: A Theological Reading of the New Testament Portraits of Jesus.* Grand Rapids: Baker Academic, 2016.

———. "A Gospel of the Eleven: The *Epistula Apostolorum* and the Johannine Tradition." Pages 189–215 in *Connecting Gospels: Beyond the Canonical/Non-Canonical Divide.* Edited by Francis Watson and Sarah Parkhouse. Oxford: Oxford University Press, 2018.

———. *Gospel Writing: A Canonical Perspective.* Grand Rapids: Eerdmans, 2013.

———. "Toward a Literal Reading of the Gospels." Pages 195–217 in *The Gospels for All Christians: Rethinking the Gospel Audiences.* Edited by Richard Bauckham. Grand Rapids: Eerdmans, 1998.

Watty, William W. "The Significance of Anonymity in the Fourth Gospel." *ExpTim* 90, no. 7 (1979): 209–12.

Weber, Max. *The Protestant Work Ethic and the "Spirit" of Capitalism and Other Writings.* Translated by Peter Baehr and Gordon C. Wells. New York: Penguin, 2002.

Webster, John. "The 'Self-Organizing' Power of the Gospel: Episcopacy and Community Formation." Pages 179–93 in *Community Formation in the Early Church and the Church Today.* Edited by Richard N. Longenecker. Peabody, Mass.: Hendrickson, 2002.

Wengst, Klaus. *Bedrängte Gemeinde und verherrlichter Christus: Der historische Ort des Johannesevangeliums als Schlüssel zu seiner Interpretation.* 2nd ed. Biblisch-Theologische Studien, 5. Neukirchen-Vluyn: Neukirchener, 1983.

Wilson, Bryan R. *Magic and the Millennium: A Sociological Study of Religious Movements of Protest among Tribal and Third-World People.* New York: Harper & Row, 1973.

Windisch, Hans. *Johannes und die Synoptiker: Wollte der vierte Evangelist die älteren Evangelien ergänzen oder ersetzen?* WUNT 12. Leipzig: Hinrichs, 1926.

Witmer, Stephen E. "Approaches to Scripture in the Fourth Gospel and the Qumran Pesharim." *NovT* 48 (2006): 313–28.

Woll, D. Bruce. *Johannine Christianity in Conflict: Authority, Rank, and Succession in the Farewell Discourse.* SBLDS 60. Chico, Calif.: Scholars Press, 1981.

Young, Frances M. "Ministerial Forms and Functions in the Church Communities of the Greek Fathers." Pages 157–76 in *Community Formation in the Early Church and the Church Today.* Edited by Richard N. Longenecker. Peabody, Mass.: Hendrickson, 2002.

Zachhuber, Johannes. "The Historical Turn." Pages 53–71 in *The Oxford Handbook of Nineteenth-Century Christian Thought.* Edited by Joel D. S. Rasmussen, Judith Wolfe, and Johannes Zachhuber. Oxford: Oxford University Press, 2017.

Zahn, Theodor, et al. *Introduction to the New Testament.* 3 vols. Edinburgh: T&T Clark, 1953 (1909).

Zelyck, Lorne R. *John among the Other Gospels: The Reception of the Fourth Gospel in the Extra-Canonical Gospels.* WUNT 2/347. Tübingen: Mohr Siebeck, 2013.

Zetterholm, Magnus. *The Formation of Christianity in Antioch: A Social-Scientific Approach to the Separation between Judaism and Christianity.* New York: Routledge, 2003.

Index of Subjects

Index of Select Authors

Index of Scripture and Ancient Texts